Communications in Computer and Information Science   **566**

Commenced Publication in 2007
Founding and Former Series Editors:
Alfredo Cuzzocrea, Dominik Ślęzak, and Xiaokang Yang

More information about this series at http://www.springer.com/series/7899

Andrzej Dziech · Mikołaj Leszczuk
Remigiusz Baran (Eds.)

Multimedia Communications, Services and Security

8th International Conference, MCSS 2015
Kraków, Poland, November 24, 2015
Proceedings

 Springer

Editors
Andrzej Dziech
AGH University of Science and Technology
Kraków
Poland

Remigiusz Baran
Kielce University of Technology
Kielce
Poland

Mikołaj Leszczuk
Department of Telecommunications
AGH University of Technology
Kraków
Poland

ISSN 1865-0929   ISSN 1865-0937   (electronic)
Communications in Computer and Information Science
ISBN 978-3-319-26403-5   ISBN 978-3-319-26404-2   (eBook)
DOI 10.1007/978-3-319-26404-2

Library of Congress Control Number: 2015954345

Springer Cham Heidelberg New York Dordrecht London

Printed on acid-free paper

Springer International Publishing AG Switzerland is part of Springer Science+Business Media
(www.springer.com)

Preface

The objective of the Multimedia Communications, Services and Security (MCSS 2015) conference is to present research and development activities contributing to many aspects of multimedia communications, systems, and security. As in previous years, we invited theoretical and experimental papers as well as work-in-progress research in the domain of audio-visual systems including novel multimedia architectures, multimedia data fusion, acquisition of multimedia content and QoE management, watermarking technologies and application content search methods, interactive multimedia applications, cryptography, and biometry. An overview of the selected subjects and publications, given below, shows that the subjects included in MCSS 2015 are current and important from the point of view of potential practical implementation.

Road Traffic Safety and Efficiency Supported by Multimedia Analysis

Optimal placement of advertisements (such as large billboards) in the proximity of roads and highways can significantly affect traffic safety. A variety of options for performing multifactorial research in this area are presented. The methodology makes it possible to conduct an objective assessment of risks arising from the presence of advertisements by roadsides.

Another aspect of road traffic analyzed at MCSS is efficient estimation of traffic parameters based on sparse measurements covering a small fraction of road segments within a large urban road network. The solution is intended to be used within dynamic maps used for route planning and traffic control. Estimation models based on fuzzy cognitive maps (FCM) formalism and applying FCM learning techniques based on the evolution algorithm to determine model parameters are also presented.

Biometric Methods for Security Purposes

In the well-explored domain of facial biometrics, methods that go beyond traditional models can lead to more robust systems. One such method, outlined in an MCSS paper, assumes following the movement of feature points over the course of an expression to make user authentication systems more secure. To do this, a new algorithm was developed using a process known as ranking, in order to describe facial expressions with low computational cost.

Behavioral biometrics such as mouse dynamics are gaining attention today by addressing the limitations of conventional verification systems. A novel method of continuous verification of users by following their mouse activity is presented. The method, based on comparing mouse activity against simple statistical profiles, can complement regular verification systems and its simplicity makes it effective for continuous verification.

Another research paper dedicated to user authentication investigates the accuracy of an identification scheme based on the sound of typing a password. The innovation of this method lies in the comparison of performance between timing-based and audio-based keystroke dynamics data in authentication and identification settings.

Cryptography

Elliptic curve cryptography (ECC) offers security levels similar to other cryptographic methods while using smaller bit key sizes. A novel mapping model for converting pixels of a plain image into coordinates of predefined elliptic curve points is proposed. The method is used in combination with existing algorithms, such as Koblitz's encoding method and chaos-driven elliptic curve pseudo-random number generator (C-D ECPRNG).

Protection of Critical Infrastructures with SCADA Systems

Protection in critical infrastructure, especially when dealing with highly dynamic and complex systems such as SCADA, requires preparation of appropriate strategies for predicting and reacting to anomalous events. However, if prediction is difficult (or even impossible), dedicated plans for dealing with such problems should be devised in order to adapt the strategies ad hoc when problems arise. Studies have been conducted into planning under uncertainty, with applications in problems such as scheduling. The work presented at MCSS 2015 discusses SCADA as a problem similar to scheduling, and constructs a system dedicated to preparing ready-to-use strategies before certain events arise.

Potential Commercial Applications of Image Analytics

DEEP by Viaccess-Orca is an example of a commercial application based, to some extent, on collaboration between industry and academic research teams. DEEP is a comprehensive new content discovery solution that combines search, recommendation, and second-screen devices into a single immersive experience. Automated generation of content for DEEP relies on structured sources of data and on multimedia databases. Using the Internet as a source of multimedia can result in the acquisition of near duplicates – visually similar images. An enhanced method of near duplicate detection for a certain type of photograph – images of celebrities – is proposed. An overview of the IMCOP system was conducted, complementing this method. It uses the innovative concept of intelligent discovering and sharing multimedia content using the Internet. As with previous MCSS conferences, this year's event was also an opportunity for all researchers focusing on the future of multimedia communications, services, and security to come together, collaborate, and share experiences. We were delighted to host this year's gathering that facilitated discussions on the future course of state-of-the-art technologies in the fields addressed by the MCSS conference.

November 2015

Andrzej Dziech
Mikołaj Leszczuk
Remigiusz Baran

Organization

The International Conference on Multimedia Communications, Services and Security (MCSS 2015) was organized by AGH University of Science and Technology in the scope of and under the auspices of the IMCOP project.

Executive Committee

General Chair

Andrzej Dziech	AGH University of Science and Technology, Poland

Committee Chairs

Andrzej Dziech	AGH University of Science and Technology, Poland
Mikołj Leszczuk	AGH University of Science and Technology, Poland
Remigiusz Baran	Kielce University of Technology, Poland

Technical Program Committee

Laurie Basta	Assystem E&OS, France
Alexander Bekiarski	Technical University - Sofia, Bulgaria
Fernando Boavida	University of Coimbra, Portugal
Eduardo Cerqueira	Federal University of Para and UCLA, Brazil
Marilia Curado	University of Coimbra, Portugal
Andrzej Czyzewski	Gdansk University of Technology, Poland
Anne Demoisy	Skynet Belgacom, Belgium
Magdalena Diering	Poznan University of Technology, Poland
Charalampos Dimoulas	Aristotle University of Thessaloniki, Greece
Andrzej Duda	Grenoble Institute of Technology, France
Krzysztof Dyczkowski	Adam Mickiewicz University, Poland
Enrico Francesconi	Legal Information Institute of the National Research Council of Italy, Italy
Apostolos Gkamas	University Ecclesiastical Academy of Vella of Ioannina, Greece
Burak Gorkemli	Argela, Research and Technology, Turkey
Michał Grega	AGH University of Science and Technology, Poland
Nils Johanning	InnoTec Data, Germany
Eva Kiktova	Technical University of Kosice, Slovakia
Marek Kisiel-Dorohinicki	AGH University of Science and Technology, Poland
Zbigniew Kotulski	Warsaw University of Technology, Poland
Anton Kummert	University of Wuppertal, Germany
David Larrabeiti	Universidad Carlos III de Madrid, Spain
Antoni Ligęza	AGH University of Science and Technology, Poland
Tomasz Marciniak	PUT, Poland

Rafael Molina	Universidad de Granada, Spain
Cecilia Occhiuzzi	University of Palermo, Italy
George Papanikolaou	Aristotle University of Thessaloniki, Greece
Anna Paulson	NTIA/Institute for Telecommunication Sciences, USA
Kamisetty Ramamohan Rao	University of Texas at Arlington, USA
Thomas Sablik	University of Wuppertal, Germany
Emanuele Salerno	ISTI-CNR, Italy
Stefano Salsano	University of Rome Tor Vergata, Italy
Ovidio Salvetti	ISTI-CNR, Italy
Irena Stange	U.S. Department of Commerce, USA
Nikolai Stoianov	Technical University of Sofia, Bulgaria
Piotr Szczuko	Gdansk University of Technology, Poland
Ryszard Tadeusiewicz	AGH University of Science and Technology, Poland
Cedric Tavernier	Assystem E&OS, France
Manuel Uruena	Universidad Carlos III de Madrid, Spain
Joerg Velten	University of Wuppertal, Germany
Jaroslav Zdralek	VSB – Technical University of Ostrava, Czech Republic

Organizing Committee

Remigiusz Baran	Kielce University of Technology, Poland
Jacek Dańda	AGH University of Science and Technology, Poland
Jan Derkacz	AGH University of Science and Technology, Poland
Sabina Drzewicka	AGH University of Science and Technology, Poland
Michał Grega	AGH University of Science and Technology, Poland
Piotr Guzik	AGH University of Science and Technology, Poland
Agnieszka Kleszcz	AGH University of Science and Technology, Poland
Paweł Korus	AGH University of Science and Technology, Poland
Mikołaj Leszczuk	AGH University of Science and Technology, Poland
Andrzej Matiolański	AGH University of Science and Technology, Poland
Piotr Romaniak	AGH University of Science and Technology, Poland
Krzysztof Rusek	AGH University of Science and Technology, Poland

Sponsoring Institutions

- Institute of Electrical and Electronics Engineers (IEEE)
- Intelligent Multimedia System for Web and IPTV Archiving. Digital Analysis and Documentation of Multimedia Content (IMCOP Project)
- Security In trusted SCADA and smart-grids (SCISSOR Project)
- AGH University of Science and Technology, Department of Telecommunications
- University of Computer Engineering and Telecommunications (WSTKT)

Contents

Biometric Applications

Experiments and Deployments

Multimedia Services

An Overview of the IMCOP System Architecture with Selected Intelligent Utilities Emphasized

Remigiusz Baran[1(✉)], Andrzej Zeja[2], and Przemyslaw Slusarczyk[3]

[1] Faculty of Electrical Engineering, Automatics and Computer Science,
Kielce University of Technology, al. 1000-lecia P.P. 7, 25-314 Kielce, Poland
r.baran@tu.kielce.pl
[2] University of Computer Engineering and Telecommunications,
ul. Toporowskiego 98, 25-553 Kielce, Poland
a.zeja@wstkt.pl
[3] Department of Computer Science, Institute of Physics, Jan Kochanowski University,
ul. Swietokrzyska 15, 25-406 Kielce, Poland
pslusarczyk@ujk.edu.pl

Abstract. The paper presents an overview of the IMCOP system which refers to the general modern idea of intelligent discovering and sharing the multimedia content using the Internet. An extended background within the framework of the subject matter is presented at the beginning. The main components of the IMCOP system as well as concept of complex multimedia objects known as the CMO objects are introduced then. Categories of applied web services with an insight into the tasks they were designated to are farther also described in details. Finally, performance aspects of the IMCOP system are reported. The conclusion includes a summary of IMCOP's advantages as well as discussion about its drawbacks with an insight into potential future improvements.

Keywords: Content discovery and data enrichment platform · Multimedia indexing · Complex multimedia objects · DEEP · Cloud computing · Content delivery

1 Introduction

The IMCOP system is an outcome of the second joint Polish-Israeli R&D project titled "Intelligent Multimedia System for Web and IPTV Archiving. Digital Analysis and Documentation of Multimedia Content" [1], which refers to the general modern idea of intelligent discovering and sharing the multimedia content using the Internet With regard to all the above, the major objectives of the IMCOP project were:

– to develop a system able to aggregate, analyze and bind various multimedia objects (mainly the text as well as still images and movies) and finally make them accessible for external entities (applications, end-users, other systems, etc.) as a subject related collections of multimedia content,

© Springer International Publishing Switzerland 2015
A. Dziech et al. (Eds.): MCSS 2015, CCIS 566, pp. 3–17, 2015.
DOI: 10.1007/978-3-319-26404-2_1

- to find a flexible and efficient representation of such a subject related collections of multimedia content with regard to the needs of their cost-and space-effective archiving as well as fast searching and sharing.

There were also other minor, although not less important goals, including:

- to ensure that the IMCOP system is platform independent and it is capable of incorporating external services to improve its efficiency and increase its intelligent facilities, for example by removing duplicate images from the database [2],
- to guarantee scalability despite huge amount of multimedia objects processed,
- to make absolutely certain that the system is legal in terms of copyright law as well as the processed objects and their content are fully protected against coping, reproducing, modifying and other forms of authentication rights violation.

It has been agreed between the project partners that the IMCOP system should comply with, and complement–especially in terms of improving the quality of multimedia content, the needs of DEEP (Data Enrichment and Engagement Platform) concept [3] developed by the Israeli partner as part of his project duties. The DEEP's content is organized in the service as a set of automatically created magazines, covering such subjects (known also as topics) as actors lives, life stories of actors or characters, buzz graphs, etc. Each magazine contains pages which are based on predefined visual templates filled with enriched data. "DEEP's magazine format turns the small tasks of search, discovery and recommendation into a process of exploration, a journey. The familiarity of the magazine format invites readers to browse the ads, as if they were in print. For example, in fashion magazines, browsing the ads has always been an integral part of the reading experience" [4].

From IMCOP's perspective, the DEEP platform can been seen as advanced and professionally realized presentation layer translating data, organized and delivered by the IMCOP system, to the application layer represented by the DEEP magazines. In that case, the DEEP platform is just an example of aforementioned external entities, which rely on subject related collections of multimedia data coalesced by the IMCOP system. In fact, due to IMCOP's architecture which is "open" to variety of data sources and diversity of its content, list of such entities is not limited anyway and can include education, libraries, museums or e.g. business related ones.

The purpose of this paper is to give a status report on the IMCOP system architecture, which, in general, is an organization of service oriented applications, where particular services are divided into few main categories. Data in the IMCOP system, despite their content form, are represented by objects of the same structure, known as Complex Multimedia Objects (CMO). CMO objects represent as well multimedia data itself as descriptive metadata about them. Selected metadata also describes relations between respective multimedia data and builds, in this way, subject related collections of multimedia content mentioned above.

For clarity of presentation, the rest of the paper is organized as follows. The current section presents some background material within the framework of the subject matter. In Sect. 2, the overall architecture of the IMCOP system including definition of the CMO objects is introduced. Categories of services are presented in detail in successive subsections of Sect. 3. In Sect. 4, the system's performance is reported and discussed. Conclusions, with an insight to potential future improvements, are drawn in Sect. 5.

1.1 Background

As it was declared at the beginning of this section, the IMCOP system refers to the general modern idea of intelligent discovering and sharing the multimedia objects of different content forms. It can be seen as a combination of content discovery and data enrichment platforms, on the one hand, and content delivery platform on the other.

As a typical content discovery platform, the IMCOP system is capable to utilize user metadata in order to discover an appropriate custom-oriented content which is then delivered to websites, mobile devices and set-top boxes. In this domain, IMCOP aspires to operate as the world's largest content discovery platforms - Outbrain [5] and Taboola [6]. Likewise these both Israeli startups, IMCOP also employs specialized and sophisticated algorithms to select the contents which is best and most relevant to customers' needs within the network. Although IMCOP applies no algorithms that could be categorized as behavioral and personal ones at the moment, it utilizes an assortment of intelligent automated multimedia indexing tools. In that case, IMCOP goes beyond content discovery platform facilities and also works as data enrichment platform. As in many examples of such platforms, its analytics engine can process and enhance social media posts [7], crawl and analyze web data, detect and recognize faces, objects, landmarks and more [8], etc.

Moreover, according to other capabilities of the IMCOP system, it can be also categorized as content delivery platform, just as in the cases of Viddler's Video Tools for Learning & Engagement [9] and IMDb's X-Ray for Movies & TV [10]. In contradistinction to the both aforementioned ones, the IMCOP delivery platform additionally employs automated indexing services, which, in conjunction with IMCOP's capability to find relations between multimedia data, enrich entrusted video sequences by adding information relevant to their content.

Thanks to all these above-mentioned facilities (as well as other ones), the IMCOP system is capable to aggregate, analyze, relate and finally share with a given client (external entity) the multimedia content which is absolutely compliant with his (its) requirements. In the case of DEEP magazines for instance, these requirements (as illustrated in Fig. 1) could include:

- a set of the highest quality and good looking subject (topic) related images of a given actor (or actress),
- relevant descriptive data taken from movies (and actors) oriented internet metadata providers,
- links to movie trailers - in IMDb for example,
- news or other descriptive information about relevant events aggregated from the internet news services,
- tweets or other posts from various social media.

Above requirements are pretty challenging, especially when thousands of different DEEP magazines are going to be generated within hours. Content discovery and enrichment are also the challenge in the case of "reading" Persona fashion magazines. A platform able to rise to this challenge, known as the IMCOP system, is presented in this paper.

Fig. 1. An exemplary screenshot from the DEEP magazine referred to Charlize Theron [3].

2   IMCOP Architecture

The IMCOP system is based on Service-Oriented Architecture (SOA), where logic and presentation layers are separated. It is also a kind of a distributed system, which is spread over several machines, at the moment. These machines are connected to each other by a fast LAN network. Each machine can run any number of IMCOP services, including the main ones:

- Data Aggregation Services (DAS) – crawlers aggregating data from the Web,
- Metadata Enhancement Services (MES) – content discovery and enrichment applications,
- Data Repository Services – software components responsible for reading from (and writing to) Data Repository (DR).

Up to particular requirements, the IMCOP services can be run in heterogeneous environments, e.g. MS Windows and Linux (as well × 32 as × 64) using the virtual machine applications. In other words, there is no need to unify the IMCOP software components. Thanks to the above, they can be easy implemented and integrated with the rest of the system. They can be written and compiled on any platform, e.g. Java, .NET, native C ++, Phyton, etc., and then, used in target Web applications.

An overall architecture of the IMCOP system is depicted in Fig. 2.

At present, the main IMCOP components (services) have been developed in Java as Spring Framework Model–view–controller (MVC) applications. They have been launched inside the Tomcat server containers.

With regard to its co-operation with external entities (clients), the IMCOP system can be seen as a provider of services in the cloud. IMCOP differs however from standard

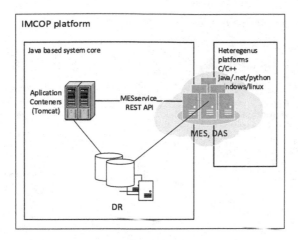

Fig. 2. The overall IMCOP system architecture.

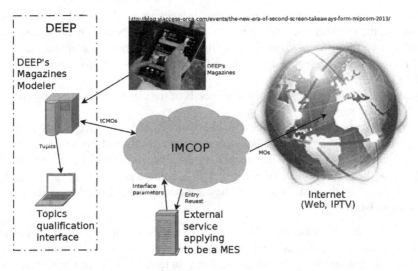

Fig. 3. IMCOP as provider of services in the cloud.

cloud computing models, which are intended in general to run client's applications. IMCOP services are activated (selectively or together) as a result of requests, which express clients' requirements within the framework of desired data. An illustration of IMCOP cloud computing model is depicted in Fig. 3, where the DEEP's Magazine Modeler (a component of the DEEP platform responsible for assembling the magazines referred to a given topic – e.g. Charlize Theron, an actress) requests the IMCOP system for collections of Theron's "red carpet" images, for instance.

Main tasks of the IMCOP Cloud in that case are as follows:

- aggregation of relevant images (in general, multimedia data objects – MOs) from the Internet or from the Data Repository (DR),

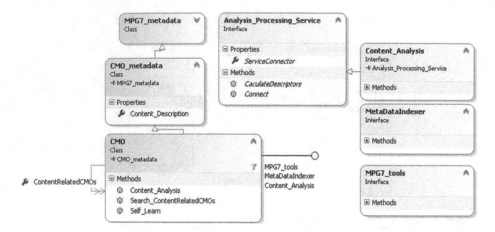

Fig. 4. Model of the complex multimedia object.

- extensive analysis of the content of these images using dedicated MES services, including the external ones (the purpose of this analysis, besides metadata enhancement, can be for instance twofold: to confirm their relevance – e.g. by face detection and recognition MES services, and to verify their quality – e.g. using noise detection MES),
- adjustment of relevant images to suit the needs of the client request (e.g. by cropping or sharpening services),
- generation response to the request in the form of the so called tCMOs objects, containing the best images together with metadata discovered from their content (in fact, client requests and IMCOP responses are exchanged using the same tCMOs objects; at the request stage, the tCMOs objects contain parameters describing client requirements; at the response stage, they are completed with selected images and their metadata).

The tCMOs as well as the MOs objects are kinds of the Complex Multimedia Objects (CMO), which, in turn, are basis structures dedicated to represent any multimedia data in the IMCOP system, despite their content form. In terms of software implementation, Complex Multimedia Object is an instance of the CMO class. Model of the CMO class is depicted in Fig. 4.

Figure 4 shows that the CMO class definition is derived from MPEG-7 standard, especially in the range of Description Schemes and Descriptors. Metadata written down to the CMO objects are however of three different categories. Metadata referred to standard (MPEG-7) Description Schemes include keywords and brief texts aggregated together with MOs from the Internet or entered by the IMCOP users (e.g. during the editing of the selected CMO objects). In turn, metadata referred to Descriptors comprise numerical descriptors generated by various transforms (e.g. SIFT or SURF ones). Metadata of this kind are serialized before they are written down to the CMO object. Serialization takes the place also in the case of metadata of the third category, addressed to represent MOs objects as themselves.

The CMO class definition extends however the MPEG-7 standard in some respects. This extension first of all refers to the so called lists of indices which are also a part of the CMO object representation. Lists of indices are created by services responsible for building relations between objects. Indices in this case, indicate objects which are related to each other in some respects.

3   Services

Main services of the IMCOP system, as has been briefly mentioned in previous Section, have been developed in Java according to the MVC software architectural pattern. They have been also organized with regard to the Representational State Transfer (REST) software architecture style for building scalable web services, known also as the RESTful Web services. In accordance to the above, each IMCOP service is a self-contained application with its own GUI and REST-based interface. Development of IMCOP services is easy and quick owing to specialized libraries which provide API, programming specifications and code examples within SDK for programmers. CMOcore and MEScore are the two the most important libraries of this kind. API for MES services for instance, lets to run them also in remote locations. In that case, they communicate with each other, or with other ones, through the Internet. A typical implementation scheme of IMCOP services is presented in Fig. 5.

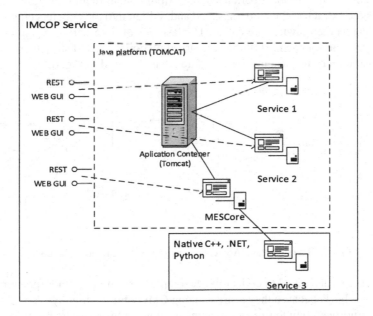

Fig. 5. A typical implementation scheme of IMCOP services.

Services in the IMCOP system can be divided into three main categories listed below:

– Data Aggregation Services (DAS),
– Metadata Enhancement Services (MES),
– specialized MES-based web-services.

Destination as well as tasks of each of above categories of services are described in detail in the following subsections, respectively.

3.1 DAS Services

Data Aggregation Services are designated to download multimedia objects (MOs) from the Internet. Each DAS service is dedicated to only one selected data source. At the moment, there are services dedicated to Wikipedia (MediaWiki) and Wikidata, Flickr, Allocine (a service organization providing information mainly on French cinema), and Twitter. Next ones, dedicated to YouTube, Getty Images and selected news agencies (as Associated Press for instance) are in progress. An extra service, dedicated to collect the data directly from the Data Repository of the IMCOP system, completes the above list of DAS services.

Multimedia data are aggregated by the DAS services in scheduled and triggered manner. In fact, multimedia data are collected not by DAS services directly but by processes which DAS services are able to run and manage. These processes are known also as crawlers. The primary task of DAS services is to receive and parse the tCMO objects to extract the metadata parameters describing client requirements. When these parameters are extracted, they are translated and written into the crawlers configuration files, whereupon the crawlers are called. The last task of DAS services is to create the CMO objects (one for each MOs object returned by crawlers) and store them in DR.

An illustration of the scheme described above is depicted in Fig. 6.

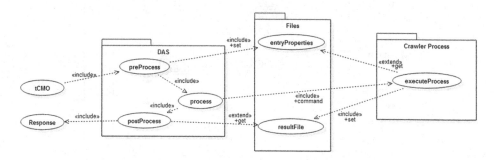

Fig. 6. The way the DAS services aggregate multimedia objects.

DAS services dedicated to collect the data directly from the Data Repository break this scheme. This is because they search among CMO objects directly.

There is no one common model of implementing DAS services. They have to be implemented and configured discretely – adequately to various data source authorization requirements, API, license conditions, protocols used in communication interfaces, etc.

In the case of Allocine service for instance, API has been implemented in C# while data-interchange is based on JSON format only. Flickr's API, in turn, supports many different languages and offers XML(REST), JSON, JSONP and PHP Serial options in which data may be returned. Similar data formats are available also in API for MediaWiki webservice.

3.2 MES Services

There are many different kinds of Metadata Enhancement Services (MES) in the IMCOP system. Majority of them is oriented on content discovery and metadata enhancement. MES Services of this kind are dedicated to perform selected operations from the scope of text and signal (image and video) processing. Text processing operations include mainly text recognition and semantically organized detection of selected keywords and phrases. The list of image and video processing operations is, in turn, much more extensive and includes inter alia:

- image transforms dedicated to detect, extract and describe various types of local features: SIFT, SURF, MSER, Piecewise-linear [11], etc.,
- algorithms dedicated to detect as well as recognize monuments, faces, bodies, skyline, nudity, etc. and e.g. to compress images (or their subregions) using selected compression schemes [12],
- procedures designed to measure the similarity between two or more images as well as evaluate selected image and video quality metrics: noise, blur, blockiness, slicing, etc. (acquired from [13, 14]),
- algorithms designated to analyze and classify faces according to various face quality traits, e.g. profile, presence of red eye, smile and facial hair (to identify Unshaved faces), etc.

MES services are components of a self-contained cloud known as Analysis and Processing Services (APS) cloud. Their activities within the APS cloud are managed by an APS manager service. The APS manager determines and schedules the manners in which particular CMO objects are interchanged and processed within the APS cloud and exchanged with remaining parts of the IMCOP system. Diagram of interactions occurring between particular IMCOP components (APS cloud, DR, DAS) and hypothetical client (the DEEP's Magazines Modeler) is depicted in Fig. 7. The flow of particular objects within the system is illustrated using arrows with different colors. Black arrows show where (between which IMCOP components) the tCMOs objects are interchanged. Gray ones picture the flow of the CMO objects. A blue one, in turn, shows where the MOs objects are passed.

MES services, as the DAS ones, are capable to run and manage other, external processes. From this perspective, MES services (as the DAS ones) are responsible for receiving and parsing the CMO objects and running the processes which, in turn, perform dedicated content discovery and metadata enhancement tasks. An activity diagram depicted in Fig. 8 shows how tasks are performed by a given MES service.

MES services are implemented on the basis of MEScore library, which is a part of the IMCOP API. MEScore library includes specifications for object classes, variables, calls, etc., needed to create and run new MES services.

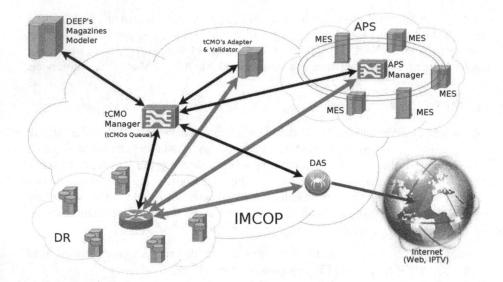

Fig. 7. Diagram of interactions occurring between particular IMCOP components.

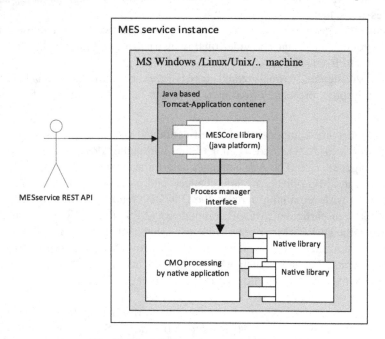

Fig. 8. The MES service activity diagram.

3.3 Specialized Services

The third category of IMCOP services has been distinguished according to specific and very specialized tasks to which they have been designated. In fact, implementation of these services is based on MEScore library, as in the case of other MES services described in previous sub-section. They also perform their tasks as the typical MES services do. However, they are not oriented on content discovery and metadata enhancement. With regard to their tasks, these specialized services can be categorized as follows:

- IMCOP Manager,
- Data Repository Services (DRS),
- Relations Building Services (RBS),
- Watermark Retrieval and Embedding Services (WRES).

In some sense, the IMCOP Manager is a primary group of IMCOP services. This is because they control the flow of CMO objects inside the system. They decide also which MES services, and in which order, participate in a given CMO object processing. The tCMOs Manager service (shown in Fig. 7) is an exemplary instance of the IMCOP Manager. In particular, the tCMOs Manager is responsible for receiving tCMOs objects from clients and then for their management within a framework of tCMOs Queue.

The DRS services are responsible for communication with the Data Repository. They take over the read, write and search requests directed to the repository and serve them. The task of the RBS services is to look for and build relations between objects in the ICMOP system. Relations are built according to descriptive metadata including keywords and brief texts as well as selected numerical metadata. The latter category of metadata includes at the moment local feature descriptors and similarity. Local feature descriptors are used to relate objects with regard to its content, e.g. to connect to each other pictures with Eiffel Tower, trees, the same models of cars [15], etc. Similarity in turn, is used to associate objects (images for instance) which are similar in the context of similarity measure. An exemplary scenario of building relations between objects according to the similarity measure is depicted in Fig. 9.

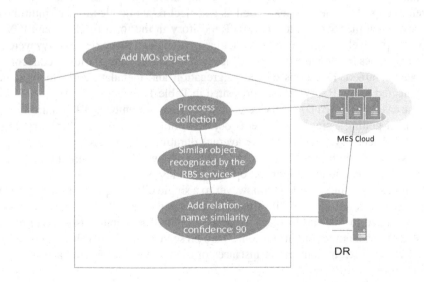

Fig. 9. A scenario of building relations according to the similarity measure.

The last group of Watermark Retrieval and Embedding Services (WRES) is designated in turn to embed as well as retrieve metadata which, in general, are hidden in multimedia data to protect them against forbidden use and manipulation. In this way, multimedia data, which have been taken for instance from licensed data sources (e.g. from Getty Images), are protected from being shared with unauthorized client. On the other hand, they are also protected in this way from being for example cropped or resized by the IMCOP services when their license doesn't allow that.

4   System Performance

The IMCOP system has to be capable to serve to a large number of clients. As each client may request for many multimedia objects of different content forms, scalability was the major challenge facing the IMCOP designers and developers. Although some of the algorithms incorporated by IMCOP services, e.g. MES services responsible for face and object detection and recognition, are computationally highly expensive, the IMCOP facilities to replicate services and to apply parallel processing in this way ensure that the IMCOP objectives can be put into practice.

Results of two tests are presented below to confirm that the IMCOP system is scalable. In both cases, the IMCOP system has been examined with regard to the DEEP platform's requirements within the framework of typical DEEP magazine preparation. In general, the IMCOP system has been obligated to receive the client request (e.g. a DEEP's Magazine Modeler request in that case), aggregate relevant multimedia data (MOs) of different content forms (mainly the text, still images and movies) and process these data to discover their content and enrich related metadata. Next, the aggregated data have been filtered (according to the noise and blur factors for instance) to return only quality multimedia data collections and only these ones which are truly relevant. The remaining data, one by one, as well as a subject related collections of multimedia data, have been then written to the Data Repository in the form of CMO and tCMOs objects, respectively. A given actor (or actress), movie and place (e.g. a city) were the exemplary topics for which the above subject related collections of multimedia content have been returned. Durations of data aggregation and metadata enrichment stages, using selected IMCOP services, are presented in Table 1.

In the case of selected DAS services, lengths of time presented in Table 1 are average durations of getting a single multimedia object within a given topics' category. In the case of MES services in turn, these are average durations of processing a single object, regardless of to which topic it refers. As Table 1 shows, the total time taken by data aggregation and metadata enrichment operations is less than 50 s.

Durations given in Table 1 refer however to a single client request (for a single actor for instance). Average durations (in minutes) referred to the case where the IMCOP system has been forced to respond to many requests submitted simultaneously (precisely, 50 request at the same time for various topics) are presented in turn in Table 2. There have been however different numbers of instances of each service configured and run in the system before examination.

Table 1. The IMCOP system performance with regard to a single client request.

Service task (Service category)	Average duration [s]
Aggregate multimedia data from Wikidata (DAS) for given actors I movies I places	3.87 I 5.96 I 10.53
Aggregate multimedia data from Allocine (DAS) for given actors I movies I places	3.87 I 5.96 I 10.53
Aggregate multimedia data from Flickr (DAS) for given actors I movies I places	1.10 I 1.56 I 1.30
Search for a given image in DR (MES)	0.4
Detect if there is a logo on an image (MES)	1.0
Detect faces on an image or video frame (MES)	1.2
Detect and recognize texts on an image or video frame (MES)	1.0
Write data into the data repository (MES)	0.5

Table 2. System performance with regard to different number of instances of IMCOP services.

The number of copies of services	Average duration [min]
Only single instances of services have been run	15
Each service has been duplicated before run	9
Each service has been tripled before run	6
Four instances for each service have been run	3
Five instances for each service have been run	1.5

Results presented in Table 2 show that the IMCOP system's average response time decreases significantly, when the number of instances of services grows. This confirms that the service-oriented architecture followed in the IMCOP system is able to match the above requirements with regard to its performance. The IMCOP system is also able to match the clients' needs according to accuracy aspects related to particular MES services. This latter issue however has not been covered by this paper.

The third reported test has been performed to verify if and how the results presented in Tables 1 and 2 are dependent on the data transfer rate of the customer line. The test consisted in aggregation of images (where the medium image size was about 80 kB) and then writing them directly to the Data Repository in the form of relevant CMO objects - no MES services have been involved. Times required to complete these tasks in various transfer rate conditions are presented in Table 3.

Table 3. Times required to fulfill the third test scenario in various transfer rate conditions.

Network type and its bandwidth	Average duration [s] with regard to the number of collected and stored images		
	100	500	1000
LAN – 100 Mbps	0.93	0.97	0.91
WAN – 20 Mbps	1.45	1.89	1.76
WAN – 1.5 Mbps	10.50	13.23	11.60

Results obtained during the third examination demonstrate that the network bandwidth has no significant impact on the IMCOP system performance when its range is from 20 Mbps to 100 Mbps (the main IMCOP components have been designated to operate in 100 Mbps LAN environment). However, when the data transfer rate of the customer line is strongly limited (up to 1.5 Mbps for instance), average durations required to accomplish tasks of the third test rise notably (more than 10 times).

5 Conclusions and Future Work

Overview of the IMCOP system architecture which is an outcome of the second joint Polish-Israeli R&D project titled "Intelligent Multimedia System for Web and IPTV Archiving. Digital Analysis and Documentation of Multimedia Content" [1] has been presented in the paper. IMCOP is a service-oriented architecture, with a huge number of differentially designated web services, which refers in general to modern vision of intelligent discovering and sharing the multimedia content using the Internet. In particular, the IMCOP system has been designed to aggregate, analyze and interrelate various multimedia content (represented mainly by text and still images and movies) to finally make them accessible for external entities (applications, end-users, other systems, etc.) as a subject related collections of multimedia.

Main advantages of the IMCOP system are listed below:

- versatility – the ICMOP system is capable to respond to various demands requested by different types of clients, including for instance the DEEP magazines and other custom-oriented content discovery and metadata enrichment platforms, dynamically created on-line multimedia presentations for schools, museums or business, etc.,
- flexibility – there is no need to build different IMCOP applications to put into practice above-mentioned versatility – it is just enough to create another instances of the ICMOP system with different configurations (only the specialized custom-related DAS services have to be extra implemented in that case)
- scalability – as shown in Sect. 4, the IMCOP system, due to its facilities to integrate external services as well as increase (via replication) the number of services being used, is capable to handle a growing amount of client requests.

Regardless of the above-mentioned IMCOP abilities to replicate services, we are going to improve the system by applying the true parallel processing model as well as by optimizing the core IMCOP services. Field tests with potential end users in order to indicate any other imperfections of the IMCOP system are also planned.

Acknowledgements. This work was supported by The Polish National Centre for Research and Development (NCBR), as a part of the EUREKA Project no. E! II/PL-IL/10/01A/2012.

References

1. http://research.wstkt.pl/?page_id=27. Accessed on 10 August 2015
2. Eshkol, A., Grega, M., Leszczuk, M., Weintraub, O.: Practical application of near duplicate detection for image database. In: Dziech, A., Czyżewski, A. (eds.) MCSS 2014. CCIS, vol. 429, pp. 73–82. Springer, Heidelberg (2014)
3. http://www.deepmagazines.com/. Accessed on 10 August 2015
4. http://www.viaccess-orca.com/resource-center/white-papers/462-going-deep-into-discovery.html. Accessed on 10 August 2015
5. http://www.outbrain.com/. Accessed on 10 August 2015
6. http://taboola.com/. Accessed on 10 August 2015
7. http://datasift.com/platform/data-enrichments/. Accessed on 10 August 2015
8. https://rekognition.com/. Accessed on 10 August 2015
9. http://www.viddler.com/. Accessed on 10 August 2015
10. http://www.imdb.com/x-ray/. Accessed on 10 August 2015
11. Baran, R., Wiraszka, D., Dziech W.: Scalar quantization in the PWL transform spectrum domain. In: Proceedings of the International Conference on Mathematical Methods in Electromagnetic Theory, pp. 218–221 (2000). http://dx.doi.org/10.1109/MMET.2000.888560
12. Slusarczyk, P., Baran, R.: Piecewise-linear subband coding scheme for fast image decomposition. Multimedia Tools Appl. (2014). doi:10.1007/s11042-014-2173-1
13. Cerqueira, E., Janowski, L., Leszczuk, M., Papir, Z., Romaniak, P.: Video artifacts assessment for live mobile streaming applications. In: Mauthe, A., Zeadally, S., Cerqueira, E., Curado, M. (eds.) FMN 2009. LNCS, vol. 5630, pp. 242–247. Springer, Heidelberg (2009)
14. Romaniak, P., Janowski, L., Leszczuk, M., Papir, Z.: Perceptual quality assessment for H. 264/AVC compression. In: Proceedings of Consumer Communications and Networking Conference (CCNC), pp. 597–602 (2012). http://dx.doi.org/10.1109/CCNC.2012.6181021
15. Baran, R., Glowacz, A., Matiolanski, A.: The efficient real-and non-real-time make and model recognition of cars. Multimedia Tools Appl. **74**(12), 4269–4288 (2013). http://dx.doi.org/10.1007/s11042-013-1545-2

Detection of Lip Synchronization Artifacts

Ignacio Blanco Fernández[1](✉) and Mikołaj Leszczuk[2]

[1] Department of Telecommunications, Polytechnic School of Engineering of Gijón,
Gijón, Spain
gncblncfrnndz@gmail.com
[2] Department of Telecommunications, AGH University of Science and Technology,
Al. Mickiewicza 30, 30059 Kraków, Poland
vq@kt.agh.edu.pl
http://vq.kt.agh.edu.pl/

Abstract. Over 10 billion hours of video are watched each month on the Internet, what, together with high definition television broadcasting and the rise in high quality video on demand makes the task of quality assessment a key one in the global multimedia market nowadays. Automating quality checking is currently based on finding major audiovisual artifacts. The Monitoring Of Audio Visual quality by key Indicators (MOAVI) subgroup of the Video Quality Experts Group (VQEG) is an open collaborative project for developing No-Reference models for monitoring audiovisual service quality. The purpose of this paper is to report the development of the audiovisual part of this project, which includes the detection of lip synchronization (also known as lip sync) artifacts.

Keywords: MOAVI · VQEG · Lip sync

1 Introduction

Automating quality checking is currently based on finding major video and audio artifacts. The Monitoring Of Audio Visual quality by key Indicators (MOAVI) subgroup of the Video Quality Experts Group (VQEG) is an open collaborative project for developing No-Reference (NR) models for monitoring audiovisual service quality. MOAVI is a complementary, industry-driven alternative to Quality of Experience (QoE), used as a subjective measure of a viewer's experiences.

Current NR QoE models, like the reported in related research work [11], followed the less useful Full-Reference (FR) models (e.g. [4]), address measuring quality of networked multimedia, using objective parametric models. Still, these models might have slight problems in predicting overall audiovisual QoE. MOAVI can be used alternatively to automatically measure audiovisual quality by using simple indicators of perceived degradation.

The goal of the project is to develop a set of key indicators (including blockiness, blur, freeze/jerkiness effects, block missing errors, slice video stripe errors, aspect ratio problems, field order problems, interlace, lip synchronization, also known as lip sync, mute, and clipping [2]) describing service quality in general

© Springer International Publishing Switzerland 2015
A. Dziech et al. (Eds.): MCSS 2015, CCIS 566, pp. 18–33, 2015.
DOI: 10.1007/978-3-319-26404-2_2

(the list is not closed, but the major artifacts are presented), and to select subsets for each potential application. Therefore, the MOAVI project concentrates on models based on key indicators contrary to models predicting overall quality.

The video signal needs some signal processing to be performed on. Quality checking can be conducted before, during, and/or after the encoding process. However, in MOAVI, no Mean Opinion Score (MOS) is provided. A binary indicator for each artifact is provided instead showing its presence or absence.

Figure 1 shows the concept of MOAVI. The audio or video stream (only video for video artifacts, only audio for audio artifacts, and both of them together if the artifact is an audiovisual one) is the input to the system. The metric of each artifact is used to determine the level of impairment that the media to be analyzed suffers. These results are converted into binary indicators using a threshold that would determine if the artifact is in a noticeable level in the video or if it is not. In that way, MOAVI obtains a key indicator for each artifact.

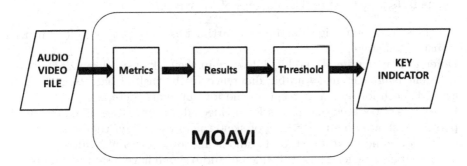

Fig. 1. Concept of monitoring of audiovisual quality

This paper is organized as follows. Section 2 describes measuring the key audiovisual indicator – presence of lip sync. Section 3 presents the video database for the assessment of the metrics. Sections 4–6 describe the algorithms and the obtained results. Section 7 concludes the paper and summarizes the results.

2   Measuring Lip Sync Artifact

In the present research the process followed for the detection of audiovisual artifacts is exposed. Therefore, this paper includes the description of both the algorithm, implementation and results of three different metrics. These metrics were developed to indicate the presence or the absence of the most frequent audiovisual problem affecting an audiovisual signal, which is lip sync problem.

Lip sync is a key parameter in interactive communication. In the case of video conferencing, streaming and television broadcasting, the uneven delay between audio and video should remain below certain thresholds, recommended by several standardization bodies. However, further research has shown that the thresholds can be relaxed, depending on the targeted application and use case [9].

In multimedia systems, synchronization is needed to ensure a temporal ordering of events. For single data streams, a stream consists of consecutive Logical Data Units (LDU). In the case of an audio stream, LDU are individual samples or blocks of samples transferred together from a source to one or more sinks. Similarly with video, one LDU may typically correspond to a single video frame and consecutive LDU – to a series of frames. These have to be presented at the sink with the same temporal relationship as they were captured giving so called "intra-stream". The temporal ordering must also be applied to related data streams, where one of the more common relationships is the simultaneous playback of audio and video with lip sync. Both media must be "in sync", otherwise the result will not be adjudged as satisfactory.

In general, "inter-stream" synchronization involves relationships between all kinds of media including pointers, graphics, images, animation, text, audio and video. In the following discussion, "synchronization" always refers to "inter-stream" synchronization between video and audio.

Some facts about the problem of lack of lip sync:

- The most common origin for lip sync artifact is the jitter produced in the transmission stage.
- Different languages make no big difference in the task of synchronizing media.
- Different languages make no big difference in the task of detecting lip sync artifact, both for human perception and for automatic detection.
- In [10] it is also stated that professional video editors and TV-related technical personnel showed a smaller level of skew tolerance. When they detected an error they could correctly state if audio is ahead of or behind video.
- Watermarks or fingerprints embedded in audio signal have been used in broadcasts to avoid this problem. However this fingerprints are not suitable for multimedia streaming through the internet.

Regarding detection thresholds, [9] refers to the large amount of different ones that authors have determined. Some authors and research groups have concluded that audio may be played up to 305 ms ahead of video and conversely video displayed up to 190 ms ahead of the audio. Both temporal skews are noticed, but can be accepted by the user without any significant loss of effect. Some authors however report a tolerance of only 4–16 ms to be acceptable.

Figure 2 shows a graphical representation of the different audio/video delay and lip sync thresholds of detectability as identified by several standard bodies and already conducted research by independent studies. The thresholds used for the metric of lip sync artifact in MOAVI are set to 100 ms when audio is delayed with respect to video and 140 ms when video is delayed versus audio. These thresholds are based on the research work we refer here [10].

3 Video Database for Assessment of Metrics

The development of experiments with the objective of analyzing the behavior and measuring the accuracy of the different metrics in this section requires the

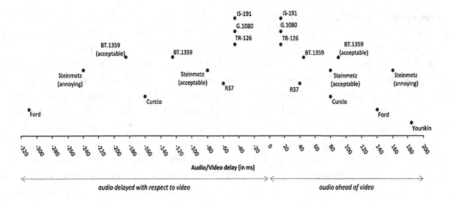

Fig. 2. Different audio/video delay and lip sync thresholds of detectability

storage of a small database of videos and some key information about them. It is a set of 15 video sequences with lengths between 13 and 37 s, coming from all kinds of media. The videos are all taken from frontal view, although some of them include several frames in which there is a profile view. Usually only the face and the shoulders are visible. Finally, only one person is seen and listened to in each video.

Some of the sources of videos are TV news shows, others come from interviews. A small group of them are videos uploaded directly to the internet.

Table 1. Characteristics of the video database for the assessment of the metrics

Video	Length (s)	View	Visible	Movement
ABERCROMBIE	19,8	FRONTAL	HALF BODY	MEDIUM
ANGIE	21,6	FRONTAL	SHOULDERS	LOW
AYALA	13,9	FRONTAL	SHOULDERS	LOW
BECKHAM	18,2	FRONTAL	SHOULDERS	LOW
DICAPRIO	18,3	FRONTAL	HALF BODY	HIGH
FOXNEWS	14,3	FRONTAL	SHOULDERS	LOW
GOOGLE	27,7	FRONTAL	SHOULDERS	LOW
HAYS	25,4	FRONTAL	SHOULDERS	MEDIUM
LARRYPAGE	24,4	FRONTAL	HEAD	LOW
LISA	26,2	FRONTAL	HEAD	MEDIUM
MORRIS	24,1	FRONTAL	SHOULDERS	LOW
RESUME	25,3	FRONTAL	SHOULDERS	MEDIUM
STOSSEL	22,2	FRONTAL	HALF BODY	LOW
USAJOBS	17,9	FRONTAL	SHOULDERS	LOW
USAJOBS2	19,9	FRONTAL	SHOULDERS	LOW

The most important characteristics of each of the videos are shown in Table 1. The audio files extracted from the videos have been stored and analyzed too, in order to use them for the tests of Voice Activity Detection (VAD).

MOAVI's indicator for lip sync is based on the lip sync metric that is explained in the next sections. In the first of the sections, the audio part of the metric is explained. Signal processing used to implement a VAD algorithm is described in this first section. In the second section, the part of the metric regarding video is exposed. The combination of techniques used to detect the movement of the lips are explained. In the third and last section, the algorithm that compares the audio and visual information between each other is described. Every section includes a results subsection and a further research subsection too that will complete the approach to the method developed to detect the delay between a visual media and an audio media.

4   Voice Activity Detector

Developing an indicator that analyzes if the audio and the video is synchronized is a challenging goal. Nevertheless, if the process is divided into small parts, it is simplified. Therefore, the first algorithm to develop is a VAD.

4.1   Algorithm

In lip sync, processing the signal in utterances consisting of speech, silence, and other background noise is needed. The detection of the presence of speech embedded in various types of non-speech events and background noise is called endpoint detection, voice detection, or VAD.

The VAD algorithm consists on basically two steps. The algorithm for the detection of voice is represented in Fig. 3. The two detectors are used complementarily to obtain better results than applying just one of them.

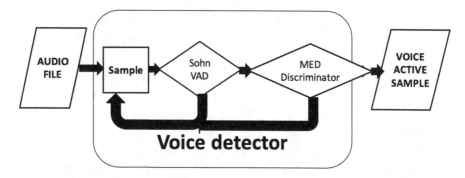

Fig. 3. Algorithm for the detection of speech instants artifact

The first step is the signal processing leading to detect the endpoints of the voice in the audio. An algorithm based on [8] was developed in MATLAB.

The second step is the analysis of the Minimum Energy Density (MED) feature which is a key distinction between music and similar waveforms and speech waveforms. The algorithm is described in the related research work [5] and based on that algorithm, the MATLAB code has been completed.

In [8], a VAD for variable rate speech coding is decomposed into two parts, a decision rule and a background noise statistic estimator, which are analyzed separately by applying a statistical model. A robust decision rule is derived from the generalized likelihood ratio test by assuming that the noise statistics are known a priori. To estimate the time-varying noise statistics, allowing for the occasional presence of the speech signal, a novel noise spectrum adaptation algorithm using the soft decision information of the proposed decision rule is developed. The algorithm is robust, especially for the time-varying noise.

In [5], MED is used in discrimination of audio signals between speech and music. This method is based on the analysis of local energy for local subsequences of audio signals. The subsequences in the proposed method will be the ones in which voice activity has been detected in the first detector. An elementary analysis of the probability density for the power distribution in these subsequences is an effective tool supporting the decision making. It is very intuitive to try to discriminate speech and music based on shape of signal's energy envelope. As Fig. 4 shows, speech signal has characteristic high and low amplitude parts,

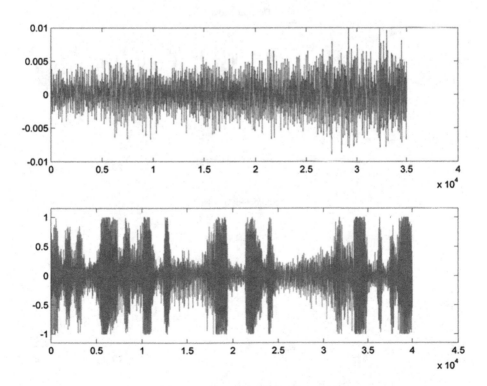

Fig. 4. Comparison between a music waveform (up) and a speech waveform (down)

which represent voiced and unvoiced speech, respectively. On the other hand, the envelope of music signal is more steady. Moreover, it's known that speech has a characteristic 4 Hz energy modulation, which matches the syllabic rate.

Considering these characteristics, a decision is taken to discriminate between speech and music subsequences using for that issue the probability density function of short time frame energy inside some time window, which we refer to as a normalization window. The window has to be long enough to capture the nature of the signal. The value of the length of the window chosen is 200 ms, when the subsequence of speech after the first discriminator is longer than that value.

As it has been explained, these two algorithms work together to make the resulting combination more robust and to improve the accuracy of the metric in order to provide a better information which will be later compared with information coming from video, and finally will provide a lip sync artifact indicator.

4.2 Results

Regarding the results of the developed VAD for MOAVI, the output of the metric would be like the one presented in Fig. 5. As it can be seen, the metric provides an accurate classification of samples. Every subsequence of 50 ms is

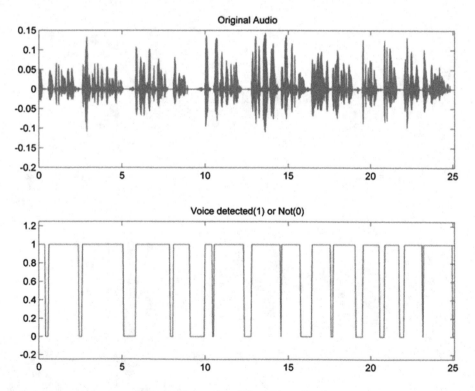

Fig. 5. Example of detection of voice

classified into two different values: voiced (1) or unvoiced (0). Thus, a binary vector is constructed to be compared with the information coming for video about endpoints of speech. The final goal would be the calculation of the delay that one of the signals may have with respect to the other. The binary vector coming from the VAD metric described above is stored.

These results have been compared with the ground truth prepared by listening to the 15 audio files and developing a small database for each sound in which every instant is classified between voiced or unvoiced with a precision of 50 ms. Table 2 shows the Hamming distance, the precision, the accuracy and the F1 metric for each of the video files stored.

Table 2. Accuracy results of the VAD algorithm in each video from the database

Audio	Hamming Distance	Precision	Accuracy	F1 Metric
ABERCROMBIE	4	0.98	0.98	0.99
ANGIE	33	0.82	0.85	0.90
AYALA	14	0.96	0.90	0.94
BECKHAM	28	0.91	0.85	0.91
DICAPRIO	24	0.96	0.87	0.92
FOXNEWS	6	0.96	0.96	0.98
GOOGLE	32	1.00	0.88	0.93
HAYS	14	0.97	0.94	0.97
LARRYPAGE	22	0.95	0.91	0.95
LISA	15	0.94	0.94	0.97
MORRIS	4	0.98	0.98	0.99
RESUME	22	0.94	0.91	0.95
STOSSEL	8	0.99	0.96	0.98
USAJOBS	16	0.96	0.91	0.94
USAJOBS2	7	0.97	0.97	0.98

Table 3 shows the same parameters describing the performance of the metric as the Table 2, but this time the data shows the results for all the videos together. It has to be highlighted that the VAD algorithm has an accuracy of 92.17 % and an F1 metric of 95.47 % regarding the measurements made based on the database.

Table 3. Accuracy results of the VAD algorithm in the whole video database

Total Frames	Hamming Distance	Precision	Accuracy	F1 Metric
3182	249	0.95	0.92	0.95

5 Lip Activity Detector

This section exposes the sub-metric of the lip sync metric based on video analysis. The combination of techniques detecting the frames with lip motion is explained.

5.1 Algorithm

In this research the video metrics are developed in OpenCV, a cross-platform library of programming functions mainly aimed at real-time computer vision.

The reason to use an OpenCV implementation is the easy and fast implementation, the fast execution of high level metrics based on optimization for multi-core systems and the advance vision research by providing not only open but also optimized code for basic vision infrastructure.

The algorithm to track and detect lips activity in this environment is explained in Fig. 6. It can be observed that for every frame, the algorithm classifies it into two different groups, e.g. frames in which the lips are moving and frames in which they are not. The block diagram represents the following algorithm:

- From the video file to analyze, the next frame is read. In case it is the first one, two frames have to be read.
- In that frame, a Haar cascade is used for the detection of the mouth region based on OpenCV implementation of Viola and Jones algorithm for face detection. The Viola and Jones object detection framework is the first object detection framework to provide competitive object detection rates in real-time. It was proposed in 2001 by Viola and Jones [12]. Although it can be trained to detect a variety of object classes [1,6], like for the mouth region in this algorithm, it was motivated primarily by the problem of face detection. The mouth region will be our Region Of Interest (ROI).
- In the ROI of the frame, we measure the motion that has appeared between the previous frame and the new one. The algorithm for estimating the amount of motion will be explained in detail in the next figure.

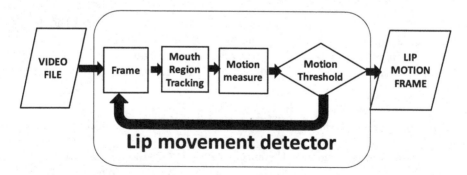

Fig. 6. Algorithm for the detection of lip movement

- A motion threshold will be compared with the calculated motion to determine if the output of the metric is lip-active. This threshold has been optimized for the final output of the metric, which is the audiovisual delay.
- The first of the two frames is released and the last frame read is used to compare with the next one, until we reach the end of the video file.

Figure 6 describes the algorithm in general. However, the key block for the detection of lip movement is the one named "motion measure". Figure 7 explain in more detail the process carried out to determine the amount of movement between two frames in the mouth ROI. The algorithm is described here:

- The inputs of the block are two consecutive frames in which the mouth region has been located.
- The optical flow between them is calculated. The implementation is based on the algorithm exposed in the related research work carried out by Farneback [3]. Optical flow estimates the quantity and direction of the motion in every corresponding point of the two consecutive frames the algorithm receives
- Once the direction and intensity of motion is estimated, the next step is to discriminate between movement of all the face and movement of the lip region independently. This has been achieved by the calculation of the edges of the optical flow output. This stands for knowing the laplacian of the motion field, and analyzing the borders. If the border is in the mouth ROI, we consider it as an indicator for the independent movement of the lips.
- The last step is to "count" how much edges of the optical flow have been discovered in the mouth region. The number of these edges is strongly correlated with the amount of lip motion in the frame.

The whole information coming from the OpenCV metric is loaded into MATLAB in order to process it and continue with the comparison with the information coming from the audio part. This means only the video part of the lip sync algorithm is implemented in OpenCV. Future plans include the full implementation of the metrics included in this research into C++ and OpenCV.

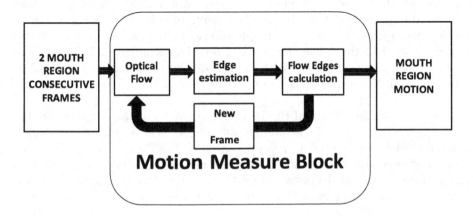

Fig. 7. Detailed block diagram for motion measure

5.2   Results

The output of the algorithm for Lip Activity Detection (LAD) should be a binary vector showing the instants in which the video information analysis provides evidence of lip movement. This binary vector should be compared with the binary vector obtained with the VAD algorithm. The comparison will be carried out using the delay calculation algorithm which will be explained in next section.

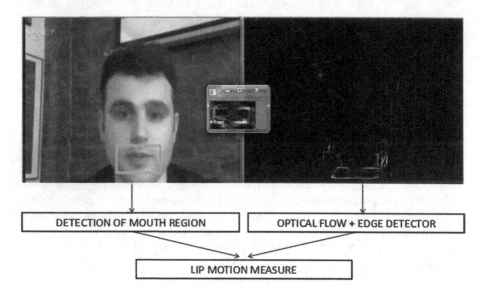

Fig. 8. Graphical output of the LAD algorithm

Being a video metric has the advantage of having the possibility of showing its behavior in an image, something not possible for audio metrics. Figure 8 shows the graphical output for a frame of the LAD metric for MOAVI. It is a frame coming from one of the audiovisual sequence, named "STOSSEL", that is included in the MOAVI database. All elements presented by OpenCV can be seen in this capture. The green rectangle shows the position of the mouth and defines the ROI of the frame. The optical flow is calculated and the edges of its output are drawn in the black and white square on the right. In the middle of the figure, it can be seen the graphical representation of the output of the metric.

In this results subsection of the LAD, some graphs of the outputs that the metrics described above provide are shown. The typical output of the motion measure block is represented in the upper graph of the Fig. 9. The binary vector determined from that information is shown in the graph situated under it. This binary vector, based on the threshold for the amount of motion, indicates which of the frames are considered active in terms of lip movement.

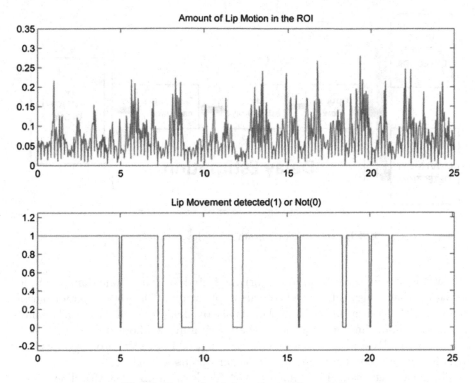

Fig. 9. Example of detection of lip activity

6   Delay Calculation

The goal of the previous algorithms, VAD and LAD, was to provide a binary vector coming from the audio information and another one from the video information. In a second step, they have to be compared with each other to obtain the delay that one of them has with respect with the other. This section explains the algorithm to carry out this comparison and shows the obtained results.

6.1   Algorithm

Some delay estimation algorithms have been implemented in time-domain. For example, the primitive but well-known delay estimation based on cross-correlation method has been tried in this application, without good results. Most advanced time delay estimation algorithms are implemented in frequency-domain; for example the generalized cross-correlation method. The problem that comes out when using frequency domain is the lack of accuracy in the spectral estimation in case of short signal segments. The delay algorithm needed in this synchronization stage will have the goal of estimating the time shift of audio with respect to video, and it must be possible to be used in short audiovisual sequences like the ones stored in the database described above.

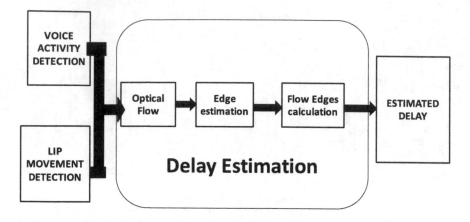

Fig. 10. Block diagram for delay estimation

For this reason, the estimation algorithm found in [7] is a time-domain implementation that satisfies the needs of this application. The proposed information theoretic delay criterion is used. The basis of the proposed algorithm relays in a time-domain implementation of the maximum likelihood method. Usually numerically motivated convergence criteria are used but in the proposed method, statistically motivated convergence criterion was used instead.

The delay algorithm is outlined in the block diagram (Fig. 10). The implementation has been done in MATLAB. The first input of the delay estimator is the binary vector from the VAD. The second input is the binary vector from the LAD. Both vectors are going to have the same length to compare them and to adjust which of the possible delays makes maximum the likelihood between the two signals. The process followed in the present algorithm is described here:

- First, a covariance matrix is constructed based on the possible delays that are assumed. In this metric, the possible delays were set to ± 2 s.
- In a second step, the criterion is build up. The goal is to establish a statistically motivated convergence criterion to make the decision.
- Finally the maximum of the criterion is calculated. The estimated delay will be the shift that corresponds to that maximum.

One of the problems of this method is that it's assumed that the audio activity and the video activity are perfectly synchronized. It's supposed that when a person is talking and the lips are visible, the viewer can see the lips moving only when some sound can be heard.

Obviously, this is not an accurate approach. The first example of lack of audiovisual speech correlation can be the *noisy, unvoiced motion* of the lips, such as smiling, or wetting lips, which are impossible to discriminate using this algorithm, although some differences are accepted and still the estimated delay will be accurate. There is luckily another example of the problems that can be easily corrected. That is the lack of complete synchronization between lip activity and voice activity even when the lip sync artifact has not occurred. It can be observed that lip activity usually starts around 300 ms in average before the voice activity starts to be perceived. This is a stationary delay that can be perfectly corrected just by taking into account this 300 ms in the estimated delay. In the next section, the results show this artificially added gap.

6.2 Results

As it can be seen in the other results sections of the lip sync indicator, the accuracy of the previous metrics is quite high. There are some specific situations in which the VAD method is not able to perfectly discriminate between human speech and other sounds, and the same happens in a few situation in the case of LAD method with lip motion for speaking and other kinds of lip motion.

In these circumstances, it is obvious that the two binary vectors used as inputs for the Delay Estimation Algorithm are not going to be active (value = 1) in the same instants, even if no delay is introduced. This is the reason why the goal of detecting Lip Sync artifact is challenging. On the other hand, this is the reason why an advanced delay estimation algorithm is used and the results of estimating the delay with this algorithm are presented in this subsection.

It is important to understand that, being the Delay Estimation Block the last of the stages for the Lip Sync Artifact Key Indicator Determination, the output of this block is going to be the Key Indicator. Therefore, if the estimated delay is over the thresholds that were determined in previous sections (140 ms), the determined Lip Sync Artifact Key Indicator will be active.

Delays of 0, 300, 500 and 800 ms are artificially introduced to analyze the delays that the metric determines. The absolute error is also calculated. An average gap of 154.8 ms is calculated for the 60 estimations carried out for the experiment. Moreover, in 80 % of the test audiovisual sequences, the binary key indicator is correct. Thus, in the 80 % of the times, this key indicator determines correctly not only if the lip sync artifact is present and the threshold is overcame if the audio is delayed with respect to the video or vice versa.

7 Limitations and Future Research

As limitations, we can list a few main aspects that would be important to improve as further research.

With respect to VAD, some sounds that should not be detected as speech because they appear without any correlation with video information are actually detected as voice active. Examples of this sounds could be speakers that are not visible in the scene (more and more frequent in today's films), background music with voice are not detectable. Further research will include audio signal processing in terms of speaker recognition to discriminate between different speakers.

With respect to LAD, some *noisy* lip movement that should not be detected as speech because they appear without any correlation with audio information are actually detected as lip active. Examples of this lip movements could be people smiling or wetting lips, which are impossible to discriminate using this algorithm. Further research will include video signal processing in terms of speaker recognition to discriminate between different people in the scene.

With respect to Delay Estimator, further research will expect to be capable of detecting both senses of delays, not only audio delayed with respect to video.

Acknowledgments. The work was co-financed by The Polish National Centre for Research and Development (NCBR), as a part of the EUREKA Project №. C 2012/1-5 MITSU.

References

1. Baran, R., Glowacz, A., Matiolanski, A.: The efficient real- and non-real-time make and model recognition of cars. Multimedia Tools Appl. **74**(12), 4269–4288 (2015). http://dx.doi.org/10.1007/s11042-013-1545-2
2. Cerqueira, E., Janowski, L., Leszczuk, M., Papir, Z., Romaniak, P.: Video artifacts assessment for live mobile streaming applications. In: Mauthe, A., Zeadally, S., Cerqueira, E., Curado, M. (eds.) FMN 2009. LNCS, vol. 5630, pp. 242–247. Springer, Heidelberg (2009)
3. Farneback, G.: Very high accuracy velocity estimation using orientation tensors, parametric motion and simultaneous segmentation of motion field. In: Proceedings of the Eighth IEEE International Conference on Computer Vision, Vancouver, Canada (2001)
4. Głowacz, A., Grega, M., Gwiazda, P., Janowski, L., Leszczuk, M., Romaniak, P., Romano, S.: Automated qualitative assessment of multi-modal distortions in digital images based on glz. Ann. Telecommun. - Ann. Telecommun. **65**(12), 3–17 (2010). http://dx.doi.org/10.1007/s12243-009-0146-6
5. Kacprzak, S., Ziółko, M.: Speech/music discrimination via energy density analysis. In: Dediu, A.-H., Martín-Vide, C., Mitkov, R., Truthe, B. (eds.) SLSP 2013. LNCS, vol. 7978, pp. 135–142. Springer, Heidelberg (2013)
6. Leszczuk, M., Baran, R., Skoczylas, L., Rychlik, M., Ślusarczyk, P.: Public transport vehicle detection based on visual information. In: Dziech, A., Czyżewski, A. (eds.) MCSS 2014. CCIS, vol. 429, pp. 16–28. Springer, Heidelberg (2014)
7. Moddemeijer, R.: On the convergence of the iterative solution of the likelihood equations. In: Schouwhamer Immink, K.A. (ed.) Ninth Symposium on Information Theory in the Benelux, May 26-27, 1988, Mierlo (NL), pp. 121-128. Werkgemeenschap Informatie- en Communicatietheorie, Enschede (NL) (1999). ISBN: 90-71048-04-7
8. Sohn, J., Sung, W.: A voice activity detector employing soft decision based noise spectrum adaptation. In: Proceedings of the 1998 IEEE International Conference on Acoustics, Speech and Signal Processing, vol. 1, pp. 365–368, May 1998
9. Staelens, N., De Meulenaere, J., Bleumers, L., Van Wallendael, G., De Cock, J., Geeraert, K., Vercammen, N., Van den Broeck, W., Vermeulen, B., Van de Walle, R., Demeester, P.: Assessing the importance of audio/video synchronization for simultaneous translation of video sequences. Multimedia Syst. **18**(6), 445–457 (2012). http://dx.doi.org/10.1007/s00530-012-0262-4

10. Steinmetz, R.: Human perception of jitter and media synchronization. IEEE J. Sel. Areas Commun. **14**(1), 61–72 (1996)
11. Venkatesh, R., Bopardikar, A.S., Perkis, A., Hillestad, O.I.: No-reference metrics for video streaming applications. In: Proceedings of the 14th International Packet Video Workshop (PV 2004), Irvine, CA, USA, 13–14 December 2004
12. Viola, P., Jones, M.: Robust real-time object detection. Int. J. Comput. Vis. **57**(2), 137–154 (2001)

Image Encryption Using Koblitz's Encoding and New Mapping Method Based on Elliptic Curve Random Number Generator

Omar Reyad[1,2]($\boxtimes$) and Zbigniew Kotulski[1]

[1] Faculty of Electronics and Information Technology, Warsaw University
of Technology, Warsaw, Poland
zkotulsk@tele.pw.edu.pl
[2] Faculty of Science, Sohag University, Sohag, Egypt
ormak4@yahoo.com

Abstract. Elliptic Curve Cryptography (ECC) has attractive advantages compared to other public-key cryptosystems that motivated cryptographers for using it. ECC offers equal security for a smaller key sizes, thereby reducing processing overhead, making it ideal for small devices, key agreement protocols and digital signature applications. Images are data types that occasionally include secret information, such as faces, places and signatures. Encryption scheme is a technique to protect images secrecy by encrypting them before transmission over public networks and unsecured channels. In this paper, we proposed an image encryption scheme which is based on computational operations (Add, Double, Multiply) on points that lie on a predefined elliptic curve (EC). For any ECC-based encryption scheme, converting a message (image pixel) to a coordinate on an affine curve is a mandatory prerequisite. The proposed image encryption scheme utilizes, both, the Koblitz's encoding method and the novel proposed mapping method to convert pixels of a plainimage into coordinates of the predefined EC-points. Then, addition of the resulting points with the points resulting from the Chaos-Driven Elliptic Curve Pseudo-random Number Generator (C-D ECPRNG) is considered for completion of the image encryption process. Discussing Koblitz's encoding method, creating the mapping table, the converting process and the encryption itself are given in detail along with their implementation. Finally, drawing EC-points is done to show changes in the distribution of points in each case.

Keywords: Elliptic curve cryptography · Image encryption · Encoding · Random number generator · Chaotic maps

1 Introduction

Cryptography is a practical means for protecting private and sensitive information. Elliptic curve cryptography (ECC) is a public-key cryptosystem first introduced in 1985 by Miller [1] and Koblitz [2]. Since then, many researchers tried

© Springer International Publishing Switzerland 2015
A. Dziech et al. (Eds.): MCSS 2015, CCIS 566, pp. 34–45, 2015.
DOI: 10.1007/978-3-319-26404-2_3

to employ ECC on different data types and improve it's efficiency by proposing various encryption techniques. The most attractive advantage that motivated cryptographers to use ECC was the well suitability of it in the constrained environments where processing power, storage, bandwidth or power consumption is of primary interest [3]. These characteristics of ECC motivated us to study the potential of using it for image encryption discipline.

Images are those data types that widely used in various areas such as science, engineering, medical, military, art, advertising, education as well as training. The fundamental issue of protecting the confidentiality, integrity as well as authenticity of images through various communication entities has become a major concern especially with the increasing use of digital techniques for transmitting and storing these images. Image encryption is the process of remodeling the plainimage into an incomprehensible one named the cipherimage. In the recent years, various image encryption schemes have been proposed and widely used by several researchers to overcome image encryption problems [4–7]. In this paper, we first encode image pixels by Koblitz's encoding method or using the proposed mapping method to convert the plainimage pixels into coordinates of EC-points before doing the image encryption itself.

Several pseudo-random number generators (PRNG) have been proposed which are using the form of elliptic curves. Since [8] methods, different approaches for extracting pseudo-randomness from elliptic curves have been proposed such as [9–12]. The key sequence generators used in this paper is based on the Chaos-Driven Elliptic Curve Pseudo-random Number Generator (C-D ECPRNG) which uses the Linear Congruential Generator on EC (EC-LCG) presented in [13] with modulation by chaotic maps. The C-D ECPRNG constructions increases randomness of the sequence generated and makes its period (theoretically) infinite since it combines positive properties of both ECPRNG and Chaotic Pseudo-random Number Generators (CPRNG) as discussed in [14].

In this paper, we propose a secure image encryption scheme using EC-points addition applied after the encoding process of the image pixels was done. The encoding (converting image pixel to a point) are done firstly by using the Koblitz's method or the proposed new mapping method. Then, the new encryption scheme completed by addition of the resulting EC-points from the encoding operation with the EC-points resulting from the C-D ECPRNG. The decryption process is done by firstly subtract (inverse addition) the resulting EC-points from the encryption scheme with the EC-points resulting from the C-D ECPRNG. Then, the decoding (converting a point to image pixel) of the resulting EC-points from the decryption process are accomplished by using the Koblitz's method or the proposed new mapping method to obtain the plainimage pixels. The simulation analysis demonstrated that the proposed scheme has large key space and can satisfy the performance requirements for the confidentiality of digital images.

The rest of the paper is organized as follows: In Sect. 2, we presented preliminaries about some related works. Also the description of EC over finite prime field, CPRNG and the C-D ECPRNG constructions, as well as the Koblitz's method for encoding messages are discussed. The proposed schemes for image encryption and decryption are discussed in Sect. 3. In Sect. 4, we discussed the proposed schemes related results while conclusions are given in Sect. 5.

2　Preliminaries

The cryptographic key is a crucial part in most cryptosystems. No matter how strong and how well designed the encryption algorithm might be, if the key is poorly chosen or the key space is too small, the cryptosystem will be easily broken. Due to this principle, additive elliptic curve method modulated by chaotic maps are chosen as a key stream generator because of their properties and easy implementation. In this paper we assume that the elliptic curve E is defined over a finite field $\mathbb{F}_p$ of prime order p which is represented by the elements of the set $[0, 1, ..., p - 1]$.

2.1　Related Works

Recently, several attempts for using ECC in image encryption has been proposed in literature. In [15,16], ECC was used only to encrypt the secret key that was used to encrypt images. The image encryption itself was done using permutation and diffusion [15] or code computing [16]. An image encryption scheme using ECC has been proposed in [17] in which every plainimage pixel is transformed into EC point with (X_m, Y_m) coordinates. In [18] proposed an EC-based key generation based on combination of linear feedback shift register (LFSR) and cyclic EC over a finite prime field. A new mapping method was introduced in [19] to convert a pixel's value to a point on an affine EC using a map table. A new scheme for image encryption based on a cyclic EC and generalized chaotic logistic map has been presented in [20]. In [21], additive and affine encryption schemes using six schemes of key sequences obtained from random EC-points were designed and investigated. Two ECC-based encryption algorithms: selective encryption of the quantised discrete cosine transform (DCT) coefficients and perceptual encryption based on selective bit-plane encryption have been presented in [22]. A secure image encryption scheme using additive EC and chaotic switching mode have been proposed in [23].

2.2　Elliptic Curve over Finite Prime Field

Let E be an elliptic curve over $\mathbb{F}_p$, $p > 3$, given by an affine Weierstrass equation of the form

$$E : y^2 = x^3 + ax + b, \tag{1}$$

where a and b are coefficients belonging to $\mathbb{F}_p$ such that $4a^3 + 27b^2 \neq 0$ (this last condition ensures that E has no singular point over $\mathbb{F}_p$). The set $E(\mathbb{F}_p)$ of $\mathbb{F}_p$-rational points is simply defined as

$$E(\mathbb{F}_p) = \{O\} \cup \{P = (x, y); x, y \in \mathbb{F}_p; y^2 = x^3 + ax + b\}, \tag{2}$$

where O represents the point at infinity. Such an elliptic curve E admits an addition law. Equipped with this addition law, $E(\mathbb{F}_p)$ becomes a finite abelian group, where O is the neutral element.

To encrypt a message, Alice and Bob pick an elliptic curve E and select an affine point $G \in E(\mathbb{F}_p)$. Plaintext m is encoded into a point P_m. Alice choose a random prime integer x and Bob choose a random prime integer y. Alice and Bob's private keys are x and y respectively. To generate the public key, Alice computes $P_A = [x]G$ and Bob computes $P_B = [y]G$. To encrypt a message point P_m for Bob, Alice chooses another random integer k and computes the encrypted message P_C using Bob's public key P_B. Then, P_C is a pair of points given by the following equation:

$$P_C = [((k]G), (P_m + [k]P_B)].\tag{3}$$

Alice sends the encrypted message P_C to Bob. Bob receives the ciphered message and multiplying his private key, y, with $[k]G$ and subtract it from the second point in the encrypted message to compute P_m. The result is the plaintext message m indicated by the following equation:

$$P_m = [(P_m + [k]P_B) - ([yk]G)].\tag{4}$$

Points addition and points doubling are the basic EC operations. Assume that $P_1 = (x_1, y_1)$ and $P_2 = (x_2, y_2)$ are two points of E, then their sum which is $P_3 = (x_3, y_3)$ can be obtained as follows:

$$P_3 = P_1 + P_2 = \begin{cases} O & \text{if } P_1 = -P_2 \\ (x_3, y_3) & \text{if } P_1 \neq -P_2 \end{cases}$$

where (in the latter case)

$$\begin{cases} x_3 = \lambda^2 - x_1 - x_2 \\ y_3 = (x_1 - x_3)\lambda - y_1 \end{cases}$$

with

$$\lambda = \begin{cases} \frac{y_2 - y_1}{x_2 - x_1} & \text{if } x_1 \neq x_2 \\ \frac{3x_1^2 + a}{2y_1} & \text{if } x_1 = x_2 \text{ and } y_1 \neq 0 \end{cases}$$

It turns out that point P_3 belongs to the curve E, and even is an element of $E(\mathbb{F}_p)$ if both P_1 and P_2 are. Recall that the computations of the algebraic quantities above are done (mod p) at each step in practice.

Using this addition law, one can compute, like in any abelian group, any multiple $[k]G$ for any $G \in E(\mathbb{F}_p)$ and any integer k, as follows:

$$[k]G = \begin{cases} \underbrace{G + ... + G}_{k \ times} & if \ k \geq 1 \\ O & if \ k = 0 \\ \underbrace{(-G) + ... + (-G)}_{k \ times} & if \ k \leq -1 \end{cases}$$

Therefore, multiplication on EC requires a scalar multiplication operation $[k]G$, defined for a point $G = (x, y)$ on EC and a positive integer k as k times addition of G to itself. This scalar multiplication can be done by a series of addition and doubling operations of G. The strength of an ECC-based cryptosystem depends on the difficulty of finding the number k of times G is added to itself to get $[k]G$ (P_A). This reverse operation is known as the Elliptic Curve Discrete Logarithm Problem (ECDLP) and is considered the core hardness of ECC [24, 25].

2.3 Chaotic Pseudo-Random Number Generator

Assume that μ is a normalized invariant measure of a dynamical system, equivalent to a Lebesgue measure. The idea of construction of CPRNG is to divide the dynamical system state space S, $\mu(S) = 1$, into two disjoint parts: S_0 corresponds to bit 0, S_1 to bit 1 such that $\mu(S_0) = \mu(S_1) = 1/2$. To obtain a pseudo-random sequence of bits we observe the iterations of the system governed by a measurable map ($\Phi : S \to S$) starting from an initial point $s \subseteq S$ and as a result of these iterations we obtain the infinite sequence of generated bits. Moreover, theoretically the period of such a CPRNG is infinite, since it is iterated over the infinite state space S [26].

In practical applications for constructing CPRNG we assume that $S = [0, 1]$ is the interval, $S_0 = [0, 0.5]$, $S_1 = (0.5, 1]$ are two subsets of the measure equal 0.5 and $\Phi : [0, 1] \to [0, 1]$ is a chaotic map with positive Lyapunov exponent λ. Such generators have good statistical properties under certain conditions [27]. In this paper, we consider chaotic dynamical system governed by the Logistic map [28] to generate the binary sequences defined as:

$$s_{i+1} = \Phi(s_i) = 4 \cdot s_i (1 - s_i), \ i = 0, 1, 2, ... \tag{5}$$

for the state space $S = [0, 1]$ and $S_0 = [0, 0.5]$, $S_1 = (0.5, 1]$.

2.4 Chaos-Driven Elliptic Curve Pseudo-Random Number Generator

For a given point $G \in E(\mathbb{F}_p)$, the C-D ECPRNG is defined as the following sequences generated by additive EC-points operation:

$$U_i = [i(1 + b_i)]G \oplus U_0 = \begin{cases} [i]G \oplus U_0 & if \ b_i = 0 \\ [2i]G \oplus U_0 & if \ b_i = 1 \end{cases}, \ i = 1, 2, ... \tag{6}$$

where $U_0 \in E(\mathbb{F}_p)$ is the "initial value" and b_i is the random bits generated by the chaotic Logistic map Φ

$$b_i = \begin{cases} 0 & if \ \Phi^i(s) \in S_0 \\ 1 & if \ \Phi^i(s) \in S_1 \end{cases}, \ i = 1, 2, ... \quad (7)$$

Using EC-points stream sequence U_i resulted from C-D ECPRNG [14] which given by equation (6), we can encrypt the encoded image pixels as will described later.

2.5   Koblitz's Method for Encoding Messages

The problem of encoding plaintext messages as points on an EC is not as simple as it was in the conventional case. In particular, there is no known polynomial time, deterministic algorithm for writing down points on an arbitrary elliptic curve $E \pmod{p}$. However, there are fast probabilistic methods for finding points, and these can be used for encoding messages. Here is one method, due to Koblitz, described as the following:

Let $E : y^2 = x^3 + ax + b \pmod{p}$ be the elliptic curve. The message m (already represented as a number) will be embedded in the x-coordinate of a point. However, the probability is only about $1/2$ that $m^3 + am + b$ is a square mod p. Therefore, we adjoin a few bits at the end of m and adjust them until we get a number x such that $x^3 + ax + b$ is a square $\pmod{p}$ [29,30].

In detailed, let K (be a large integer so that a failure rate of $1/2^K$ is acceptable when trying to encode a message as a point. Assume that m satisfies $(m + 1)K < p$. The message m will be represented by a number $x = mK + j$, where $0 \le j < K$. For $j = 0, 1, ..., K - 1$, compute $x^3 + ax + b$ and try to calculate the square root of $x^3 + ax + b \pmod{p}$. If there is a square root y, then we take the point $P_m = (x, y)$; otherwise, we increment j by one and try again with the new x. We repeat this until either we find a square root or $j = K$. If j ever equals K, then we fail to map a message to a point. Since $x^3 + ax + b$ is a square approximately half of the time, we have about a $(1/2^K)$ chance of failure. In order to recover the message from the point $P_m = (x, y)$ we simply calculate m by

$$m = [x/K], \quad (8)$$

where $[x/K]$ denotes the greatest integer less than or equal to x/K.

Example 1. Let $p = 179$ and suppose that our elliptic curve is $y^2 = x^3 + 2x + 7$. If we are satisfied with a failure rate of $1/2^{10}$, then we may take $K = 10$. Since we need $mK + K < 179$, we need $0 \le m \le 16$. Suppose our message is $m = 5$. We consider x of the form $mK + j = 50 + j$. The possible choices for x are $50, 51, ..., 59$. For $x = 51$ we get $x^3 + 2x + 7 \equiv 121 \pmod{179}$, and $11^2 \equiv 121 \pmod{179}$. Thus, we represent the message $m = 5$ by the point $P_m = (51, 11)$. The message m can be recovered by $m = [51/10] = 5$.

3   Proposed Image Encryption Scheme

The generated EC-points sequence named C-D ECPRNG discussed in Sect. 2.4 along with the two encoded methods presented here can be used for image encryption process. The two encoded methods for image encryption process using various EC-points sequences are designed and implemented as well as image encrypted is done. As every image consists of pixels, the proposed schemes used 256×256 grayscale Lena image in which each pixel has a 8-bit value of between 0 and 255. The proposed schemes are also applicable to color images in which each pixel represented by 3 octet values indicate the Red, Green and Blue (RGB) with changing the size of p value of the elliptic curve E to represent all image pixel values.

3.1   Koblitz's Method Implementation for Image Pixels Encryption

In Koblitz's method mentioned in Sect. 2.5, for encoding image pixels (each pixel has an 8-bit value of between 0 and 255) the maximum possible value for m is 255. Suppose that value of $K = 40$. Now the minimum value of x is $mK + K < p$ (i.e. $x = 255 * 40 + 40 < 10240$) to represent all pixel values. To get a point on the curve whose x-coordinate is above 10240, we need to select an elliptic curve E with p value not less than 10240. From this, it is clear that depending on the value of K, the curve parameters can be selected. So we consider the following curve parameters for our experiment:

$$E : y^2 = x^3 + x + 4 \tag{9}$$

over $\mathbb{F}_{10247}$, where the order of E is $N = \#E(\mathbb{F}_p) = 10262$.

In Table 1 are presented results of Koblitz's encoding method for Lena image pixels. The first column represent image pixel values as $m = 0, ..., 255$ and the second column shows how x values are encoded according to $x = m * 40 + j$ with $0 \leq j < 40$. In the third column, the EC encoded points are resulted for all image pixels values with successful iteration of j. To encrypt the EC encoded points resulted from Table 1, we utilize EC-points sequence generated from C-D ECPRNG mentioned in Sect. 2.4. In this case, we choose generator point $G = (501, 146)$ and initial value $U_0 = (8, 2419)$ belong to E defined in (9) and the random bits b_i generated from the Logistic map defined in Sect. 2.3 with an initial value $s_0 = 0.6701$.

In Table 2 are shown how the encryption process works and the EC encrypted points obtained. Rows (1,2) represent pixel indexes and the corresponding pixel values respectively. Rows (3,4) represent EC encoded points resulted from Table 1 and EC-points resulted from C-D ECPRNG respectively. The EC encrypted points are presented in row (5).

3.2   The Mapping Method Implementation for Image Pixels Encryption

To encrypt grayscale image with each pixel has an 8-bit value of between 0 and 255 using ECC, we must encrypt 256 numbers. In this case, each pixel should

Table 1. Koblitz's encoding method for Lena image pixels

Pixel value	$x = mK + j$	Encoded point
0	$x = 0$	$(0, 2)$
1	$x = 40$	$(40, 5123)$
2	$x = 80$	$(80, 3342)$
3	$x = 120$	$(120, 3144)$
4	$x = 162$	$(162, 1756)$
5	$x = 200$	$(200, 2792)$
6	$x = 241$	$(241, 4485)$
$\vdots$	$\vdots$	$\vdots$
255	$x = 10202$	$(10202, 5030)$

Table 2. Encryption for Lena image pixels encoded by Koblitz's method

Pixel index	1	2	3	$\cdots$	256×256
Pixel Value	136	136	136	$\cdots$	71
Encoded Point	$(5440, 2256)$	$(5440, 2256)$	$(5440, 2256)$	$\cdots$	$(2842, 2152)$
C-D ECPRNG	$(9584, 8114)$	$(5592, 5499)$	$(9120, 7433)$	$\cdots$	$(8384, 4084)$
Encrypted Point	$(1251, 6895)$	$(7732, 9516)$	$(7643, 1698)$	$\cdots$	$(7769, 3493)$

be considered as a message and mapped to a point on a predefined EC. The mapping method proposed in this paper is based on a map table. To create this table, an elliptic curve E with at least 256 points, which is all possible points on the finite field, is generated first. Then, we find point G of order ℓ equal at least 257 and as close to 257 as possible on E. The order of point G is ℓ, that is we have different points $G, [2]G, [3]G, ..., [k]G$ with $[\ell]G = O$ is infinity point and k is integer. The row indexes start from 0 and end with 255 where each row stands for a pixel intensity value as listed in Table 3.

Starting from the first pixel in the plainimage, the corresponding point with the intensity value in the table is mapped to this pixel and continues to the last pixel. So, we encode image pixels as points of E assigning all pixels to all points as the following:

$$0 \Longrightarrow G, 1 \Longrightarrow [2]G, 2 \Longrightarrow [3]G, 3 \Longrightarrow [4]G, \cdots, 255 \Longrightarrow [256]G. \quad (10)$$

After mapping all pixels to their related points, the next step is to encrypt these points using the stream of EC-points from our C-D ECPRNG by adding the mapped points (encoding pixels) with EC-points from C-D ECPRNG. Finally, we obtain the sequence of EC encrypted points, being iterations of point G. In our experiment, in order to define the implementation process clearly, we used the following EC equation:

$$E : y^2 = x^3 + 4x + 5 \quad (11)$$

over $\mathbb{F}_{1013}$, where the order of E is $N = \#E(\mathbb{F}_p) = 1028$. We also select generator point $G = (502, 23)$ of order $\ell = 257$ for our mapping method.

Table 3. Mapping method for Lena image pixels

Pixel value	$[k]G$	Mapped point
0	$[1]G$	$(502, 23)$
1	$[2]G$	$(930, 850)$
2	$[3]G$	$(683, 174)$
3	$[4]G$	$(681, 281)$
4	$[5]G$	$(471, 33)$
5	$[6]G$	$(116, 408)$
$\vdots$	$\vdots$	$\vdots$
255	$[256]G$	$(502, 990)$

In Table 3 are presented results of the mapping method for Lena image pixels. The first column represent image pixel values as $m = 0, ..., 255$ and the second column shows how x values are mapped according to $[k]G$ with $k = 1, ..., 256$. In the third column, the EC mapped points are resulted for all image pixels values with successful iteration of k. To encrypt the EC mapped points resulted from Table 3, we utilize EC-points sequence generated from C-D ECPRNG. In this case, we choose the same generator point $G = (502, 23)$ and initial value $U_0 = (4, 386)$ belong to E defined in (11) and the random bits b_i generated from the Logistic map defined in Sect. 2.3 with an initial value $s_0 = 0.6701$.

Table 4 showed how the encryption process works and the EC encrypted points obtained. Rows (1,2) represent pixel indexes and the corresponding pixel values respectively. Rows (3,4) represent EC mapped points resulted from Table 3 and EC-points resulted from C-D ECPRNG respectively. The EC encrypted points are presented in row (5).

Table 4. Encryption for Lena image pixels encoded by mapping method

Pixel index	1	2	3	$\cdots$	256×256
Pixel Value	136	136	136	$\cdots$	71
Mapped Point	$(184, 243)$	$(184, 243)$	$(184, 243)$	$\cdots$	$(508, 670)$
C-D ECPRNG	$(220, 766)$	$(97, 873)$	$(111, 407)$	$\cdots$	$(898, 14)$
Encrypted Point	$(516, 449)$	$(28, 828)$	$(605, 231)$	$\cdots$	$(639, 714)$

4   Results and Discussion

It is important to ensure that EC encrypted points obtained in each of the proposed image encryption methods are distributed uniformly on the predefined

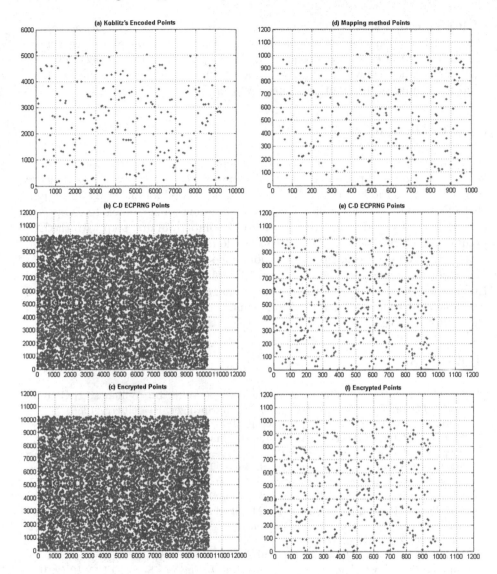

Fig. 1. Resulted EC-points

elliptic curves over a finite field of p elements. Figure 1(a – f) show plotting of the obtained points in each case. The encoded EC-points resulted from Koblitz's method are shown in Fig. 1(a) and EC-points resulted from it's C-D ECPRNG are shown in Fig. 1(b) while the encrypted EC-points resulted in this case are shown in Fig. 1(c). In Fig. 1(d), the mapped EC-points resulted from our mapping method are shown and the EC-points resulted from it's C-D ECPRNG are shown in Fig. 1(e) while the encrypted EC-points resulted in this case are shown in Fig. 1(f).

It is clear that adding EC-points resulted from C-D ECPRNG in each of the proposed image encoded methods improves the distribution of EC encrypted points resulted in each case as shown in Fig. 1(c) and Fig. 1(f) respectively. For each of them it is shown that the resulting EC-points encrypted sequences have good uniformity of distribution properties over E.

5   Conclusions

In this paper, we have presented a new scheme for image encryption based on EC-points addition applied after encoding process of image pixels was done by two encoding methods. Firstly, Koblitz's method is used for encoding image pixels to EC-points or the mapping method for mapping image pixels to EC-points as well. Secondly, addition of the resulted EC-points from first step with the EC-points resulted from the C-D ECPRNG are done to obtain EC-points encrypted sequences. The decryption process is done vice-versa. The two methods implementation was done and the encrypted EC-points was obtained. The obtained EC-points from each step in the proposed image encryption scheme are plotted demonstrated that the encrypted EC-points are uniformly distributed on the used elliptic curves.

References

1. Miller, V.S.: Use of elliptic curves in cryptography. In: Williams, H.C. (ed.) CRYPTO 1985. LNCS, vol. 218, pp. 417–426. Springer, Heidelberg (1986)
2. Koblitz, N.: Elliptic curve cryptosystems. J. Math. Comput. **48**, 203–209 (1987)
3. Gura, N., Patel, A., Wander, A., Eberle, H., Shantz, S.C.: Comparing elliptic curve cryptography and RSA on 8-bit CPUs. In: Joye, M., Quisquater, J.-J. (eds.) CHES 2004. LNCS, vol. 3156, pp. 119–132. Springer, Heidelberg (2004)
4. Gao, T., Chen, Z.: Image encryption based on a new total shuffling algorithm. J. Chaos Solitons and Fractals **38**, 213–220 (2008)
5. Patidar, V., Pareek, N.K., Sud, K.K.: Modified substitution-diffusion image cipher using chaotic standard and logistic maps. J. Commun. Nonlinear Sci. Numer. Simul. **15**, 2755–2765 (2010)
6. Ismail, I.A., Amin, M., Diab, H.: A digital image encryption algorithm based a composition of two chaotic logistic maps. Int. J. Network Secur. **11**, 1–10 (2010)
7. Indrakanti, S.P., Avadhani, P.S.: Permutation based image encryption technique. Int. J. Comput. Appl. **28**, 45–47 (2011)
8. Kaliski, B.S.: One-way permutations on elliptic curves. J. Cryptology **3**, 187–199 (1991)
9. Gong, G., Berson, T.A., Stinson, D.R.: Elliptic curve pseudorandom sequence generators. In: Heys, H.M., Adams, C.M. (eds.) SAC 1999. LNCS, vol. 1758, pp. 34–48. Springer, Heidelberg (2000)
10. Caragiu, M., Johns, R., Gieseler, J.: Quasi-random structures from elliptic curves. J. Algebra Number Theory Appl. **6**, 561–571 (2006)
11. Farashahi, R.R., Schoenmakers, B., Sidorenko, A.: Efficient pseudorandom generators based on the DDH assumption. In: Okamoto, T., Wang, X. (eds.) PKC 2007. LNCS, vol. 4450, pp. 426–441. Springer, Heidelberg (2007)

12. Reyad, O., Kotulski, Z.: On pseudo-random number generators using elliptic curves and chaotic systems. J. Appl. Math. Inf. Sci. **9**, 31–38 (2015)
13. Shparlinski, I.E.: Pseudorandom number generators from elliptic curves. Contemp. Math. Am. Math. Soc. **477**, 121–141 (2009)
14. Reyad, O., Kotulski, Z.: Statistical analysis of the chaos-driven elliptic curve pseudo-random number generators. In: Kotulski, Z., Księżopolski, B., Mazur, K. (eds.) CSS 2014. CCIS, vol. 448, pp. 38–48. Springer, Heidelberg (2014)
15. Gupta, K., Silakari, S.: Efficient hybrid image cryptosystem using ECC and chaotic map. Int. J. Comput. Appl. **29**, 1–13 (2011)
16. Zhao, Z., Zhang, X.: ECC-based image encryption using code computing. In: Yang, G. (ed.) Proceedings of the ICCEAE2012. CCIS, vol. 181, pp. 859–865. Springer, Heidelberg (2013)
17. Gupta, K., Silakari, S., Gupta, R., Khan, S.A.: An ethical way of image encryption using ECC. In: First International Conference on Computational Intelligence, Communication Systems and Networks, pp. 342–345. IEEE, Indore (2009)
18. Maria, S., Muneeswaran, K.: Key generation based on elliptic curve over finite prime field. Int. J. Elect. Sec. Digital Forensics **4**, 65–81 (2012)
19. Soleymani, A., Nordin, M.J., Hoshyar, A.N., Zulkarnain, M.A., Sundararajan, E.: An image encryption scheme based on elliptic curve and a novel mapping method. Int. J. Digital Content Technol. Appl. **7**, 85–94 (2013)
20. El-Latif, A.A.A., Niua, X.: A hybrid chaotic system and cyclic elliptic curve for image encryption. Int. J. Electron. Commun. **67**, 136–143 (2013)
21. Sathyanarayana, S.V., Kumar, M.A., Bhat, K.N.H.: Symmetric key image encryption scheme with key sequences derived from random sequence of cyclic elliptic curve points. Int. J. Netw. Secur. **12**, 137–150 (2011)
22. Tawalbeh, L., Mowafi, M., Aljoby, W.: Use of elliptic curve cryptography for multimedia encryption. IET Inf. Secur. **7**, 67–74 (2013)
23. Reyad, O., Kotulski, Z., Abd-Elhafiez, W.M.: Image encryption using chaos-driven elliptic curve pseudo-random number generators. J. Appl. Math. Inf. Sci. (to appear)
24. Menezes, A.: Elliptic Curve Public Key Cryptosystems. Kluwer Academic, Dordrecht (1993)
25. Silverman, J.H.: The Arithmetic of Elliptic Curves. Springer, New York (2009)
26. Cornfeld, L.P., Fomin, S.V., Sinai, Y.G.: Ergodic Theory. Springer, Berlin (1982)
27. Szczepanski, J., Kotulski, Z.: Pseudorandom number generators based on chaotic dynamical systems. J. Open Syst. Inf. Dyn. **8**, 137–146 (2001)
28. Phatak, S.C., Rao, S.S.: Logistic map: a possible random-number generator. J. Phys. Rev. E **51**, 3670–3678 (1995)
29. Trappe, W., Washington, L.C.: Introduction to Cryptography with Coding Theory. Pearson Education Inc., Upple Saddle River (2006)
30. Padma, B.H., Chandravathi, D., Roja, P.P.: Encoding and decoding of a message in the implementation of elliptic curve cryptography using Koblitz's method. IJCSE **2**, 1904–1907 (2010)

Ranking Based Approach for Noise Handling in Recommender Systems

R. Latha[⊠] and R. Nadarajan

Department of Applied Mathematics and Computational Sciences,
PSG College of Technology, Coimbatore, India
{lathapsg,nadarajan_psg}@yahoo.co.in

Abstract. Collaborative filtering (CF), one of the successful social recommendation approaches, makes use of history of user preferences in order to make predictions. Even though this characteristic of Recommender System has attracted many applications, the quality of recommendations is still inclined by the unreliability of user provided data. In most Recommendation Systems (RS), users are asked to rate items explicitly or their behavior is monitored to collect their preferences. But in the real scenario, users may not provide genuine rating for all items of the data set. A genuine user must be knowing about the highly popular items of the domain. So the proposed approach assigns lesser popularity score to users who are not giving good ratings for highly popular items. Users with a popularity score less than a threshold are identified as noisy users. The experiments are conducted on real world data sets Movielens and Jester. The results claim that the proposed approach is effective in identifying and handling noisy users in the rating database.

Keywords: Collaborative filtering · Popularity · Ranking · Noise

1 Introduction

Recommender Systems [RSs] are software techniques that provide suggestions to support various decision-making processes, such as what items to buy, what music to listen or what news to read, etc. [15].

According to [1], RSs are based on one of the two strategies, namely Content based filtering (CB) and Collaborative filtering (CF). CB creates a profile for each user or product to characterize its nature. The profiles are used to associate users with matching products [14]. An alternative to CB is CF which relies only on past user behavior in the form of previous transactions or product ratings [4]. Collaborative filtering analyzes relationships between users and inter-dependencies among products to identify new user-item associations.

User preferences can be collected in a RS either implicitly or explicitly. In the implicit approach, user behavior, user actions or consumption patterns are observed to infer user preferences. On the other hand explicit feedback gets user preferences in the form of ratings. Even though explicit feedback has some

© Springer International Publishing Switzerland 2015
A. Dziech et al. (Eds.): MCSS 2015, CCIS 566, pp. 46–58, 2015.
DOI: 10.1007/978-3-319-26404-2_4

practical difficulties like user availability, user's mood and user's behavior at different circumstances, it is commonly used since such feedback is thought to be reliable [2]. RSs based on explicit user feedback are built under the assumption that user ratings constitute the ground truth about the users' likes and dislikes.

Basically noisy ratings are introduced in the system in two ways. First, some users may provide random values when they are not really interested in rating items out of boredom. In social network sites the users are interested in playing tricks and as a result noise is introduced in the system. Second, in case of cold start problem, in order to have sufficient rating for user and item vectors, the RS generates random ratings which may result in noise in the system.

Great efforts are being carried out to improve accuracy of predictions, but little attention has been made to analyze noisy ratings. Moreover noise is due to the ratings provided by users unintentionally. So identification of its presence in RS databases becomes a challenging task. It is well understood that prediction accuracy can also be improved by removing noise in the system.

Trust is a major concern for all online systems and applications [12]. As large number of users are allowed to contribute their ratings to RSs towards the preferences of items, accuracy and diversity of predictions would improve a lot but at the same time it gives room for getting unreliable ratings [12]. Since as user preferences are collected in an open manner they are still vulnerable to noise. As CF techniques depend on the data provided by users in the form of tags, reviews and ratings to infer user preferences, the performance of recommendations is susceptible to the truthfulness of user contributed data.

The objective of the paper is

- to assign popularity score to users of the database based on their ratings for popular items
- to identify noisy users and discard them from prediction process in order to improve the quality of predictions

Since noise is introduced unintentionally in the rating database, they do not follow any standard pattern. Therefore it is difficult to model noise ratings. We adopt an approach with an objective to quantify noisiness for each user of the data set. If a user is not aware of popular items of the domain, then he is expected to be a noisy user. At the same time if the user knows only the popular items, then he has no novelty in giving preferences. The popularity score of the user is computed based on both the above aspects. The user profiles with popularity score less than a preset threshold are identified as noisy users and they are discarded from prediction computations. Two real-world recommendation data sets are used to empirically test the proposed approach of noise removal. The experimental results show that the proposed method improves quality of predictions.

The remainder of the paper is organized as follows: Sect. 2 discusses about neighborhood based CF techniques and Sect. 3 reviews the related work available in the literature for noise identification and handling in RS. Section 4 discusses the proposed approach of user noise identification, Sect. 5 discusses about the experimental evaluations and Sect. 6 gives conclusions and possible future extensions.

2   Neighborhood Based CF Techniques

In Collaborative Filtering systems, the prediction is based on a database of past purchases, or ratings made by the system users [14]. The ratings given by users for various items are available in the system. Each rating shows how much an item is liked by a particular user. The task of a CF based recommender system is to predict how much a user likes an item which is currently unrated. The most common form of CF is the neighborhood-based approach (also known as k Nearest Neighbors) [8]. The neighborhood CF techniques can be user based or item based [7]. These kNN techniques identify items that are likely to be rated similarly or like-minded people with similar history of rating or purchasing, in order to predict unknown relationships between users and items. Merits of the neighborhood-based approach are intuitiveness, sparing the need to train and tune many parameters, and the ability to easily explain to the user the reasoning behind a recommendation [3].

Most popularly used neighbourhood method is Item based Collaborative Filtering method [18]. Given a target item, we consider items which share similar ratings with the target item and use those ratings to predict the unknown ratings of target user. Most commonly used metric for calculating similarity between items is adjusted cosine similarity and is formulated as

$$Sim_{i,j} = \frac{\sum_{u \in U(i) \cap U(j)} (r_{u,i} - \bar{r}_u) \times (r_{u,j} - \bar{r}_u)}{\sqrt{\sum_{u \in U(i) \cap U(j)} (r_{u,i} - \bar{r}_u)^2} \times \sqrt{\sum_{u \in U(i) \cap U(j)} (r_{u,j} - \bar{r}_u)^2}} \tag{1}$$

where U(i) is the set of users who rated for item i, $r_{u,i}$ is the rating provided by user u for item i and $\bar{r}_u$ is the average rating of user u. $Sim_{i,j}$ can be between -1 and +1. Predictions can be made based on the weighted average of known ratings as defined in (2)

$$P_{u,i} = \frac{\sum_{j \in S(i)} Sim_{i,j} \times (r_{u,j})}{\sum_{j \in S(i)} Sim_{i,j}} \tag{2}$$

where $P_{u,i}$ is the predicted value of user u and item i and $S(i)$ is the set of top k similar items of item i.

3   Related Work

In [12], O'Mahony et al. classified noise in social recommender systems into two categories:

- Malicious noise, noise introduced into the system intentionally by an attacker to bias the recommendation result
- Natural noise, given by users un-intentionally and can affect recommendation results

In spite of large body of existing work to fight against attacks available in literature for RS, little work is done to identify and handle noisy users. There are not many references available in the literature for noise identification and detection. Even though natural noise has significant effect on quality of predictions, it is less researched till now. Identification of natural noise is more difficult than that of malicious noise as it is generated by different sources. Moreover, natural noisy user profiles do not match any patterns.

In [12], O'Mahony et al. attempted to determine whether an individual rating contains natural noise or is noise-free by measuring the consistency between the observed and predicted rating scores for a test rating. A rating is deemed to represent noise if the mean absolute error (MAE) is greater than a preset threshold.

Herlocker et al. [9] discussed about the noise in user ratings in their review of evaluating methods for RS. [17] projected about the concept of the "magic barrier" which is created by natural variability in ratings. The authors highlighted the significance of analysing the inherent variability in recommender data sets.

Amatriain et al. [2] proposed an approach to capture user rating consistencies from multiple trials. It requires users to rate items in multiple trials (e.g., three times) at different time points, and then measures the rating noise based on the correlation between different trials. This approach has a practical difficulty like user unavailability in getting multiple ratings from users for same items.

Bin Li et al. [10], uses the term 'self contradictions' to mean when a user does not give preference to items which are highly correlated with the item he has rated. i.e., when a genuine user rates an item and does not rate items in the close neighbourhood of that item, then the user is said to make self contradiction with respect to the item. They proposed an approach to capture self contradictions which is modeled as quadratic optimization problem with slack variables.

We propose a novel approach to detect noisy users without needing any additional information. The framework of the proposed approach is shown in Fig. 1. It includes two steps namely

- Identification of popular items: The proposed approach determines popular items from the rating database based on random walk approach
- Noisy user detection and removal: Popularity score is assigned to a user based on the popular items he rated. If a user does not rate highly popular items of the domain then his popularity score is less and so he is expected to be a noisy user. Moreover if a user rates only the popular items, then he has no novelty in rating. So his popularity score is discounted if he rates only the popular items. The users with popularity score less than a threshold are identified as noisy users and they are removed from the training set. Remaining user profiles are used for prediction computations.

4   ItemRank Based User Noise Identification

This section discusses about the proposed approach for noisy user identification and removal from the data set. The description of the two phases of the framework

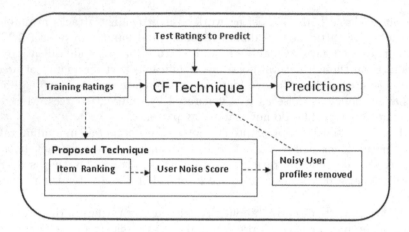

Fig. 1. Proposed framework

namely 'Identification of Popular Items' and 'Noisy User Detection and Removal' is given below:

4.1　Identification of Popular Items

To detect noisy users, we initially perform ranking of items based on users ratings. The data model for ranking of items is described below.

Definition 1. User-Item Matrix R

If there are m users who have given ratings for n items, then ratings data can be represented as an $m \times n$ matrix with rows representing users and columns representing items. The matrix is called user-item matrix R. Each element $r_{u,i} \in R$ is an ordinal value ranging from R_{min} to R_{max}. Unrated entries of the matrix are considered to be zero.

For example Table 1 shows a rating matrix, consisting of ratings provided by five users for six items.

Let U be the set of users and I be the set of items available in the system. And let U_i be the set of users who rated for item i and $U_{i,j}$, set of users who co-rated the items i and j.

$$U_{i,j} = \begin{cases} U_i \cap U_j : & r_{u,i} > 0, \ r_{u,j} > 0, \quad i \neq j, \ u \in U, \ i \in I \\ \emptyset : & otherwise \end{cases} \tag{3}$$

As we have different degree of correlations between users on social network, there exist different degree of correlations between items. If two items are co-rated by more number of users with high ratings then the items are considered to be highly correlated items.

Table 1. User-Item rating matrix R

	I1	I2	I3	I4	I5	I6
			Items			
U1	0	5	4	4	3	2
U2	0	0	1	0	5	0
U3	5	1	0	2	4	3
U4	0	4	2	0	4	0
U5	2	0	0	5	0	0

Definition 2. Item Correlation Rating Matrix, ICM

ICM is a $|I|X|I|$ correlation rating matrix that records the number of users who co-rated each pair of items of the rating database R. Each entry of ICM is formed by $U_{i,j}$.

ICM is a symmetric matrix. $U_{i,j}$ is same as $U_{j,i}$ but if item i is rated by many users and item j is rated by less users, then they should be different. So we normalize ICM into Normalized ICM, $NICM$. Item Correlation Matrix, ICM of the given rating matrix R is shown in Table 2.

Table 2. ICM of the rating matrix R

	I1	I2	I3	I4	I5	I6
			Items			
I1	0	1	0	2	1	1
I2	1	0	2	2	3	2
I3	0	2	0	1	3	1
I4	2	2	1	0	2	2
I5	1	3	3	2	0	2
I6	1	2	1	2	2	0

Definition 3. Normalized Item-Item Correlation Matrix, NICM

$NICM$ is a matrix that records relationship between each pair of items as the ratio of number of users who co-rated them and the number of users who co-rated other pair of items.

$NICM$ is computed based on the formula

$$NICM_{i,j} = \frac{ICM_{i,j}}{\sum_j ICM_{i,j}} \qquad (4)$$

$NICM$ is not a symmetric matrix. The sum of the each row of the matrix is 1. So it can be treated as a stochastic matrix. Normalized Item Correlation Matrix, $NICM$ of R is shown in Table 3.

Table 3. NICM of the rating matrix R

	Items					
	I1	I2	I3	I4	I5	I6
I1	0	1/5	0	2/5	1/5	1/5
I2	1/10	0	2/10	2/10	3/10	2/10
I3	0	2/7	0	1/7	3/7	1/7
I4	2/9	2/9	1/9	0	2/9	2/9
I5	1/11	3/11	3/11	2/11	0	2/11
I6	1/8	2/8	1/8	2/8	2/8	0

Normalized correlation between items of the rating database is modeled as a weighted directed graph called correlation graph. The nodes of the correlation graph are items and normalized correlation between items are considered as edges of the graph. The edge weights are the corresponding correlation values. The correlation graph of NICM is shown in Fig. 2.

The next step is to rank the nodes(items) of the correlation graph based on a ranking strategy. The ranking strategy proposed here is based on PageRank algorithm which assigns ranks to nodes based on popularity of web pages(nodes) in the web graph. Popularity scores assigned to items in the correlation graph are used for noisy user identification. The vertex ranking algorithm is based on PageRank [13] algorithm. PageRank is one of the most popularly used algorithm for ranking nodes in a graph. It is being used in many domains. PageRank value of a node is proportional to its parent node's PageRank values, but at the same time, the score is inversely proportional to its parent node's out degrees. The process of calculating PageRank values is modeled as random walks in graph. Random walks are considered as Markov-chain and the stationary distribution of a random walker is assigned as PageRank scores of nodes of the graph. The random walker either follows a random outgoing edge with probability α or restarts the walk to a random node with probability $1-\alpha$. The proposed ranking strategy follows two rules:

- if an item i is linked by highly ranked items with high weights, then i will also have high rank and
- an item has to transfer its rank throughout the graph

The PageRank score [13] for node n is defined as

$$PR(n) = (1 - \alpha)\ \frac{1}{|V|} + \alpha \sum_{q:(q,e)\in E} \frac{PR(q)}{O(q)} \qquad (5)$$

where $O(q)$ is the out degree of node q and α is the decay factor. ItemRank value for a node i_n is calculated as

$$ITEMRANK(i_n) = (1-\alpha)ITEMRANK(i_n) + \alpha \sum_{i_k:(i_k,i_n)\in E} \frac{ITEMRANK(i_k)}{O_w(i_k)}$$

(6)

where

$$O_w(i_k) = \frac{\sum_{i_m:(i_k,i_m)\in E} W_{i_k,i_m}}{W_{i_k,i_n}}$$

(7)

that is

$$O_w(i_k) = \frac{\sum_{i_m:(i_k,i_m)\in E} NICM_{i_k,i_m}}{NICM_{i_k,i_n}}$$

(8)

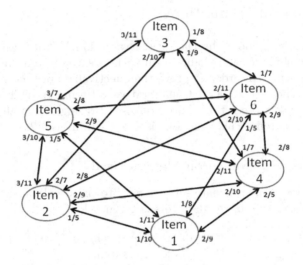

Fig. 2. Correlation graph of NICM

4.2 Noisy User Detection and Removal

This section provides the detailed description of user noise computation. Items of data set are ranked based on the item popularity (ItemRank) scores. Items with popularity score exceeding a preset threshold are considered to be popular items. It is assumed that all the users (including the new users) are aware of those items of the domain. So in general if a user does not rate any of the popular items of the domain then he is considered to be a noisy user. At the same time if a user rates only the popular items then he has no novelty in his ratings. Therefore the proposal considers both the above aspects to assign popularity score to users. User popularity score $popularity\_score_u$ is calculated by the formula as given below

$$popularity\_score_u = \frac{|PI_u|}{|PI|} \times \log \frac{|I_u|}{|PI_u|}$$

(9)

where PI is the set of popular items, PI_u is the set of popular items rated by user u and I_u is the set of items rated by user u. The first component of *popularity_score_u* is for considering how the user rates popular items, whereas the second component is for checking whether he rates unpopular items also. *popularity_score* is higher for users who rated more popular items. At the same time if he rates only the popular items his *popularity_score* is reduced. In practice, the user profiles are sorted in the increasing order of *popularity_score* and remove top n user profiles of the training set (User profiles with less popularity score) for prediction computations. It is expected that users with less popularity score are noisy users, so they are discarded from prediction computations.

5   Experimental Evaluations

This section discusses about the Data set, Evaluation Metrics, Effectiveness of noise handling techniques and Comparison with other noise removal approaches cited in the literature. In order to prove the effectiveness of the proposed noise handling approaches Item Based Collaborative Filtering ItemCF [18] is used. The algorithm makes predictions based on user's ratings for highly correlated items of the target item. This technique is discussed in Sect. 2.

5.1   Data Sets and Evaluation Metrics Used

Two real world recommender data sets are used to empirically test the proposed method. The description of the data sets is given below:

- MovieLens [16], A movie rating dataset comprising of 1,00,000 ratings (rating scores in [1...5]) given by 943 users for 1682 items.
- Jester, A jokes rating dataset comprising of 73,42,100 ratings (rating scores in [-10...10]) given by 73421 users for 100 items. The ratings are converted in to the range [1..5]

From Movielens dataset 900 users and from Jester dataset 4000 user profiles are randomly selected for performing the experiments. These users are used to build train and test data sets as mentioned in [19]. That is, from the data set, randomly select some percentage of items n_u to hide for each user. These hidden items will be the test set and the remaining items are the train set. For each user we select 60 % of the items to the training set and 40 % to the test set.

In order to measure accuracy of the predictions, two most popularly used statistical metrics namely, MAE (Mean Absolute Error), RMSE (Root Mean Square Error) and decision theoretic metric F1 are used. MAE is the average absolute deviation between predicted rating and actual rating. MAE for a user u is formulated as given below

$$MAE_u = \frac{\sum_{i=1}^{n} |p_i - a_i|}{n} \tag{10}$$

where p_i and a_i are the predicted ratings and actual rating of the test user u. MAE of the entire system is calculated as the average MAE values of all test users. $RMSE$ computes the square of the difference between predicted and actual ratings. It emphasizes larger errors compared to MAE measure. $RMSE$ is defined as

$$RMSE_u = \sqrt{\frac{\sum_{i=1}^{n}(p_i - a_i)^2}{n}} \tag{11}$$

$RMSE$ of the entire system is calculated as the average $RMSE$ values of all test users. Lower the values of MAE and $RMSE$, better the prediction quality. The third measure $F1$ is a combination of *Precision* and *Recall* as given in [7]. *Recall* and *Precision* measure the degree to which the system presents relevant information by computing the portion of both preferred and recommended items from the total number of preferred and recommended items [19] respectively. $F1$ is defined as

$$F1 = \frac{2 * precision * recall}{precision + recall} \tag{12}$$

A relevance threshold $= 4$ for $F1$ metric is set. An item is assumed to be relevant if it exceeds the threshold, otherwise it is assumed to be non-relevant.

5.2   Effectiveness of the Proposal in ItemCF Approach

This section describes about the impact of the proposed technique as a pre-processing step in prediction computations of *ItemCF* approach. Parameters considered here are the threshold for identifying popular items (α) and noisy users (β). The (α) values of Movielens and Jester are 250 items and 25 respectively. The (β) values of Movielens and Jester are 100 users and 300 users respectively. Parameter values are set based on experiments. In both the data sets less than 10 % of the users are removed to improve the results. Effectiveness of noisy user removal is shown in Tables 4 and 5 for Movielens and Jester data sets respectively. Both the tables shows that error in prediction quality namely MAE and $RMSE$ decreases and accuracy in predictions namely $F1$ increases when noisy users are removed from the data set. In both the data sets, *ItemCF* performs better when noisy users are removed as per the three metrics. This shows that the proposed approach is effective in removing noisy users.

Table 4. Effect of noise removal on MovieLens data set for ItemCF

Data Set	MAE	RMSE	F1
Baseline data	0.7723	0.9978	.0578
Noise removed data	0.7574	0.9812	.0629

Table 5. Effect of noise removal on Jester data set for ItemCF

Data Set	MAE	RMSE	F1
Baseline data	0.7850	0.9810	.0256
Noise removed data	0.7642	0.9645	.0312

5.3 Comparison with Other Techniques

Section 2 presented the approaches available in the literature for noise removal in Recommender Systems. Specifically the methods proposed by Li et al. [10] [NNMU] and O'Mahony [12] are used for comparison of results. Further the proposed work is compared with approaches proposed by [6] [RDMA], and [5] [WDMA], [WDA]. The techniques NNMU, RDMA, WDMA, WDA assigns noise score to users and rank them based on noise score. Those methods set Topk noisy users and remove the ratings provided by them from the training set and the original test set. The predictions for those users in the test set are calculated by global rating bias as given in [11].

Comparison of various noise handling methods with respect to MAE for Movielens and Jester data set is shown in Fig. 3. In the figures each method is

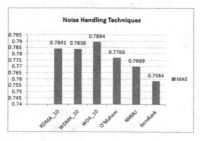

(a) MovieLens data set

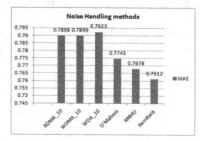

(b) Jester data set

Fig. 3. MAE based comparison of Noise handling techniques

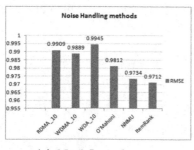

(a) MovieLens data set

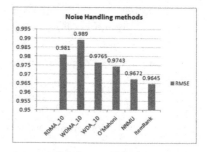

(b) Jester data set

Fig. 4. RMSE based comparison of Noise handling techniques

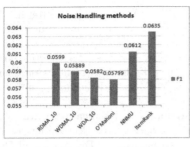

(a) MovieLens data set

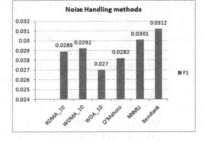

(b) Jester data set

Fig. 5. F1 based comparison of Noise handling techniques

represented as a bar with the format method-k (RDMA-60, WDA-10 and so on), where k is the value associated with the highest accuracy of the method [19].

Comparison of various noise handling methods with respect to RMSE on both datasets is shown in Fig. 4. Figure 5 shows the comparision of various noise removal approaches for F1 on Movielens and Jester data sets. The above results shows that the proposed method of noise removal is effective in *ItemCF* approach with respect to all the three metrics on both the data sets.

6   Conclusion

Trust in social recommendation is becoming a significant topic now-a-days. This work proposes a novel approach to handle natural noise in Recommender systems. The success of any noise removal approach should improve accuracy of predictions. Experimental results show that removal of noisy users results in better predictions. Noise identification technique proposed here are based on how a user provides preferences for popular items in the domain. This approach identifies noisy users and discards the entire profiles of the noisy users. Future work in this direction can be to remove only the noisy ratings in user profiles instead of removing the entire profiles. Another notable research direction is to improve novelty of the system by removing noisy users. The proposed approach can be examined for other Recommendation approaches namely Matrix Factorization based techniques.

References

1. Adomavicius, G., Tuzhilin, A.: Toward the next generation of recommender systems: A survey of the state-of-the-art and possible extensions. IEEE Trans. Knowl. Data Eng. **17**(6), 734–749 (2005)
2. Amatriain, X., Pujol, J.M., Oliver, N.: I like it.. i like it not: evaluating user ratings noise in recommender systems. In: Houben, G.-J., McCalla, G., Pianesi, F., Zancanaro, M. (eds.) UMAP 2009. LNCS, vol. 5535, pp. 247–258. Springer, Heidelberg (2009)

3. Bell, R.M., Koren, Y.: Improved neighborhood-based collaborative filtering. In: KDD Cup and Workshop at the 13th ACM SIGKDD International Conference on Knowledge Discovery and Data Mining (2007)
4. Breese, J.S., Heckerman, D., Kadie, C.: Empirical analysis of predictive algorithms for collaborative filtering. In: Proceedings of the Fourteenth Conference on Uncertainty in Artificial Intelligence, pp. 43–52. Morgan Kaufmann Publishers Inc. (1998)
5. Burke, R., Mobasher, B., Williams, C., Bhaumik, R.: Classification features for attack detection in collaborative recommender systems. In: Proceedings of the 12th ACM SIGKDD International Conference on Knowledge Discovery and Data Mining, pp. 542–547. ACM (2006)
6. Chirita, P.A., Nejdl, W., Zamfir, C.: Preventing shilling attacks in online recommender systems. In: Proceedings of the 7th Annual ACM International Workshop on Web Information and Data Management, pp. 67–74. ACM (2005)
7. Gunawardana, A., Shani, G.: A survey of accuracy evaluation metrics of recommendation tasks. J. Mach. Learn. Res. **10**, 2935–2962 (2009)
8. Herlocker, J.L., Konstan, J.A., Borchers, A., Riedl, J.: An algorithmic framework for performing collaborative filtering. In: Proceedings of the 22nd Annual International ACM SIGIR Conference on Research and Development In Information Retrieval, pp. 230–237. ACM (1999)
9. Herlocker, J.L., Konstan, J.A., Terveen, L.G., Riedl, J.T.: Evaluating collaborative filtering recommender systems. ACM Trans. Inf. Syst. (TOIS) **22**(1), 5–53 (2004)
10. Li, B., Chen, L., Zhu, X., Zhang, C.: Noisy but non-malicious user detection in social recommender systems. World Wide Web **16**(5–6), 677–699 (2013)
11. Mazurowski, M.A.: Estimating confidence of individual rating predictions in collaborative filtering recommender systems. Expert Syst. Appl. **40**(10), 3847–3857 (2013)
12. O'Mahony, M.P., Hurley, N.J., Silvestre, G.: Detecting noise in recommender system databases. In: Proceedings of the 11th International Conference on Intelligent User Interfaces, pp. 109–115. ACM (2006)
13. Page, L., Brin, S., Motwani, R., Winograd, T.: The pagerank citation ranking: bringing order to the web. Stanford InfoLab (1999)
14. Pazzani, M.J.: A framework for collaborative, content-based and demographic filtering. Artif. Intel. Rev. **13**(5–6), 393–408 (1999)
15. Ricci, F., Rokach, L., Shapira, B.: Introduction to recommender systems handbook. In: Recommender Systems Handbook, pp. 1–35. Springer (2011)
16. Riedl, J., Konstan, J.: Movielens dataset (1998)
17. Said, A., Jain, B.J., Narr, S., Plumbaum, T.: Users and Noise: the magic barrier of recommender systems. In: Masthoff, J., Mobasher, B., Desmarais, M.C., Nkambou, R. (eds.) UMAP 2012. LNCS, vol. 7379, pp. 237–248. Springer, Heidelberg (2012)
18. Sarwar, B., Karypis, G., Konstan, J., Riedl, J.: Item-based collaborative filtering recommendation algorithms. In: Proceedings of the 10th International Conference on World Wide Web, pp. 285–295. ACM (2001)
19. Toledo, R.Y., Mota, Y.C., Martínez, L.: Correcting noisy ratings in collaborative recommender systems. Knowl.-Based Syst. **76**, 96–108 (2014)

Intelligent Monitoring

Agent-Based Multi-variant Crisis Handling Strategies for SCADA Systems

Grzegorz Dobrowolski, Aleksander Byrski, and Leszek Siwik$^{(\boxtimes)}$

Department of Computer Science, AGH University of Science and Technology,
Kraków, Poland
{grzela,olekb,siwik}@agh.edu.pl

Abstract. Unpredictable changes in the problem parameters, especially when dealing with highly dynamic and complex systems like SCADA, should be predicted and appropriate strategies prepared accordingly. However, if the prediction is hard or impossible, one can consider preparing dedicated plans with dealing with these problems, in order to adapt the strategies ad-hoc when the problems arise. Such planning under uncerntainty has already been studied, and applied e.g. in the case of scheduling problems. The paper discusses SCADA as a problem similar to scheduling and constructs a system dedicated to prepare ready-to-use strategies before certain events arise. The solution is implemented in AgE platform and preliminary results are presented and discussed.

1 Motivation

The distributed nature of SCADA environments often requires the application of unconventional monitoring and control strategies being able to adapt to unexpected changes and situations, especially when their nature is hard to predict, and . the resiliency of the system and its fault tolerance has to be taken into consideration. In such environments, the occurrence of the hardware or software breakdowns should be considered when preparing dedicated plans ready-to-use for such unexpected problems, so when they occur, a dedicated strategy exists, that can be further adapted ad-hoc and used to handle the problem.

Unpredictable changes in the problem parameters can be addressed with approaches defined as *planning under uncertainty*. The methods assume that a planner does not have complete knowledge required to calculate a plan or the knowledge is uncertain. The solutions to this class of problems have to address an issue of uncertainty modeling [10]. An interesting example of a solution for mobile robot motion planning is presented in [12]. The planing algorithm handles sensing and motion uncertainty and optimizes motion plan with the complexity of $O[n^6]$ in a search space of n dimensions. Such methods cannot be applied for real-time motion planning when a group if independent vehicles is considered.

Planning in dynamic environments is also studied in the case of scheduling problems, e.g. Job Shop and similar ones, where it is necessary to receive new, unplanned jobs in certain time periods, and/or deal with potential machinery breakdowns. Such a procedure was usually called a rolling horizon procedure

© Springer International Publishing Switzerland 2015
A. Dziech et al. (Eds.): MCSS 2015, CCIS 566, pp. 61–71, 2015.
DOI: 10.1007/978-3-319-26404-2_5

where a rolling time window is introduced and newly arriving jobs are included in the prediction window. Based on the predictions, schedules are prepared (sub-problems of Job-Shop Scheduling Problem (JSSP) [3] are solved) and final schedule is integrated in the current global solutions [4,13]. In these cases, a shifting bottleneck heuristic is used for scheduling and rescheduling [11]. Such heuristics are of course very useful, and usually good-enough for the manual solving of such problems, but in the approach presented here, we would like rather to use a general-purpose evolutionary algorithms (in particular Evolutionary Multi-agent System EMAS [2]) to schedule the JSSP, however none of other possible heuristics are excluded and they may be considered in the future.

The proposed concept of predictive multi-variant planning is based on the idea of using computational power before the need for particular plan occurs. Obviously, the characteristics of the problem prevent the planner from predicting the future state of the system. Therefore, multiple variants of the future have to be considered and the planner has to prepare variants of plans or a single plan most suitable in all possible situations. The computation required for preparing such multi-variant plans can be relatively simply parallelized.

In this paper, an idea of realization of such planning environment to support SCADA-like systems is shown. After the description of the idea, the similarity of SCADA environment to scheduling problems is leveraged and a dedicated system for solving JSSP problem, being here a benchmark, is described. Its realization based on AgE platform[1] is described and first results are presented.

2   The Idea

Agent based systems turned out to be a trustworthy tool for realization of different simulation and computing tasks especially in complex and distributed environments. They seem to be especially well-suited for applying for dynamic and unpredictable domain. Agent is located and works inside the environment. It influences, controls or just monitors the system and at the same time its decisions and actions are influenced by the state of the environment itself. It seems that agent-based systems can be easily integrated into SCADA, and used for monitoring, reporting but also for reaction for unexpected events arising in such systems.

In the proposed approach the agency is considered on two levels:

- Firstly, agents reside in the PLCs distributed over the monitored network and store all crucial data regarding the system state and efficiency.
- Secondly, agents are the part of the controlling and managing unit and they are responsible for:
  - on-line data analysis,
  - predicting and simulating different possible situations including hardware and software breakdowns,
  - preparing a multi-variant system management and optimization strategies.

---

[1] http://age.agh.edu.pl.

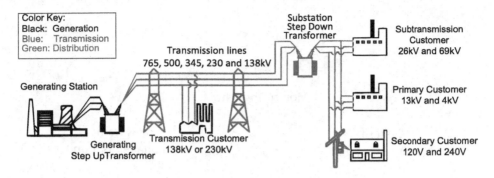

Fig. 1. The sample schema of energy production and distribution system

To visualize the idea let us imagine an energy production, transmission and distribution system as presented in Fig. 1. Important here is that the system is complex, distributed and consists of many cooperating subsystems.

So first, we are able to equip the system with **Monitoring Agents (MAg)** implemented for instance as PLC modules installed on every single important part of the system.

MAgs are responsible for capturing and storing data describing system state and efficiency. They are using their local data and the **Central Monitoring Database (CMD)** as presented in Fig. 2.

On the basis of Monitoring Agents and the data they capture and store we are able to introduce two crucial modules i.e. **Crisis handling and managing engine** and **Prediction and variant scenario engine** as presented in Fig. 3.

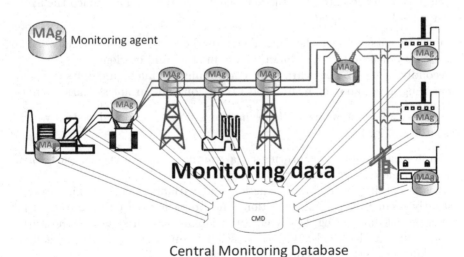

Fig. 2. Monitoring agents

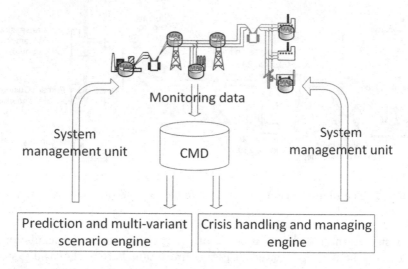

Fig. 3. Monitoring agents

The main task of the variant scenario engine is:

- predicting and simulating different possible situations including:
  - different possible failures i.e. hardware and software breakdowns
  - demand / requests peaks and calms
- preparing possible reactions (e.g. rescheduling of the tasks, reducing the throughput of the system etc.).

In Fig. 4 the complete idea of agent-based monitoring and crisis-handling system has been presented. As one may see in the proposed approach the agency is considered on two levels:

- Firstly, agents reside in the PLCs distributed over the monitored network and store all crucial data regarding the system state and efficiency
- Secondly, agents are the part of the controlling and managing units (i.e. Crisis handling and managing engine and Prediction and variant scenario engine)

So now, we can imagine the following work-flow of proposed system which is presented in Fig. 4 i.e.:

- Monitoring agents are capturing data coming from the crucial parts of the system (and cooperating systems)
- Agents working inside the Prediction and variant scenario engine are constantly predicting possible situations and preparing possible variants of production schedule taking the current situation and captured data as the starting point but considering also different possible failures i.e. hardware and software breakdowns, demand / requests peaks and calms etc.
- Agents working inside the Managing and crisis handling engine are assigning upcoming jobs and reacting on any changes in the system. So, when the new job comes they are selecting the best schedule plan prepared by agents of

Prediction and variant scenario engine. Also when some failure happen the are looking for best solution (taking good-enough schedule, rescheduling of the tasks, reducing the throughput of the system etc.)

– decisions made by agents of Managing and crisis handling engine changes the situation in the system so agents of Prediction and variant scenario engine start their predicting and multi-variant optimization tasks taking new data captured by monitoring agents into account etc.

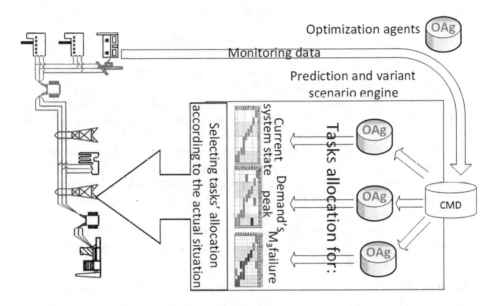

Fig. 4. Monitoring agents

3   Multi-variant Scheduling

Job-shop scheduling problem (JSSP) [3] consists in search for optimal assignment of jobs (in particular, the operations that jobs consists of) to particular machines, of which the machine park consists. The whole strategy of optimization aims at minimizing of the makespan (computed as the total time of the processing of all jobs and thus all operations on the available machines). Solving JSSP can be treated as looking for an optimal control of in such way defined SCADA system, making an interesting benchmark for the problem of optimal control of a complex system.

The solving strategy of JSSP are quite easy to implement, but finding exact solution is very resource and time demanding (as JSSP belongs to NP-hard problems [8]). Its complexity requires applying of general-purpose metaheuristics instead of brute-force or deterministic approaches. Evolutionary algorithm (EA) is an example of such strategy, and can be realized as follows [1]:

- the jobs (or operations) can be encoded into a genotype using several popular encodings (e.g. permutational [1], Lehmer [7] or random key [5]), in this work we are focusing on permutational encoding,
- the mutation operator switches two neighbouring genes in a genotype,
- the one-point crossover operator chooses part of the genotype of one parent, removes conflicting genes from the genotype of the other parent and attaches the remaining genes at the end,
- the selection can be defined randomly (we chose the tournament selection [9]),
- the fitness is defined of course as the makespan.

This problem gets even more interesting and complex, when dealing with dynamic situation. Namely, the jobs can be delivered in specific time moments, and the system should be able to properly adapt to newly delivered job, for example by scheduling anew (or rescheduling of the current operations assignment). Proper handling of incoming jobs is very important, taking into consideration the fact, that these jobs can differ from the ones already received before. Thus the adaptation of the system plays a crucial role in such setting. Moreover, other problems may arise (e.g. certain machines can become broken). In the literature, such problems were solved using so called rolling-horizon JSSP rhp1,rhp2.

As rescheduling can take time and lead to unwanted delays in production, we may prepare ourselves for the changes of the jobs and operations. In such case we can image a system trying to predict the next-to-come job, or to prepare itself for possible next-to-come josb or operations, by having at hand different schedules, ready to be implemented. Thus a multi-variant optimization system can be defined, consisting of:

- **Master** dealing with possible variants of the incoming jobs, based on a first schedule. The agent computers different possible sets of incoming jobs and delegates the optimization of the new schedules to one of the slaves. Later it collects the answers (schedules) from the slaves and chooses the best one (by comparing them to the received jobs).
- **Slave** realizing the optimization of particular variant of the problem, by running the above-mentioned evolutionary algorithm. The stopping condition is strongly dependent on the predicted time of the next incoming jobs, as the Master must select by this time the best of available schedules in order to properly reschedule the work.

4   Results

The multi-variant scheduling system has been implemented using PyAge agent-oriented framework [6]. The framework supported the authors with implementation of a notion of computing agent that was adapted to create an efficient implementation of Master and Slave agents. The system consists of one Master and many slaves agents. Master agent is responsible for exchanging information with external world e.g. he receives upcoming jobs and makes the final decision about assigning tasks to machines. Master agent is also responsible for dispatching optimization tasks among Slaves agents. Optimization tasks can be both: our predicted or real jobs to be optimized and scheduled. In the system there can be any number of Slaves agents. Theoretically the more Slaves agents in the system the better chance to match exactly predicted and real jobs – but the complexity of the system grows at the same time. So, as usually there is the typical trade-off between exactness and the complexity. Obviously slaves-agents can be run locally or can be distributed over different workstations–it is realized by PyAge framework.

When the real job comes–Master agent asks Slaves for their predictions and scheduling plan. When the prediction was successful and we have ready-to-use schedule it is taken and Master agent assigns tasks to machines and Slaves-agents starts next prediction and scheduling task (taking into account last assignments).

If we don't have exact matching between predicted and real jobs the "good–enough" matching is taken. If it is not possible (there is neither exact nor good-enough prediction) Master-agent assigns tasks without optimization or with ad-hoc scheduling depending on the configuration.

4.1 Simple Verification

The first experiment illustrates the simplest possible case i.e. the situation when upcoming jobs consist of only short tasks (short task means the task shorter than predicted).

In such a situation we have many "blank spaces" on machines since the predicted schedule assumed that the task will be longer (and the machine will be occupied for a longer time whereas the real task lasted much shorter. In Fig. 5 such a situation is illustrated.

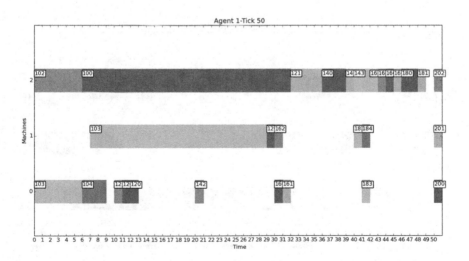

Fig. 5. Sample scheduling when short tasks come

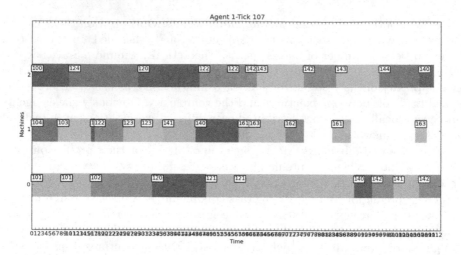

Fig. 6. Sample scheduling with exact prediction

Intuitively, we feel that occupancy of machines should be much better when the prediction was successful and the duration of real tasks is close to predicted ones. The situation is presented in Fig. 6. As one may see, in this case machines are tightly loaded what means that they are effectively (and optimally) used.

Obviously the problem arises when the real jobs consist of tasks (much) longer than predicted. In such a situation production plan has to be rescheduled. In the consequence the task can be moved among machines (according to new schedule) but there will be probably a long unproductive periods. The situation of this type is presented in Fig. 7 where task 160 is much longer than predicted, so the plan

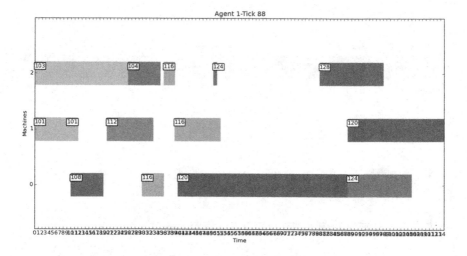

Fig. 7. Sample scheduling with exact prediction

was rescheduled and the task was moved from machine 1 to machine 2 but there finally there was a pretty long unproductive periods.

4.2 Dependency on the Number of Agents

Interesting aspect to be discussed is the influence of the number of working agents on the quality of results. The influence depends on the distribution of tasks duration. When the duration of particular tasks are coherent then smaller number of working agents are able to predict upcoming jobs and prepare high-quality schedule. The situation changes when the distribution of tasks' duration (the value of σ coefficient) grows. In such a case the higher number of working agents are required to obtain high-quality prediction (and schedule). Below, mentioned situation are illustrated experimentally.

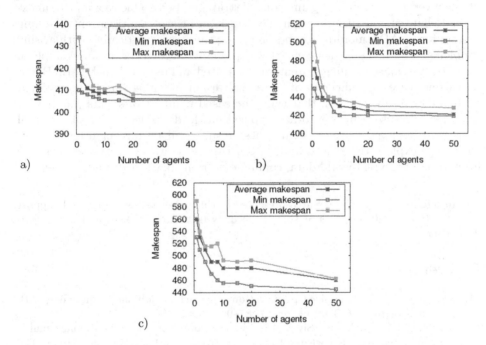

Fig. 8. Dependency of make-spans obtained on the number of working agents with distribution of tasks equals to (a) $\sigma = 0.1$, (b) $\sigma = 0.3$ (c) $\sigma = 0.5$

As one may see, the higher is the distribution of tasks' duration the more important is the number of (Slave)agents working in the system. When distribution has been set to 0.1 only 10 agents was absolutely enough to obtain high-quality results. That is why lines on Fig. 8 are relatively flat. Increasing the number of working agents from 10 to 20 allows to improve the make-span by 0.27 % only. Further increasing the number of working agents from 20 to 50 allows to improve the make-span by 0.42 %.

The situation is slightly different when the distribution of tasks' duration grows to 0.3. In this case increasing number of working agents is much more important and allows to obtain much better results. This time increasing number of working agents from 1 to 10 allows to obtain make-span improved by 9.18 %, from 10 to 20 agents improves the make-span by 0.68 %, from 20 to 50 agents improves make-span by 1.15 %.

The observation is confirmed when distribution is increased to 0.5. This time increasing the number of working agents form 1 to 10 allows to improve the make-span by 13.79 %, from 10 to 20 – 0.48 % and from 20 to 50 3.56 %.

5   Conclusions

The distributed nature of SCADA environments often requires the application of unconventional monitoring and control strategies being able to adapt to unexpected changes and situations. In this paper an idea of multi-variant planning system for SCADA monitoring and preparing the strategies dealing with arising problems, leveraging agency concept was presented. Moreover, as an example of SCADA system, scheduling system was presented and used as benchmark. Based on this use case, the efficiency of the multi-variant planning was evaluated, and preliminary results showed, that using increased numbers of agents (i.e. having more ready-to-use plans for ad-hoc application) leads to decreasing of the total makespan observed in the system. These results will be further used in order to further explore the scheduling problems use case and to move towards the evaluation of the real-world data, coming e.g. from smart-grids class systems.

Acknowledgments. The research presented in this paper received financial support from EU Horizon 2020 project SCISSOR: Security In trusted SCADA and smart-grids 2015-1017.

References

1. Bierwirth, C.: A generalized permutation approach to job shop scheduling with genetic algorithms. OR Spektrum **17**, 87–92 (1995)
2. Byrski, A., Dreewski, R., Siwik, L., Kisiel-Dorohinicki, M.: Evolutionary multi-agent systems. The Knowledge Engineering Review **30**(2), 171–186 (2015). The original publication is available at http://dx.doi.org/10.1017/S0269888914000289
3. Cheng, R., Gen, M., Tsujimura, Y.: A tutorial survey of job-shop scheduling problems using genetic algorithms, part ii: hybrid genetic search strategies. Comput. Ind. Eng. **36**(2), 343–364 (1999)
4. Fang, J., Xi, Y.: A rolling horizon job shop rescheduling strategy in the dynamic environment. Int. J. Adv. Manuf. Technol. **13**(3), 227–232 (1997)
5. GonSalves, J., Resende, M.: Biased random-key genetic algorithms for combinatorial optimization. J. Heuristics **17**(5), 487–525 (2011)
6. Kaziród, M., Korczynski, W., Byrski, A.: Agent-oriented computing platform in python. In: Proceedings of the 2014 IEEE/WIC/ACM International Joint Conferences on Web Intelligence (WI) and Intelligent Agent Technologies (IAT), WI-IAT 2014, vol. 03, pp. 365–372. IEEE Computer Society, Washington, DC (2014)

7. Lehmer, D.: Teaching combinatorial tricks to a computer. In: Proceedings of the Symposium on Applied Mathematics Combinatorial Analysis, vol. 10 (1960)
8. Malakooti, B.: Operations and Production Systems with Multiple Objectives, p. 1114. John Wiley & Sons, Chichester (2013). ISBN: 978-1-118-58537-5
9. Michalewicz, Z.: Genetic Algorithms + Data Structures = Evolution Programs, p. 387. Springer, Berlin Heidelberg (1996). ISBN: 978-3-540-60676-5
10. Mula, J., Poler, R., García-Sabater, J., Lario, F.: Models for production planning under uncertainty: A review. Int. J. Prod. Econ. **103**(1), 271–285 (2006)
11. Pinedo, M.: Planning and Scheduling in Manufacturing and Services, p. 536. Springer, New York (2009). ISBN: 978-1-4419-0909-1
12. Van Den Berg, J., Patil, S., Alterovitz, R.: Motion planning under uncertainty using iterative local optimization in belief space. Int. J. Rob. Res. **31**(11), 1263–1278 (2012)
13. Wang, B., Li, Q.: Rolling horizon procedure for large-scale job-shop scheduling problems. In. 2007 IEEE International Conference onAutomation and Logistics, pp. 829–834, August 2007

A Multi-agent Approach for Intrusion Detection in Distributed Systems

Agostino Forestiero[(⊠)]

CNR - ICAR, Institute for High Performance Computing and Networking,
National Research Council of Italy, Via Pietro Bucci, 41C, 87036 Rende (CS), Italy
forestiero@icar.cnr.it

Abstract. Detecting anomalous data is essential to obtain critical and actionable information such as intrusions, faults, and system failures. In this paper an agent-based clustering algorithm to detect anomalies in a distributed system, is introduced. Each data object, independently of which source it arrives, is associated with a mobile agent following the flocking algorithm, a self-organizing bio-inspired computational model. The agents are randomly disseminated onto a virtual space where they move in order to form a flock. Thanks to a tailored *similarity function* the agents that are associated with similar objects form a flock, whereas the agents that are associated with objects dissimilar (outliers/anomalies) to each other do not group in flocks. Preliminarily experimental results confirm the validity of the proposed approach.

Keywords: Anomaly detection · Multi-agents · Self-organizing · Distributed systems

1 Introduction

Outlier/anomaly detection is a fundamental operation to obtain critical and actionable information such as intrusions, faults, and system failures. So, it is possible to take actions, such as execute a recovery program or notify an administrator. Some significant fields and applications are [17]: (i) sensor monitoring and surveillance, network traffic, Web logs and Web page click streams; (ii) trend of workload in an e-commerce server, which can help in fine tuning the server dynamically in order to obtain better performance; (iii) to analyze meteorological data, by observing how spatial-meteorological points evolve over time; and (iv) the evolution of the spread of illnesses, finding how system evolution can identify sources responsible for the spread of illness. These systems continuously produce a huge amount of data often as data streams that can change over time. Achieving systems that can handle the endless flow of data by being incremental, has been addressed so far. They are fast and clever enough to approximate results with a fixed level of accuracy, but an important challenge is to detect the unusual objects in the data stream without storing all data. There are several methods to detect anomalies, [23] groups outlier detection techniques in into four

© Springer International Publishing Switzerland 2015
A. Dziech et al. (Eds.): MCSS 2015, CCIS 566, pp. 72–82, 2015.
DOI: 10.1007/978-3-319-26404-2_6

categories: (i) statistical approaches; (ii) distance-based methods; (iii) profiling methods; and (iv) model-based approaches.

Clustering-based approaches have also been used to detect outliers either as an algorithm to individuate points that do not belong to clusters or as clusters that are significantly smaller than others [21]. Using clustering algorithms to analyze data stream and detect anomalies in data, has evolved as a new form of online data analysis where the information in the data tends to change over time. These algorithms perform cluster analysis of data streams to monitor the results in real time. The aim of the algorithm is to recognize the evolution and provide a result that adapts dynamically to the data. The algorithm can examine data only once, as it arrives, and it must take into account data evolution. It is necessary to design a mechanism to remember old data, such as compression or summarize old information. Novel algorithms that are able to produce models of the data in an online way, are required to analyze the data flow. These algorithms look at each datum only once and within a limited amount of time. Standard data analysis algorithms are a useful starting point, but they must be adapted to work in the stream environment. A possible way to perform data stream analysis is to execute clustering of data streams able to produce results in real time. The area is still new and it has many open problems, even though researchers have successfully tackled many of the issues that are of major concern regarding data-streams.

In data stream applications, data objects arrive with very high rates, which means that the analysis must be performed very rapidly and efficiently. In such applications, data volumes are huge, so it is not always possible to keep all the data in memory. A sliding window strategy can be used to maintain a percentage of the data in memory. Sliding windows strategy can be based on two concepts: (i) a count-based window in which the n most recent objects are maintained, and (ii) a time-based window in which all objects arriving in the last t time intervals are stored. Objects maintained during the sliding window are named active objects. The object that leaves the window is deleted from the collection of active objects. So, the algorithms must be designed for outlier monitoring, considering the sliding window. The stream-based algorithms must consider the memory space required for auxiliary information and the storage consumption must be as low as possible. Possibly, they should be able to enlarge the sliding window, to accommodate more objects.

Here a clustering method based on the flocking algorithm to detect anomalies in distributed systems, is introduced. The approach was already proposed as a clustering algorithm of data streams in [14]. The agents work together following the flocking model [8]. The flocking model is a bio-inspired computational model to simulate a group of entities that mimic a flock of birds. In this model each entity makes movement decisions without any communication with others. The agents follow a small number of simple rules based on their neighboring entities and the obstacles present in the environment. The complex global behavior of the entire group emerges from the interaction of these simple rules. The flocking rules are: **alignment** rule, which gives an agent the capability to align with other nearby agents contained in its visibility range; **separation** rule, which gives an agent the capacity to maintain an established distance from others nearby. This prevents agents from crowding too closely together, allowing them to scan a wider area; and **cohesion** rule, provides an agent with the ability to approach and form a group with other agents. Steering for cohesion can be computed by finding all agents in the local neighborhood and computing the average position of the nearby agents. In addition to the basic flocking rules, a *similarity rule* was introduced. When an agent encounters other agents in its visual radius, it evaluates the similarity measure and then it decides whether to form the flock or not. The anomalies/outliers will be represented by: (i) data associated with agents belonging to flocks whose number of components does not exceed a fixed threshold and (ii) data associated with agents that do not belong to a flock. In the following, Sect. 2 discusses a set of related works; Sect. 3 introduces the flocking algorithm and how it can be exploited to detect anomalies; and finally, in Sect. 3.1 some experimental results are shown.

2   Related Work

Several approaches have been designed for discovering unusual objects in a set of data. In [1] an algorithm to find outliers in high-dimensional data, was proposed by Aggarwal. The approach considers a point as outlier if it is present in some lower dimensional projection in a local region of irregularly low density. While, Cutsem and Gath in [7], propose a method based on fuzzy clustering, where two hypotheses are used to test the absence or presence of outliers. However, the hypotheses do not account for the possibility of multiple clusters of outliers. Another clustering-based technique that involves fixed-width clustering with a fixed radius was proposed in [10]. Researchers have started to analyze data in large-scale dynamic networks. The aim is to develop techniques that are asynchronous, scalable, and robust when the characteristics of the network change. For example, in [18], an asynchronous, deterministic technique for computing an average over a large, dynamic network was developed, while Boyd et al. [3] and Kempe et al. [16] introduced a gossip-based randomized algorithms. In [15] a decentralization method in which the nodes of the network make decisions about communication and processing of the data, was proposed. In this approach, the node/sensors only send information to the leader node if the detected value is outside the normal range, so as to reduce bandwidth consumption.

Algorithms based on swarm intelligence paradigms have been designed to solve real world problems in a decentralized fashion such as the clustering problems [9,11,20], distributed systems management [12,13] and outliers detection [2,19]. In [2] a novel swarm intelligence based clustering technique for anomaly detection, called Hierarchical Particle Swarm Optimization Based Clustering, was proposed. The technique consists in performing Hierarchical Agglomerative Clustering where a swarm of particles evolves through different stages to identify outliers and normal clusters. The outlier detection problem is converted into an optimization problem in [19]. An improved version of the Particle Swarm Optimization (PSO) approach is used to optimize the distance measures. Cui et al.

in [5] use the flocking model to cluster streams of documents. Each agent carries a feature vector of data point, in this case a document. The periodical changing of the feature vector of each agent, simulates the stream of documents. But, they neither summarize nor take into account the past information. Old documents are just discarded and the new documents are considered to generate new clusters.

3   Anomaly Detection Through Flocking Agents

An example of emergent collective behavior without a global control, is the flocking model. Flocking behavior emerges from the local interactions of independent entity. Each entity interacts and attracts the elements which are inside its limited visibility range. The distance between two agents cannot be less than a prefixed value. In [22], Raynolds proposes a flocking model to simulate the behavior of birds on a computer. In this basic model the author referred to each individual as a *boid*. The basic flocking rules are depicted in Fig. 1, where R is the visibility range, r is the minimum distance between two agents, with $R > r$.

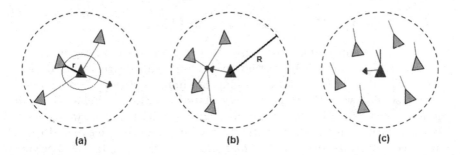

Fig. 1. Flocking behavior rules of Reynolds: (a) separation; (b) cohesion; and (c) aligment.

Each boid executes three simple rules: the **separation** rule which gives an agent the capacity to maintain an established distance from others nearby. This prevents agents from crowding too closely together, allowing them to scan a wider area; the **cohesion** rule which provides an agent with the ability to approach and form a group with other agents; and the **alignment** rule, which gives an agent the capability to align with other nearby agents contained in its visibility range. The agent can compute the steering for alignment by finding all agents in the local neighborhood and averaging together the 'heading' vectors of the nearby agents. The boids are not influenced by entities outside of its visibility range.

Flocking behavior among heterogeneous population of agents, *Multiple Species Flocking*, was modeled in [6]. The authors added, in this model, a similarity rule that allows each boid to discriminate among its neighbors and to group only with those similar to itself. The similarity rule enables the flock to organize groups of heterogeneous entities into homogeneous subgroups consisting only of individuals of the same species. The model proposed here, instead, simply modifies the basic flocking rules to take into account the similarity of an entity with its neighbors. In particular, if there are two dissimilar agents, the separation rule overrides the cohesion rule and the alignment rule. Whereas, if two agents are similar, all the rules are applied with the aim of forming a flock composed only of similar agents.

The virtual space V_s where agents move according to the flocking rules is a two dimensional Cartesian space, let $\mathcal{R}^2$, while the data stream point are represented in a n-dimensional feature space, let $\mathcal{R}^n$. For the sake of simplicity, the virtual space is assumed to be discrete and not continuous, and it is implemented as a two-dimensional toroidal grid of fixed size. Each agent is featured by a *velocity vector* $\vec{v} = (m, \theta)$ with magnitude m and direction determined by the angle θ formed between $\vec{v}$ and the positive x axis. We assume that the magnitude is constant for all the boids and it is equal to 1. This means that in the virtual space a boid moves one cell at a time. The overall flocking behavior will be expressed by a linear combination of the velocities calculated by all the rules that represent the velocity vector of the agents in the virtual space:

$$V = V_{alignment} + V_{cohesion} + V_{separation} \tag{1}$$

Each object coming from any source is associated with an agent, and the agent randomly spread on the virtual space. The loaded agents move following the flock rules trying to form a group of similar entities. Two agents are considered similar when the respective associated objects are similar. The *similarity function* is a function that quantifies the similarity between two associated objects. Similarity functions can be the Euclidean distance, the squared Euclidean distance, the cosine similarity or the Manhattan distance. In the experiment shown in this paper, the Euclidean distance to measure the similarity between two data items, is applied. Two agents, $A1$ and $A2$, are similar if their Euclidean distance of the associated object $d(obj1, obj2) \leq \epsilon$. The agents that carry a new object and moves itself in order to form a flock of similar agents, which is a group of agents with similar data item associated, are named *basic agents*.

When the process starts and for all first time units, only *basic agents* are present on the virtual space. After the first time unit, i.e. a fixed number of iterations, all the objects associated with the agents grouped in a flock can be replaced by a single virtual object associated with a *virtual agent*. The groups are composed of similar agents, i.e. with similar objects, and then the they can be replaced by means an unique summarizing virtual object. From the second time unit, *basic agents* and *virtual agents* move in the same virtual space following the flocking rules and trying to form new groups of similar entities. Figure 2 shows the virtual space at the first time unit and at a successive generic iteration.

It is possible to note how similar *basic agents* and *virtual agents* form a group, whereas dissimilar agents, that is outlier objects, move alone. This algorithm can be profitably applied to analyze the information that changes dynamically.

(a)   (b)

Fig. 2. Snapshots of the virtual space: (a) at first time unit; (b) at a generic successive time unit.

In fact, since the agents check the similarity function continuously when encounter other agents, they can move themselves among flocks. The virtual object representing the whole group of similar object is created in accordance with the concepts illustrated in [4]. The idea of a micro-cluster was borrowed to represent a group of data points through a unique data point. In this way, it is possible to employ a restricted amount of memory to store the value of old data points. In fact, for each flock of similar agents only one virtual object will be stored for the successive iterations. The operation of summarization is executed after a prefixed number of iterations (agents' movements) because during the movement an agent can leave the current group and join to another more similar group.

3.1 Experimental Results

The model was implemented in Java in order to investigate its effectiveness on a two kinds of data stream. The first a data stream, namely stream1, was generated using the synthetic datasets shown in Fig. 3.

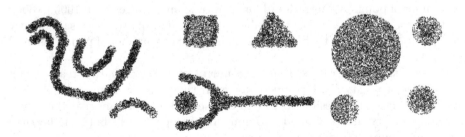

Fig. 3. The datasets used to generate the data stream stream1.

Each of them contains 10000 points, and to generate the data stream, each dataset was randomly chosen 10 times, thus generating an evolving data stream of total length 100000. The second data stream, namely stream2, consists of a combination of three Gaussian distributions with uniform noise for a total number of 100000. The right composition of *virtual agents* can be evaluated by considering the average *purity* and their *normalized mutual information*, since the true data label is known. The average purity P is defined as:

$$P = \frac{\sum_{i=1}^{Nv} \frac{|N_{similar}(i)|}{|N_{total}(i)|}}{Nv} * 100\,\%; \tag{2}$$

where Nv indicates the number of *virtual agents* for each time interval, $|N_{similar}|$ indicates the number of points really similar in *virtual agent* **i**, and $|N_{total}|$ indicates the total number of points in *virtual agent* **i**.

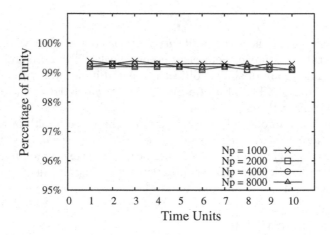

Fig. 4. The average purity for `stream1` data stream, when the values of the number of points analyzed for each time units N_p, ranges from 1000 to 8000.

Figure 4 shows the values of average purity for `stream1` data stream, when the number of points N_p, introduced for each time unit, ranges from 1000 to 8000 points. It should be noted that the values of average purity are very satisfactory and constant independently both of the time and of the number of points inserted in each time unit N_p.

Figure 5 shows the values of average purity or `stream2` data stream, when the number of points N_p, introduced for each time unit, ranging from 1000 to 8000 points. It is also possible to note in this second data stream that the values of average purity are very good and constant independently both of the time and of the number of points inserted each time unit N_p.

The *normalized mutual information* (NMI) is a well-known information theoretic measure that assesses how similar two clusterings are. Given the true clustering $A = \{A_1, \ldots, A_k\}$ and the grouping $B = \{B_1, \ldots, B_h\}$ obtained by a clustering method, let C be the confusion matrix whose element C_{ij} is the number of records of cluster i of A that are also in the cluster j of B. The normalized mutual information $NMI(A, B)$ is defined as:

$$NMI(A, B) = \frac{-2 \sum_{i=1}^{c_A} \sum_{j=1}^{c_B} C_{ij} log(C_{ij} N / C_{i.} C_{.j})}{\sum_{i=1}^{c_A} C_{i.} log(C_{i.}/N) + \sum_{j=1}^{c_B} C_{.j} log(C_{.j}/N)} \tag{3}$$

where c_A (c_B) is the number of groups in the partition A (B), $C_{i.}$ $(C_{.j})$ is the sum of the elements of C in row i (column j), and N is the number of points. If $A = B$, $NMI(A, B) = 1$. If A and B are completely different, $NMI(A, B) = 0$.

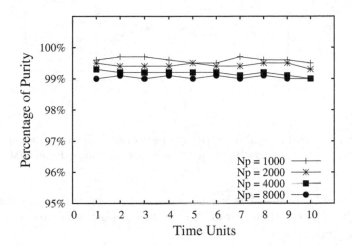

Fig. 5. The average purity for `stream2` data stream, when the number of points processed for each time units ranges from 1000 to 8000.

Figure 6 shows the values of normalized mutual information for `stream1` data stream, when the number of points N_p, introduced for each time unit, ranges

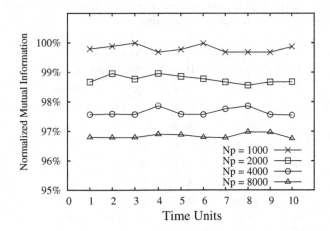

Fig. 6. The normalized mutual information for `stream1` data stream, when the values of the number of points analyzed for each time units N_p, ranges from 1000 to 8000.

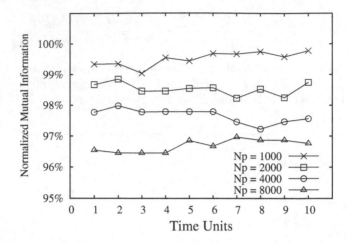

Fig. 7. The normalized mutual information for `stream2` data stream, when the values of the number of points analyzed for each time units N_p, ranges from 1000 to 8000.

from 1000 to 8000 points. The values of normalized mutual information, independently both of the time and of the number of points inserted in each time unit N_p, are very positive.

Figure 7 shows the values of normalized mutual information for `stream2` data stream, when the number of points N_p, introduced for each time unit, ranges from 1000 to 8000 points.

The same things can be noted for this second data stream, indeed, the values of normalized mutual information are very good and constant independently both of the time and of the number of points inserted in each time unit N_p.

Table 1. Precision and Recall for `stream1` end `stream2` data streams, when the number of points analyzed N_p is set to 5000 for each time unit.

Time	stream1		stream2	
Units	Precision	Recall	Precision	Recall
1	99.80	99.80	99.60	99.90
2	99.90	99.80	99.40	99.80
3	99.60	99.80	99.70	99.00
4	99.90	99.80	99.70	99.80
5	99.80	99.70	99.90	99.80
6	99.80	99.80	99.70	99.80
7	99.80	99.70	99.70	99.80
8	99.90	99.80	99.90	99.80
9	99.80	99.80	99.60	99.70
10	99.90	99.90	99.90	99.70

Successively, two measures, namely Precision and Recall, were used to further validate the algorithm. Precision represents the fraction of the values reported by algorithm as outliers that are true outliers. Recall represents the fraction of the true outliers that the algorithm identified correctly. Table 1 reports the values of Precision and Recall for both data streams, `stream1` and `stream2`, when the number of points analyzed N_p is set to 5000 for each time unit. Notice that the values obtained by the model for both data streams are very satisfactory. Indeed the results, both the fraction of the true outliers and the fraction of the true outliers that the algorithm identified correctly, are very encouraging.

4 Conclusion

To detect anomalies in a distributed system, a bio-inspired algorithm has been proposed. The features to discriminate among similar/non-similar agents was added to the model to enhance the basic flocking rules. The algorithm proposed in this paper is very scalable and suitable for large data stream thanks to features such as adaptivity, parallelism, asynchronism, and decentralization. Preliminary experimental results on synthetic data streams confirm the validity of the approach proposed and encourage to study the approach on real life data streams.

References

1. Aggarwal, C.C., Yu, P.S.: Outlier detection for high dimensional data. In: Proceedings of the 2001 ACM SIGMOD International Conference on Management of Data, SIGMOD 2001, pp. 37–46 (2001)
2. Alam, S., Dobbie, G., Riddle, P., Naeem, M.A.: A swarm intelligence based clustering approach for outlier detection. In: 2010 IEEE Congress on Proceedings of Evolutionary Computation (CEC), pp. 1–7. IEEE (2010)
3. Boyd, S., Ghosh, A., Prabhakar, B., Shah, D.: Gossip algorithms: design, analysis and applications. In: Proceedings of 24th Annual Joint Conference of the IEEE Computer and Communications Societies, Proceedings of IEEE, vol. 3, pp. 1653–1664. IEEE (2005)
4. Cao, F., Ester, M., Qian, W., Zhou, A.: Density-based clustering over an evolving data stream with noise. In: Proceedings of the 2006 SIAM International Conference on Data Mining, pp. 328–339 (2006)
5. Cui, X., Gao, J., Potok, T.E.: A flocking based algorithm for document clustering analysis. J. Syst. Archit. **52**(8), 505–515 (2006)
6. Cui, X., Potok, T.E.: A distributed agent implementation of multiple species flocking model for document partitioning clustering. In: Klusch, M., Rovatsos, M., Payne, T.R. (eds.) CIA 2006. LNCS (LNAI), vol. 4149, pp. 124–137. Springer, Heidelberg (2006)
7. Cutsem, B.V., Gath, I.: Detection of outliers and robust estimation using fuzzy clustering. Comput. Stat. Data Anal. **15**(1), 47–61 (1993)
8. Eberhart, R.C., Shi, Y., Kennedy, J.: Swarm Intelligence. Morgan Kaufmann, San Francisco (2001)

9. Ellabib, I., Calamai, P.H., Basir, O.A.: Exchange strategies for multiple ant colony system. Inf. Sci. **177**(5), 1248–1264 (2007)
10. Eskin, E., Arnold, A., Prerau, M., Portnoy, L., Stolfo, S.: A geometric framework for unsupervised anomaly detection: detecting intrusions in unlabeled data. In: Applications of Data Mining in Computer Security, Kluwer (2002)
11. Folino, G., Forestiero, A., Spezzano, G.: An adaptive flocking algorithm for performing approximate clustering. Inf. Sci. **179**(18), 3059–3078 (2009)
12. Forestiero, A.: Self organization in content delivery networks. In: 2012 IEEE 10th International Symposium on Parallel and Distributed Processing with Applications (ISPA), pp. 851–852. IEEE (2012)
13. Forestiero, A., Mastroianni, C., Spezzano, G.: A multi agent approach for the construction of a peer-to-peer information system in grids. Self-Organiz. Auton. Inform. (I) **135**, 220–225 (2005)
14. Forestiero, A., Pizzuti, C., Spezzano, G.: Flockstream: a bio-inspired algorithm for clustering evolving data streams. In: ICTAI. pp. 1–8. IEEE Computer Society (2009)
15. Huang, L., Nguyen, X., Garofalakis, M., Jordan, M.I., Joseph, A., Taft, N.: In-network PCA and anomaly detection. In: Advances in Neural Information Processing Systems, pp. 617–624 (2006)
16. Kempe, D., Dobra, A., Gehrke, J.: Gossip-based computation of aggregate information. In: Proceedings of the 44th Annual IEEE Symposium on Foundations of Computer Science, pp. 482–491. IEEE (2003)
17. Khalilian, M., Mustapha, N.: Data stream clustering: challenges and issues. CoRR abs/1006.5261 (2010)
18. Mehyar, M., Spanos, D., Pongsajapan, J., Low, S.H., Murray, R.M.: Asynchronous distributed averaging on communication networks. IEEE/ACM Trans. Netw. **15**(3), 512–520 (2007)
19. Mohemmed, A.W., Zhang, M., Browne, W.N.: Particle swarm optimisation for outlier detection. In: GECCO, pp. 83–84. ACM (2010)
20. Monmarch, N., Slimane, M., Venturini, G.: On improving clustering in numerical databases with artificial ants. In: Floreano, D., Mondada, F. (eds.) ECAL 1999. LNCS, vol. 1674, pp. 626–635. Springer, Heidelberg (1999)
21. Pokrajac, D., Lazarevic, A., Latecki, L.J.: Incremental local outlier detection for data streams. In: CIDM, pp. 504–515. IEEE (2007)
22. Reynolds, C.W.: Flocks, herds and schools: a distributed behavioral model. In: Stone, M.C. (ed.) SIGGRAPH, pp. 25–34. ACM, Anaheim (1987)
23. Tang, J., Chen, Z., Fu, A.W.C., Cheung, D.W.: Capabilities of outlier detection schemes in large datasets, framework and methodologies. Knowl. Inf. Syst. **11**(1), 45–84 (2007)

A Reconfigurable Prototyping Platform for iBeacon Service

Janusz Tomasiak, Michał Bernat, and Zbigniew Piotrowski[✉]

Faculty of Electronics, Military University of Technology,
Kaliskiego 2 street, 00-908 Warsaw, Poland
janusztom@o2.pl,
{michal.bernat,zbigniew.piotrowski}@wat.edu.pl

Abstract. The paper describes the results of tests of the iBeacon reconfigurable hardware platform using the BLE112 module. The platform is used in UUID broadcasting. Based on the unique UUID address broadcast by a radio transmitter, it is possible to determine the distance from it using an application installed on a smartphone. The article presents the results of prototype tests of the electronic module, among others, the estimation of the maximum working time of a battery powered device and the estimation of the accuracy of determining the distance.

Keywords: iBeacon · BLE 112 · Bluetooth low energy · Location-based services · Indoor positioning system

1 Introduction

The iBeacon technology was developed by Apple, and presented to potential customers and producers in 2013. Since then, there have been many cases of implementation of this standard. The operating systems based on this technology [1–5] are used to locate the miniature transmitters commonly referred to as iBeacons, which are the radio-frequency tags of a given place or product. These transmitters are installed in stores, commercial buildings, on products, etc. By broadcasting its unique identifier in the form of an UUID address, they inform the receiver of their position. The iBeacons allow in particular the location of shops and objects inside buildings (indoor). The iBeacon is an uncomplicated transmitting or transmitting-receiving system working in the Bluetooth 4.0 Low Energy, BLE standard. By definition, it is a device optimised in terms of the energy consumption, which means long periods of use on a single battery at the expense of a smaller range of 50-80 [m], as well as a low bandwidth of useful data. However, by using dedicated antennas you can get the range of up to 250 [m], but usually the iBeacons work on miniature antennas mounted on the PCB.

The iBeacon continuously broadcasts its UUID identifier within a given interval, without the need to receive confirmations or establishing relations with devices receiving the transmitted frames. Many iBeacons which can be received by the smartphone can work in a given area. A person who is in range of the iBeacon broadcast, and has a smartphone with Bluetooth 4.0 technology, running a suitable application can, for example, receive

© Springer International Publishing Switzerland 2015
A. Dziech et al. (Eds.): MCSS 2015, CCIS 566, pp. 83–94, 2015.
DOI: 10.1007/978-3-319-26404-2_7

personalised messages about products in the store or the way to the correct terminal at the airport. On the basis of, among others, the radio signal strength determined by the Received Signal Strength Indication (RSSI) coefficient, a smartphone located within the iBeacon range can estimate the distance from the transmitter. In the context of determining the distance, developers define three ranges of distance: close (2–10 cm), medium (3–10 [m]) and far (10–70 [m]). The iBeacon technology is therefore an interesting alternative to the NFC technology, which works only in direct contact of devices.

2   Implementation of a Selected iBeacon System Module in the BLE Hardware Module

2.1   Development Environment for BGScript Language

The programming of the BLE112 module was implemented using dedicated Bluegiga BGScript1 language. However, the module can also be programmed in ANSI C language in the IAR Embedded Workbench SDK environment. In accordance with the manufacturer's instructions, the editing of the software files was carried out using the Notepad ++ text editor, version 6.4.5 with the additional plug-in enabling highlighting the script language syntax, provided by Bluegiga [6]. The compilation of the project was carried out using Bluegiga BLE SW Update Tool application, version 1.3.2-122 [7].

Programming in script language involves constructing short blocks of code that are performed depending on the occurrence of a specific event, e.g. reset after the detection of an interruption, establishing or breaking the connection with another module. In addition to the implementation of the logic of programme operation, there is also a possibility to change the module parameters specified in the file describing the hardware. BGScript language specification is available on the manufacturer's website [8]. The project of the software consists of a set of files that must be created manually and edited in the Notepad ++ editor:

- a file with the *.bgproj extension – the main file of the project, which includes:
- a list of files that will be compiled and the name of the *.hex resulting file;
- a gatt.xml file – specifying the configuration, UUIDs of characteristics and services offered by the programmed module and visible in mobile applications;
- a hardware.xml file – describing the settings of electrical parameters, such as the data rate of the USART port, USB parameters, power of the transmitter, oscillator operating mode;
- scripts.xml – file describing the logic of the programme operation using a dedicated script language.

2.2   Description of the Hardware Platform with a BLE112 Module

The hardware platform, hereinafter referred to as BLE112 module was built based on the commercially available pre-prepared Bluetooth ble112-A system of the Bluegiga company, (Fig. 1) soldered to the designed and made [9] base printed circuit board shown in Fig. 2. This circuit board has support functions for the wireless system, intended to ensure power supply, remove the programmer/debugger interface and signal the system status via LEDs.

Fig. 1. Bluegiga BLE 112-A module

Fig. 2. Appearance of the BLE112 module

After programming the radio system and loading the developed software implementing the iBeacon functionality, the board requires only providing the power supply via USB or debugger connector shown in Fig. 2.

The Ble112A system is a radio device of the Bluetooth LE 4.0 family equipped with a programmable microcontroller. The radio parameters of the system are as follows: Bluetooth 4.0 Low Energy receiver/transmitter; transmitter power: +3 [dBm] max; receiver sensitivity: -92 [dBm]; integrated antenna or U.FL connector; peak power consumption of the transmitter: 27 [mA] (with the power of 0 [dBm]); current consumption in the sleep mode: 0.4 [μA]. The parameters of the Bluetooth module: L2CAP, ATT, GATT, GAP and Security Manager; Bluetooth Smart profiles; Master and Client modes; ability to maintain 8 connections in Master mode; The parameters of the base board: SPI, I2C, PWM, UART, GPIO, USB host; ADC 12-bit; supply voltage: 2.0–3.6 [V]; temperature range: -40 to +85 [°C]; 8051 microcontroller; 8 [KB] of RAM; 128 [KB] Flash.

The developed software of the BLE112 module is designed to configure the microcontroller system controlling the radio system in such a way as to hold the function of

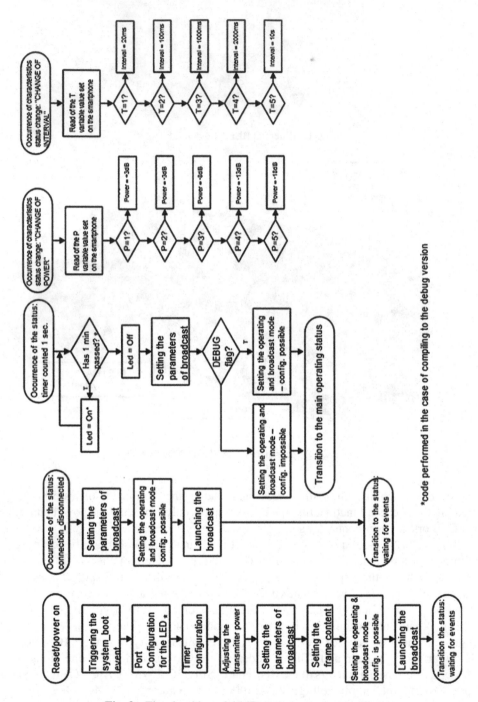

Fig. 3. The algorithm of the iBeacon program operation

the iBeacon. The BLE112 module programmed in this way operates as a standalone device visible to other devices working in the Bluetooth 4.0 standard.

The described hardware module implements the full functionality of iBeacon by sending its identifier. This module has the ability to configure the power and interval of the broadcast via radio. The broadcast starts always automatically after power is provided and after a reset. For the purpose of the module configuration a service with the 1d5688de-866d-3aa4-ec46-a1bddb37ecf6 UUID signature with two UUID characteristics aa20fbac-2518-4998-9af7-af42540731b3 to configure power, and UUID bb20fbac-2518-4998-9af7-af42540731b3 to configure the time interval of the broadcast, have been implemented. The record of the values from 1 to 5 for these characteristics via mobile application changes the parameters of the iBeacon. Both characteristics have the Read/Write attribute, and after their setting, you can also perform the read to verify the settings. All settings made in this way are stored in the volatile memory and are lost when power is removed or reset. For the purposes of the study, the ability to define the DEBUG = 1 flag in the *.bgs file was provided. Defining the flag activates the LED and blocks entering into the non-reconfigurable mode after 1 min since providing power. An illuminating LED indicates whether the module is in configuration mode or not. The configuration can be changed within 1 min after switching on the module, because after that time the iBeacon enters the mode preventing configuration. The implementation is modelled on the examples provided on the company's forum at: https://blue-giga.zendesk.com. The algorithm of the program operation is shown in Fig. 3.

3   Tests of the Developed Module

The studies presented in this section were aimed at determining the parameters of the designed device in different operating conditions.

3.1   Estimation of the Maximum Operation Time on the Battery

The measurement of the current consumption was made using Tektronix TDS7154B oscilloscope with a TCA-1MEG amplifier and a P6139A probe. The measurement was performed by connecting the 9.7 [Ohm] resistor in series into the line no. 9 of the CC Debugger tape power supplying the BLE112 module. The oscilloscope was connected to the terminals of the standard resistor. The current measurements were carried out for the iBeacon transmitter power of -18 [dBm] (txpower power parameter = "3"). The bundles of pulses registered by the oscilloscope which were used to determine the current consumption are shown in Fig. 4.

Analysing the oscillograms, we read that a single transmission consists of a main part in which the 3 broadcast frames with parameters t = 0.9 [ms] I = 35 [mA] (340/9.7) are sent, and the auxiliary (preparatory and ending the transmission) part with parameters t = 1.5 [ms] I = 21.7 [mA] (210/9.7). Calculating the energy for such transmission, we get 17.8 [nAh] in one transaction. Dividing the CR2477T battery capacity by the energy consumed for one transaction, we obtain the total number of 56200000 transactions (1 [Ah] /17.8 [nAh]).

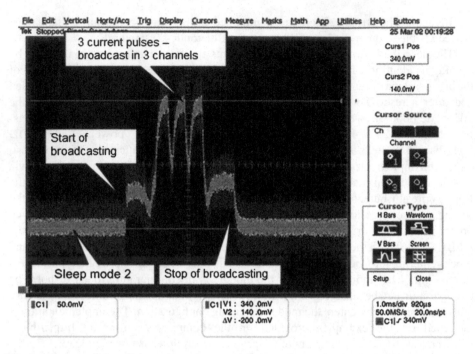

Fig. 4. Characteristics of the voltage drop on the measuring resistor – the voltage cursors are visible

Assuming that the iBeacon sends 10 frames per second, we obtain 864,000 transactions per day (10 * 60 * 60 * 24). Hence, it is easy to calculate that the device would work 65 days on the battery. It is true only for the assumption that the transmission break in between the transactions is zero. In the present case there is a high current leakage, which would significantly decrease the battery life.

The current in a sleep state consumed by the system amounted to 14.4 [mA] (140 mV /9.7). The obtained value is more than an order of magnitude greater than that the one provided by the manufacturer for a similar hardware configuration described in [10]. This is probably due to the presence of the R13 resistor-jumper connecting the P1_0 port to VDD and the connection of the signal lines of the P1 port to the programmer socket, which powered the module.

Assuming that the value of the quiescent current is 0.9 [uA], and adjusting the value read from the oscillogram (subtracting 14 [mA] from the calculated current values), we would get 135 days of work time. Such an operation time is realistic and similar to the operation time of the Estimote device (Table 1).

Table 1. Estimated operation time after the additional current leakage adjustment

Battery type	Transmission parameters	Estimated operation time
CR2477: 1000 [mAh]	Power -18 dBm, Interval 100 ms	135 days

3.2   Test of Accuracy of Determining the Distance from the iBeacon Emitter Using Mobile Applications

The study was carried out in the hall of an underground garage which did not have windows, and it was located under the ground at the -2 level. No vehicles or people were moving in the room during the measurements. The vertical space between the iBeacon and the smartphone had the height of approx. 2.5 [m] and was limited from the bottom by a reinforced concrete floor and from the top by a reinforced concrete ceiling, under which the electrical systems (lighting, fire protection, visual monitoring), central heating pipes, and metal ventilation ducts were routed. The horizontal measurement surface had a width of about 8 [m], and it was limited on both sides by reinforced concrete walls. Cars were parked on both sides along the walls and perpendicular to them, occupying about 50 % of the parking spaces.

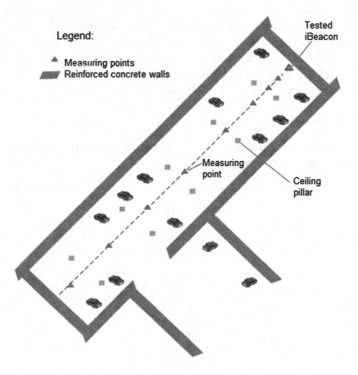

Fig. 5. Sketch of the measurement area in the underground garage.

No other devices in the 2.4 GHz band (Wi-Fi, microwave ovens, Bluetooth devices) worked at the place of the measurement performance. The tested iBeacon was placed at a height of 1.5 [m] above the floor, about 50 [cm] from the wall in such a way that the main radiation direction was perpendicular to the wall. The study was performed using a smartphone as described in paragraph 2.1.1 held in the hand at a height of 1.5 [m] above the floor. The tests with the use of mobile applications were performed using the

Samsung Galaxy SIII Mini GT-I8190 N phone. The Android software in this phone was adapted, and the 8 GB microSD card and a SIM card with access to the internet were installed. The phone with the original software does not allow to carry out experiments with BLE devices; it was necessary to install a newer OS. In this case, the CyanogenMod 12 software available on the internet, based on the Android software, version 5.0.2 was used. The Beacon Scanner & Logger mobile application was launched on the phone. It is the application used, among others, to capture and save the iBeacon frame to the file. You can import the text file with data, e.g. to an Excel spreadsheet. The person performing the measurement for all measuring points was facing the iBeacon transmitter, and the smartphone was held in a horizontal position, face up, with the speaker facing the iBeacon transmitter. The measuring application recorded 1 frame per second. The test was performed for the measuring points arranged as shown in Fig. 5. Bearing in mind the significant fluctuations of the RSSI coefficient values for the iBeacon transmitter, it was assumed that for each measuring point 100 RSSI measurements would be performed and then a median of RSSI values will be determined for each point. The values for calibration of the model were A = -72.13 [dB], n = 1.6102 respectively. The average value of the RSSI measurement results depending on the distance are shown in Table 2. The ranges of distances including the measurements for certain points, assumed by developers are defined in Table 2, in the last column.

Table 2. Average values of the RSSI coefficient for each of the measuring points.

No.	Distance of measuring point from the iBeacon [m]	RSSI median [dBm]	Distance range
1	1	-73	average
2	2	-74.7	
3	3	-82	
4	5	-80.7	
5	7	-95	far
6	10	-90.2	
7	15	-96.2	
8	20	-83.7	
9	25	-102	
10	30	-92.9	
11	40	-101	
12	50	-100.3	

Having a set of the RSSI measurements for various distances, using a simple exponential model of propagation [11] it is possible to determine the approximated RSSI values for any distance:

$$P_0 = RSSI = P\left(d_0\right) - 10n \log \frac{d}{d_0} \qquad (1)$$

Assuming in the formula that: $d_0 = 1$ [m], and $P(d_0) = A$, we obtain a formula for the distance:

$$d = 10^{\frac{A-RSSI}{10n}} \qquad (2)$$

The A and n parameters for the above formulas shall be determined for the location in which the measurements are carried out. In our case the A parameter value is an average RSSI value determined at a distance of 1 [m] from the iBeacon. The parameter n was calculated separately for each measuring point, and then the average was determined, and this value was used in the formula for approximation of the RSSI for the chart below. The chart below presents the course of the approximated course of the RSSI (black) and the measurement results obtained for each measurement with the logarithmic approximation (green).

Analysing the RSSI course, it can be seen that with increasing distance the slope of the curve decreases, which in practice means a weaker accuracy of determining the distance on the basis of an observable change in the RSSI for longer distances (Table 3).

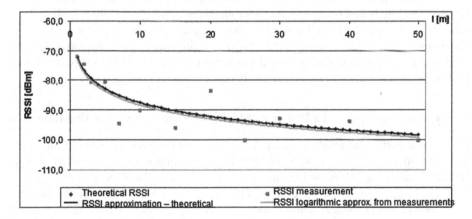

Fig. 6. Approximation of the distance from the iBeacon transmitter and the results of measurements of the RSSI in the function of the distance (Color figure online)

The table below presents a summary of the results of determining the distance and errors for all measurement points.

Table 3. Accuracy of calculating the distances for individual measuring points

No.	d [m]	Calculated d [m]	Relative error [%]	Absolute error [m]
1	2	1,45	27,5	0,5
2	3	3,42	13,5	0,4
3	5	3,39	32,3	1,6
4	7	24,78	254	17,8
5	10	13,34	33,4	3,3
6	15	31,09	107	16,1
7	20	5,24	73,8	14,8
8	25	55,82	122	30,5
9	30	19,54	34,9	10,5
10	40	22,45	43,9	17,6
11	50	55,82	11,6	5,8

The analysis of the results, while rejecting the results of items 4, 6, and 8, being regarded as extremely unrealistic, shows that the relative error for all points was in the range from 0.4 [m] to 14.5 [m], corresponding respectively to 27.5 % and 73.8 %. In order to determine the causes of these errors, the measurements should be carried out in different conditions and using different instruments to verify the results e.g. the Nexus smartphone, the use of which Bluegiga refers to the examples. Bearing in mind the very stable results obtained by using the SmartRF Studio 7 device (paragraph 3.3), it is assumed that the errors in determining the distance could be related to the properties of the Bluetooth receiver in the tested smartphone.

3.3 Test of RSS Values at a Distance of 1 [M] for Various Broadcasting Channels

The test was performed for the purposes of determining the RSSI required to add to the iBeacon frame to the Measured power field. This test is important because at the manufacturing stage of the iBeacon the one determined value of the RSSI power level at a distance of 1 [m] from the device is entered to the broadcast frame, although the iBeacon broadcasts in three channels with numbers 37, 38, 39. In order to avoid measurement errors for each test, after setting the initial parameters, 100 consecutive frames were recorded using SmartRF Studio 7 tool, which automatically calculates and displays the average RSSI value.

The tests were performed for all power levels implemented in the iBeacon (i.e. -18, -13, -8, -3, 3 [dBm]) for the constant broadcast interval value equal to 100 [ms]. The power level while carrying the examination was changed using a BLE Scanner mobile application, while the power level measurement was performed using the ble112 module and SmartRF Studio software. The choice of tools was dictated by the chosen environment that enabled automated recording of a series of frames (e.g. 100) along with the calculation of the average RSSI or BER. The RSSI values for each channel at the fixed power differ significantly, as shown in Fig. 6.

The collected data were compiled in the form of a chart and shown in Fig. 6. The X-axis indicates the subsequent values of power set in the tested module, and the Y-axis indicates the RSSI power level measured at a distance of 1 [m]. The RSSI measurements for the three broadcasting channels were carried out for each power setting and they were distinguished in the chart by using different colours (Fig. 7).

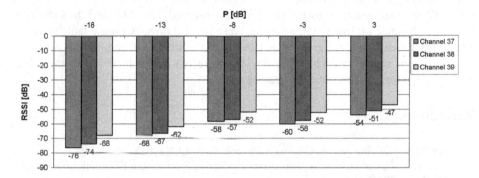

Fig. 7. Characteristics of the effects of the set transmitter power on the RSSI level for different channels

The chart shows that at the set broadcast power the RSSI value for the different channels may vary by up to 8 [dB] – as it is for the first series of data, plotted for -18 [dBm]. The second characteristic and repetitive property which can be observed is a decrease in the RSSI, along with the increase of the channel number at the set broadcast power. The analysis of the charts also confirms the growth of the RSSI values along with the increase of the set transmitter power. By the set power of -18 [dBm], the average value of RSSI was on average -73 [dB] and for the power of 3 [dB] an average value of the RSSI was -51 [dB]. It could be observed when performing these measurements that the placement of any object in the Fresnel zone affected the level of the measured RSSI power very strongly. When placing a hand or a smartphone in this area, it was observed that the signal level decreased from a few to several [dB].

4   Conclusions

The article describes the dedicated, reconfigurable iBeacon transmitter based on the BLE 112 module. The system was tested during the examination carried out in the hall of the underground garage. The determined distance values calculated on the basis of the RSSI signal levels for the individual measuring points were compared with the characteristics determined based on the exponential model of propagation. The relative error for the BLE112 module for all points was in the range from the 0.4 [m] to 14.5 [m], which corresponded with 27.5 % and 73.8 % respectively. Signals of such quality are completely sufficient for applications in which it is necessary to estimate the distance from the potential receiver to the iBeacon. Comparing the accuracy of the obtained measurements as described in the article [11], the results obtained here are burdened with a relatively big error. In order to determine the causes of these errors, the measurements in different conditions and using different tools (e.g. a higher class smartphone) should be carried out to verify the results.

In the course of the research on the RSSI signal level at a distance of 1 [m] from the iBeacon, the signal levels for the three broadcasting channels were measured and compared. In the case of the ble112 module, the RSSI discrepancies depending on the test channel up to 8 [dB] were obtained. A significant effect of distribution of iBeacons on the RSSI level measured by the scanner was observed during the test. In a study of RSSI at a distance of 1 [m], when devices were located directly on the table made of chipboard, the decrease of the RSSI on the scanner of up to a dozen dB was noted, in comparison to the test in which the devices were placed 30 [cm] above the table, providing the free space within the Fresnel zone.

References

1. Gast, M.S.: Building Applications with iBeacon. OREILLY (2015)
2. Townsend, K., Carles Cufi, A., Davidson, R.: Getting Started with Bluetooth Low Energy. OREILLY (2014)
3. Bluetooth. http://bluetooth.com
4. http://www.itu.int/en/ITU-T/asn1/Pages/UUID/uuids.aspx
5. http://www.itu.int/rec/T-REC-X.667-201210-I/en
6. Bluegiga.   https://www.bluegiga.com/protectedstore/8pHYFByrRbCfvauWLt5CMQ/ Fy7zP-M6WtLgoq90YqmVMw/4HjebXhW8xcGV8kz18VSS2evbojnAxnSNwDxSJo VkhtzUmMZjpUf/BGScript_Syntax_highlighting_for_Notepad%2B%2B.zip
7. Bluegiga.   https://www.bluegiga.com/protectedstore/8pHYFByrRbCfvauWLt5CMQ/ FOq1vu3eHkfZ74TQHi5FKA/_49oTHY5sAr9kf_OYCyJsNktS9-SmR3X7iA3LU8- bAMmu3fuo7mf/ble-1.3.2-122.zip
8. Bluegiga.   https://bluegiga.zendesk.com/attachments/token/jddX2mGRIYxgDAtme YlWbEYdU/?name=Bluetooth_Smart_Software_v1.3.1_API_Reference.pdf
9. Bernat, M., Piotrowski, Z.: Mobile recorder for electrical activity of the heart. In: Progress in Electromagnetics Research Symposium, PIERS 2015, 6–9 July, Prague, pp. 713–717 (2015). ISSN: 1559-9450
10. Bluegiga forum. https://bluegiga.zendesk.com/entries/24740576–BGScript-min-current- Low-power-baseline-reference-project
11. Radecki, K., Kosiło, T., Marski, J.: iBeacon–nowe zastosowanie standardu. In: KKRRiT 2015 (2015)

Modeling and Analysis of Spatial Conflicts with Layered Competitive Cellular Automata

Bernadetta Stachura-Terlecka[✉] and Antoni Ligęza

AGH University of Science and Technology in Krakow,
al. Mickiewicza 30, 30-059 Kraków, Poland
{bstachur,ligeza}@agh.edu.pl
http://www.agh.edu.pl

Abstract. The paper presents a new approach to modeling and analysis of conflicting spatial phenomena. The proposal is based on an extension of Cellular Automata. A new approach, namely Layered Competitive Cellular Automata for modeling of spatial conflicts of dynamic nature is put forward. The idea of this approach consists in building two or more levels of the grid with competitive automata and defining influences about them. A first implementation is presented and application example illustrating the approach is provided.

Keywords: Cellular Automata · Conflicts · Layered Competitive Cellular Automata · Spatial modeling

1 Introduction

Since *Spring and Autumn* period of ancient China, people have known how grave is war and conflict. Sun Tzu[1] said, that war was the greatest thing of the state. In modern World practically all types of conflicts are omnipresent; in fact they are part of everyday life. In practice, all people observe, are involved in or actively participate in conflicts. This happens in at ours work or at school, in private life, in public life and in politics, in international situation, often with involvement of army. Hence, modeling and analysis of conflicts becomes very important issues; for dealing with them both theory and tools must be developed.

Conflicts can be modeled and analyzed with a variety of tools, more or rather less formal. In fact, conflicts are investigated in domains such as psychology, sociology, economy, game theory, operations research, theory of combat, etc. The tools used for modeling range from natural language, through visual modeling to some mathematical models such as equation (e.g. the Lanchester Models of

---

A. Ligęza—AGH Research Contract No.: 11.11.120.859.

[1] Chinese military general, strategist, and philosopher who lived in the *Spring and Autumn* period of ancient China. According to him: *War is the greatest thing of the state, the basis of life and death, Tao survival or destruction. It must be carefully considered and analyzed.*
(Sun Tzu: The Art of War).

A. Dziech et al. (Eds.): MCSS 2015, CCIS 566, pp. 95–109, 2015.
DOI: 10.1007/978-3-319-26404-2_8

Combat), game-theoretical models (tables, graphs), to simulation models incorporating use of specialized programming languages.

In this paper the main focus is on modeling *spatial, dynamic phenomena* (such as fire or terrorism) and *spatial conflicts* among such phenomena. The models incorporate the Cellular Automata (CA) approach. CA is a popular tool for modeling dynamic spatial phenomena, both of continuous and discrete nature [2, 16, 21]. Classical CA are used to modeling a single phenomenon, typically with homogeneous, uniformly spread cells over a predefined rectangular grid. The presented approach is aimed at providing an important extension: two (or more) *conflicting* or *competitive* CA, are introduced. These CAs fight each against the other.

For intuition, such an approach can be used for modeling contradictory environments, each of them influencing the other. In the example (see Sect. 6) the phenomenon of fire and the firemen with extinction tools (resources of water) form two sides of the conflict. By changing the initial conditions and environment parameters (e.g. strength and direction of wind, amount of water used, etc.) one can simulate, visualize and analyze behavior of such a dynamic system. A nice feature is the conflict visualization tool allowing for transparent presentation of the dynamically changing situation.

The approach proposed in this paper is build around a new concept: the *Layered Competitive Cellular Automata*, or LCCA for short. The Automata involved in the modeling are organized in two (or more) layers. They are described by:

- type and parameters of the cells in use (different cells maybe used at different layers),
- spatial location of the cells (placement over the predefined grid),
- interaction among cells (of the same layer as well as cross-layers).

Such an approach allows for modeling a variety of conflicting and competitive phenomena of dynamic, spatial nature. In fact, the cellular automata of the LCCA type are best fitted for simulation and modeling of spatial phenomena, where two (or more) conflicting phenomena influence (e.g. fight against) each other. Some typical example applications may include:

- conflicts of spatial nature (military and non-military),
- problems of international and internal safety and security, including
- migrations of refugees vs. contractions of local authorities and forces,
- terrorism: initial centers, spread of, effects of counteraction,
- natural disasters such as fire, flooding, avalanches, etc.,
- broadening epidemics and contraction,
- disasters of critical infrastructure, e.g. propagation of damages of a network and influence of undertaken actions [19, 20].

The proposed approach captures both the spatial aspects of the modeled phenomena and the dynamics of each of the medium itself and the conflict as well. In the next subsection we present some concepts used in this paper at the intuitive level.

1.1   A Brief Outline of LCCA: How It Works

Let us briefly present the basic ideas about the Layered Competitive Cellular Automata — a tool for modeling dynamic, spatial, conflicting phenomena. The basic concept here is a *cell* — almost exactly as in the classical Cellular Automata [2]. Such a cell models the phenomenon of interest at a specific point; the location is described with classical Cartesian coordinates x and y. The cells are located in an rectangular space on a regular grid. The environment itself is defined in an analogous way. The rules of interaction are predefined and implemented in the simulation engine.

For illustration, consider a simple map as presented in a following figure (see Fig. 1). The map is located in the top-left corner. It contains:

- trees — to be denoted with 1,
- grass — to be denoted with 2,
- concrete (walls, pavement) — to be denoted with 3,

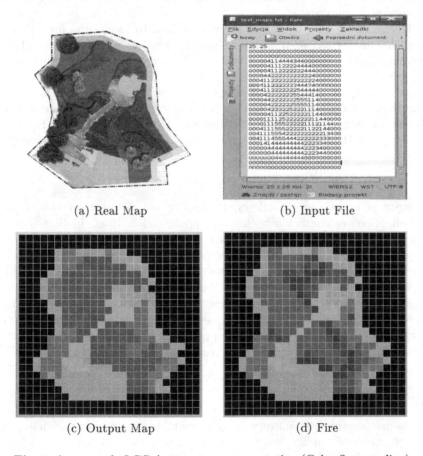

(a) Real Map   (b) Input File

(c) Output Map   (d) Fire

Fig. 1. An example LCC Automaton representation (Color figure online)

– sand — to be denoted with 4, and
– water — to be denoted with 5.

Such a map is represented as a numerical matrix defining the *environment*. The appropriate matrix in shown in the figure, right to the original map. The above components are represented with respective numbers, while 0 denotes empty space.

Having defined the environment, represented as layer 0 (the basic level) one can define next active layers for representation of the spatial phenomena to be simulated. For example, here we define the fire. It is modeled with Object Oriented approach; each cell is defined as specific object, and there are numerous cells in a single layer, so that the predefined grid is covered one-to-one.

The cells are initialized by static assignment of type of a cell (in fact the type defines a specific behavior, e.g. fire) and some value (intensity or wear) — representing the level of the phenomenon at the respective cell (location). In the figure, the bottom-left picture is a visualization of the initial state. The dark-green color represents the grass, the green represents the trees, and the blue pixels represent the water.

In this example only one extra layer is defined to model the fire. The cells representing fire form a separate layer (layer 1). Fire is visualized with red color, and its hue denotes its intensity. A state of the fire is visualized in the bottom-right picture.

In an analogous way new layers can be added. They can represent other (conflicting) phenomena. The interaction among phenomena allocated at different levels are defined with rules of operation. In this way competitive spatial phenomena and their interactions can be modeled, visualized and analyzed.

1.2   Organization of the Paper

The paper is organized as follows. In Sect. 2 an overview of theory, tools and applications of conflict modeling are presented in brief. In Sect. 2 a brief overview of the selected approaches to modeling conflicts is presented. We refer to Lanchester models, game-theoretical approaches and some work of Z. Pawlak. The next Sect. 3 recapitulates some essential notes on classical Cellular Automata. Section 4 is entirely devoted to presentation of the proposed approach: the concept of Layered Competitive Cellular Automata (LCCA). In the next Sect. 5 some details of implementation in the Python programming language are reported in brief. Some application of the proposed approach is presented in Sect. 6. Finally, concluding remarks are given in Sect. 7.

2   Conflict Modeling

Conflicts are omnipresent in everyday life, politics, economy, work. There exists many definitions of conflict, but for the purposes of this paper we use definition of sociological dictionary:

Definition 1. *Conflict situation occurs between two or more sides, where one of the sides (an individual or a group) preclude other group from reaching the target [15].*

So, a conflicting situations is one where two or more agents are confronted and having mutually exclusive goals.

2.1 Lanchester Model of Combat

Most of the simulations and models of modern battlefield [1,3,10] are based on the concepts of English mathematician F.W. Lanchester [8]. In 1914, Lanchester formulated the Lanchester Laws, with which one can analytically determine the course of the battle. Lanchester Laws allow at any time to estimate the number of individual parties of the conflict and the level of losses incurred.

Nowadays, there are also common opinions that Lanchester models [6] are no longer valid, because they seem inadequate to the modern battlefields. The basic Lanchester model presupposes the existence of two sides fighting, to be labeled A and B. Loss factors are known to both sides fighting denoted by S_A and S_B.

At the time t the number of fighting units of A-side is described as $a(t)$, the number of fighting units B side is described as $b(t)$, the initial number of sides are a_0 and b_0.

Lanchester Laws describing the battle take the form of the following systems of ordinary differential equations:

$$\frac{da}{dt} = -S_A b \tag{1}$$

$$\frac{db}{dt} = -S_B a \tag{2}$$

with the following initial conditions: $a(0) = a_0$ and $b(0) = b_0$, and assuming $S_A > 0$ and $S_B > 0$.

Factor S_A is determined by the ability of the forces B for the destruction forces A, analogously ratio S_B depends on the power to destroy a force B. These equations are known as the square Lanchester Law; they describe known from economies effect of scale. This effect is associated with size of the fighting forces and its impact on the potential to destroy the enemy forces. There are also equations of homogeneous type of combat (e.g. infantry vs. infantry), in which both sides have the same weapons and have equal firepower and the battlefield (the so-called First Lanchester Law) and in the case of the known area of fighting, but ignorance of the exact location of hostile forces, which can lead to erroneous elimination of own units one can use second linear law of Lanchester.

The main problem with the models such as Lanchester Laws is that they are very compound; in fact no spatial characteristics are taken into account. Moreover the dynamics once defined stays not changed despite of the changes in conditions and environment.

2.2   Conflicts in Game Theory

The area of interest in game theory [7] are problems with decisions in systems with more participants (agents, players), each of which has some of its preferences, defining its mode of action (within the set of rules) and its winning situations. It is assumed that all players behave rationally, which in the game theory means that each player tries to maximize his own winnings, regardless of what are doing other players.

Each player makes decisions about the movements that are consistent with the rules of the game and that maximize his winnings. Game theory has found wide applications in economics, evolutionary biology, sociology, political science, and in computer science. In all these areas, game theory serves as a tool for examining models of optimal decisions (strategy) in situations involving at least two players also in such situations when individual players are not sure of the actions that take other players.

2.3   Conflicts with Agents

Around 1984, Z. Pawlak proposed a model of conflict situations based on information systems and the theory of Rough Sets [11]. Since that time, it is being developed by various authors (e.g. [4,5,14]). Pawlak's model describes the conflict situation in the steady state in which the agents decided to analyze the conflict peacefully by voting on given conflict cases. In addition to that description of the conflict situation Pawlak considering a solution to the conflict basis on the division of the spoils (power solution and with common accord) [12].

In the conflict involved sides are called agents. The agents define their positions by assigning the opinion of each selected case. In Pawlak's model the relationship between the agent and with the case (attribute) are presented in the form of a table where agents are corresponding to rows of the table and affairs correspond to attributes in columns.

The values assigned for each agent and attribute come from the trivalent set $-1, 0, 1$, where -1 means that the agent is against, 0 is neutral and 1 means approval for the case. Formally, the table creates an information system defined as follows.

Definition 2. *The information system which is modeling conflicts is a pair $I = (U, A)$, where: U - is a non-empty, finite set called the universe; elements of the set are objects - here called agents, A - is a non-empty, finite set of attributes (cases). Each attribute $a \in A$ is a mapping $a : U \rightarrow V_a$, where V_a is a set of attribute a values. The elements of the set V_a are the opinions of the agent ag about the case a. The sets values of attributes for Pawlak's conflicts model are limited to three values: $-1, 0, 1$, which represent opposition, neutrality approval.*

Relations between agents are defined by their views on issues under consideration [11,14]. Relation of consent is an equivalence relation [13], agents belonging to the class of equivalence defined by this relationship in the coalition are determined by the attribute a.

3   Cellular Automata

John von Neumann is considered as the father of the theory of cellular automata. The foundations of the theory laid by J. von Neumann became useful in clarifying and modeling complex situations present in the real world [9]. Cellular automata are complex systems of cell networks representing mathematical models to assist in the analysis and modeling of physical systems [22]. The value of the machine is described by the values which are the cells in the grid. Changes in the cells during simulation follow in accordance with established rules of automata and depend on their neighbors states in the previous step. The most popular neighborhoods for 2D automata are: (Fig. 2)

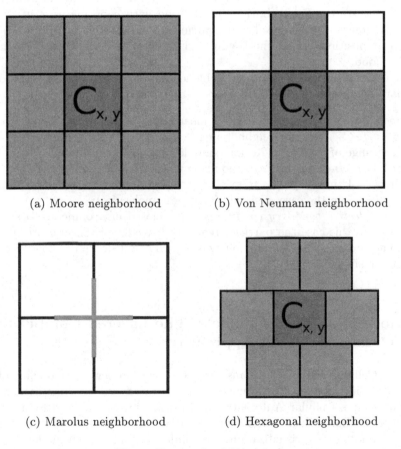

(a) Moore neighborhood   (b) Von Neumann neighborhood

(c) Marolus neighborhood   (d) Hexagonal neighborhood

Fig. 2. Types of neighborhood

There are of course other types of neighborhoods like Marolus neighborhood and hexagonal one.

Cellular automata rules are selected for mapping the changes in the simulated system [16]. To make this possible, there are types of automata for adopting continuous values by the automata (Fuzzy Cellular Automata). For explanation of the rules of automata, consider the following example: we consider the 2D automata $C_{x,y}$ - single cell with coordinates x, y and $\phi_{x,y}(t)$ denoting the state of the cell $C_{x,y}$ at time $t \in 0, 1, 2, \ldots, N$ – the range of state of the cell (for finite N).

Having defined the basic concepts we can move on to the definition of rules that describe the automata:

$$\phi_{x,y}(t+1) = F(\phi_{x,y}(t), N_{x,y}(t)) \tag{3}$$

where: $\phi_{x,y}(t+1)$ – - state of the cell with coordinates x, y at the time $t + 1$, $N_{x,y}$ — the states of neighboring (to the one with coordinates x, y) at time t, F — a function that specifies a change in the cell that accepts a state of the cell at position x, y at the time t and the states of the cells being in her neighborhood.

For the description of automata behavior one needs also specification of the boundary conditions. We can divide them as follows:

- *periodic* - these types of conditions means grid bonding, cell located on the shore, e.g. $C_{0,5}$ has the neighbor in the vicinity of von Neumann cell $C_{20,5}$ with a range of $x \in 0, \ldots, 20$ (an example is the game of life);
- *closed absorbing* - in this transition rule when the cell reaches the shore then in time $t + 1$ the cell ceases to exist (with the boundary condition most often we deal with in the case of simulation of gas molecules);
- *closed reflective boundary conditions* - are closed environments to simulate research in this case the particles reaching the edge of the grid are reflected off in accordance with the previously designed conditions (such conditions can meet the simulation HPP).

4   Modeling Spatial Conflicts: The Layered Competitive Cellular Automata Approach

With use Cellular Automata because with CA one can perform modeling of real phenomena of irregular, spatial nature and characterized by some dynamically changing shape. Cellular Automata build on a grid can be used for modeling diversified media, such as water flow, gas flow, fire propagation, etc. Simultaneously, almost direct visualization is possible. In reality, such modeling seems very useful, since using numbers for modeling the *level of intensity* one can model continuous, or even fuzzy spatial objects.

The approach based on Layered Competitive Cellular Automata is dedicated to modeling spatial phenomena which are in conflict with one another. Some basic characteristics of the application areas are as follows:

- 2-D environment, such as land or other 2-D space in which we encounter a conflict,
- each of participating phenomena has its own dynamics defined,
- when in contact (the same coordinates) or enough close to (at some predefined, small distance) the conflicting environments influence each other,
- typically, winning environment removes the cells of the other one, and spreads out in according to predefined rules.

For intuition, with use of the LCCA we can model and analyze conflicts in following areas:

- safety and security national and international,
- crisis situations,
- damage to critical infrastructure,
- spotted terrorism acts, terrorism propagation over certain territories,
- natural disasters, such as fire, flooding.
- armed conflict,
- politics cooperate,
- other natural phenomena (e.g. propagation of weeds and effects of active weeding.

A Layered Competitive Cellular Automata is system consisting of several layers of cells allocated according to predefined grid. Each layer is responsible for representing a certain phenomenon involved in the simulation.

Definition 3. *A single-level cell $C_{x,y}$ is defined by the following tuple:*

$$C_{x,y} = (x, y, (s, v)), \tag{4}$$

where x and y are the cell coordinates defining its location on the rectangular grid, s defines the type (sort) of the cell, and v is the value defining level of intensity (or state) of the considered phenomena at the location defined by x and y.

An example cell defining fire, can be as follows:

$$C_{7,13} = (7, 13, (fire, 30\%))$$

The above formula represent a cell of type *fire*, located at position $(7, 13)$ with the intensity level equal 30% of the maximum.

In order to enable representation of different phenomena interacting at some position, several layer must be used. This leads to the definition of a *multi-layered cell*.

Definition 4. *A multi-layered cell incorporating k levels is defined*

$$MC_{x,y} = (x, y, k, (1, v_1), (2, v_2), \dots (k, v_k)) \tag{5}$$

In the definition above the sequence $(1, v_1), (2, v_2), \ldots (k, v_k)$ defines as a natural extension of single-level cell all the necessary layers; definition of each layer is composed of its type and current value (which can further change over time). The number k defines how many layers are there. The most typical case, i.e. modeling of two conflicting phenomena requires used of two layers of CA ($k = 2$), and the zero-level layer defining the environment.

Finally, we come to the definition of a Layered Competitive Cellular Automata.

Definition 5. *A Layered Competitive Cellular Automata, LCCA, of k-levels is defined as:*

$$LCCA = (N_x, N_y, k, D, \delta, \{MC_{x,y} : x = 1, 2, \ldots, N_x, y = 1, 2, \ldots, N_y\}, F, G), \quad (6)$$

where N_x and N_y are positive integers defining the size of the grid (identical to all levels), k is the number of active levels (recall that the environment is represented by level 0), D is a domain of some basic accessible elements of the environment, δ is a mapping:

$$\delta : \{1, 2, \ldots, N_x\} \times \{1, 2, \ldots, N_y\} \to D$$

defines the zero-level environment (see the example in Sect. 1.1), and $MC_{x,y}$ multi-level cells assigned to positions over the whole grid, $MC_{x,y}$ are the k-level cells, $F = \{F_1, F_2, \ldots, F_k\}$ are the functions of type (3) defining the behavior of the CA of level k, and, finally, G is a function defining the inter-level dynamics (the competitive behavior),

$$G : (\delta(x, y), \phi^1_{x,y}(t), \phi^2_{x,y}(t), \ldots, \phi^k_{x,y}(t)) \mapsto (\phi^1_{x,y}(t+1), \phi^2_{x,y}(t+1), \ldots, \phi^k_{x,y}(t+1))$$

i.e. function G updates the states of the competitive cells located in different layers at the same coordinates. Note also that, contrary to classical CA, even in a single layer there can be cells of different type! This means that a single layer can, in fact, represent non-homogeneous environment. A practical example

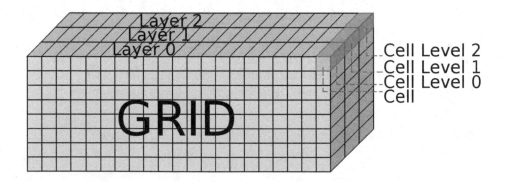

Fig. 3. Graphic presentation for grid use in LCCA

is that the fire extinction level can contain firemen, water, and perhaps other extinction means.

The resulting multi-level grid is schematically presented in Fig. 3.

Each automaton in the proposed approach is modeled with use of Object Oriented programming. It is a user-defined object, having the coordinate attributes and several (e.g. 3) levels allowing for definition of its state and wear.

5 Example Implementation

The current implementation is in Python programming language [23]. Python aroused late in '80. In 2015 Python is located within the seven most popular languages [18]. En example definition of a class for representing cells is as follows:

```
class Cell:
    def __init__(self):
        self.level = [CellLevel(), CellLevel(), CellLevel()]
    def replace_cell(self):
        return self
```

The output map (bottom-left) (see Fig. 1) is visualization-based internal representation (top-right) implemented as the following method:

```
def readMaps(self):
    map_ = open("test_maps.txt", "r")
    lines = map_.readlines()
    self.width = int(lines[0].split(' ')[0])
    self.height = int(lines[0].split(' ')[1])
    self.grid = [[Cell() for x in range(self.width)] for y in
                range(self.height)]
    for x in range(0, self.width):
        for y in range(0, self.height):
            self.grid[y][x].level[0].state = int(lines[x + 1][y])
            self.grid[y][x].level[0].wear = 100
    for x in range(0, self.width):
        for y in range(0, self.height):
            if self.grid[x][y].level[0].state == 0:
                self.grid[x][y].level[0].state = EmptyCellState()
            elif self.grid[x][y].level[0].state == 1:
                self.grid[x][y].level[0].state = TreeCellState()
            elif self.grid[x][y].level[0].state == 2:
                self.grid[x][y].level[0].state = GrassCellState()
            elif self.grid[x][y].level[0].state == 3:
                self.grid[x][y].level[0].state = WallCellState()
            elif self.grid[x][y].level[0].state == 4:
                self.grid[x][y].level[0].state = SandCellState()
            elif self.grid[x][y].level[0].state == 5:
                self.grid[x][y].level[0].state = WaterCellState()
            else:
                self.grid[x][y].level[0].state = EmptyCellState()
```

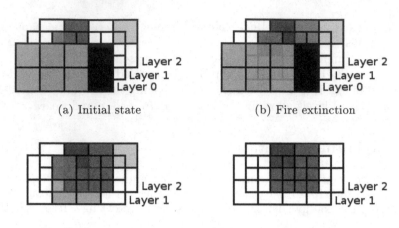

(a) Initial state

(b) Fire extinction

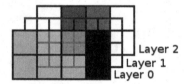

(c) Competitive layers

(d) State of the automaton when values in Layer 2 are greater than values in Layer 1 (Layer 0 hidden)

(e) State of the automaton when values in Layer 2 are greater than values in Layer 1 (with Layer 0)

Fig. 4. Presentation of rules

The visualization of LCCA is performed with use of PyQT 4.8 [17]; en example definition of a window is as follows: (Fig. 4)

```
class LccaWindow(QMainWindow):
    def __init__(self):
        super(LccaWindow, self).__init__()
        uic.loadUi('LCCA.ui', self)
        self.gridView = GridView()
        self.horizontalLayout.addWidget(self.gridView)
        self.grid = Grid()
        self.grid.readMaps()
        self.gridView.setModein base of predefined rulesl(self.grid)
        self.show()
        self.timer = QTimer()
        self.timer.setSingleSin base of predefined ruleshot(False)
        self.timer.setInterval(10)
        QObject.connect(self.startButton, SIGNAL("clicked()"), \
```

```
self.timer.start)
QObject.connect(self.stopButton, SIGNAL("clicked()"), \
self.timer.stop)
```

6   Example Application: Fire Modeling

In this section a generic application example of modeling two conflicting phenomena is presented. The first phenomenon is fire. Its model is located in layer 1. It is a set of homogeneous cells (Fig. 5).

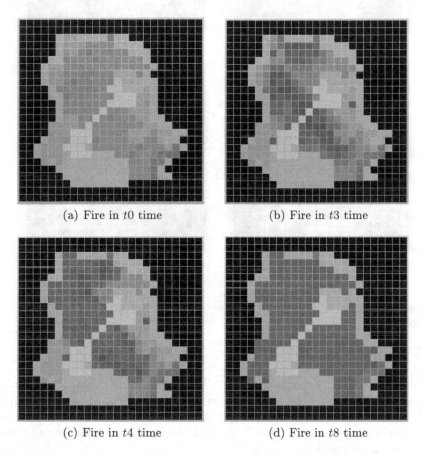

(a) Fire in $t0$ time   (b) Fire in $t3$ time

(c) Fire in $t4$ time   (d) Fire in $t8$ time

Fig. 5. An example LCCA application for modeling fire: four subsequent stages are visualized in turn

The second phenomenon represents the active fight against the fire. It comprises of two types of objects: the firemen and their water facilities. At start time we see only fire in the map, at the second step firemen appear and start taking part in the conflict. The fire is growing on the base of predefined rules. Firemen move according to predefined rules too (Fig. 6).

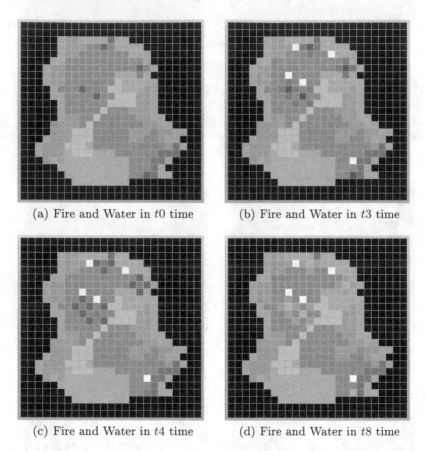

(a) Fire and Water in $t0$ time   (b) Fire and Water in $t3$ time

(c) Fire and Water in $t4$ time   (d) Fire and Water in $t8$ time

Fig. 6. An example LCCA application for modeling fire: four subsequent stages are visualized in turn

7   Conclusions

Modeling conflicts and competition in case of spatial and dynamic phenomena requires sophisticated tools. In this paper a proposal of the Layered Competitive Cellular Automata (LCCA) was put forward. Both theoretical foundations and example implementation were discussed. An example application of generic character was supplied.

The presented proposal seems to constitute an original and simultaneously generic approach. At present, it is in an initial stage of implementation and testing. Each particular application requires both precise, case-dependent definition of functions F and G, as well as adequate parameters tuning. On the other hand, the proposal seem to be of general nature, and possible applications may cover various phenomena.

It seems that the proposed approach can be used a generic tool for modeling, analysis and visualization of dynamic, spatial, conflicting phenomena. As such, it can become a valuable tool in the fight with natural disaster or in military applications.

References

1. Bowen, K.C., McNaught, K.R.: Mathematics in warfare: lanchester theory. In: Fletcher, J. (ed.) The Lanchester Legacy. A Celebration of Genius, vol. 3. Coventry University Press, Coventry (1996)
2. Cecherrini-Silberstein, T., Curnaert, M.: Cellular Automata and Groups. Springer, Heidelberg (2010)
3. Davis, P.K.: Distributed interactive simulation in the evolution of DoD warfare modeling and simulation. Proc. IEEE 83(8), 1138–1155 (1995)
4. Deja, R.: Conflict analysis. In: Proceedings of the Fourth International Workshop on Rough Sets, Fuzzy Sets and Machine Discovery, The University of Tokyo, vol. 6–8, pp. 118–124, November 1996
5. Deja, R.: Conflict model with negotiation. Bull. Pol. Acad. Sci. Techn. Sci. 44(4), 475–498 (1996)
6. Epstein, J.M.: The Calculus of Conventional War: Dynamic Analysis without Lanchester Theory. Brookings Institution, Washington (1985)
7. Garg, R.: An Introduction to Game Theory. Oxford University Press, Chicago (2004)
8. Lanchester, F.W.: Aircraft in Warfare: The Dawn of the Fourth Arm. Constable and Co Ltd., London (1916)
9. Mitchell, M.: Nonstandard Computation. Verlagsgesellschaft, Weinheim (1998)
10. Moffat, J.: Mathematical modelling of information age conflict. J. Appl. Math. Decis. Sci. 2006, 15 (2006)
11. Pawlak, Z.: On Conflicts. Int. J. of Man-Mach. Stud. 21, 127–134 (1984)
12. Pawlak, Z.: O Konfliktach. Państwowe Wydawnictwo Naukowe, Warszawa (1987)
13. Pawlak, Z.: Anatomy of Conflicts. Bull. EATCS 50, 234–246 (1993)
14. Pawlak, Z.: An inquiry into anatomy of conflicts. J. Inf. Sci. 109, 65–78 (1998)
15. Ratajczak, S.: Porównanie wybranych definicji symulacji. In: Symulacja Systemów Gospodarczych, Prace Szkoły Antaływka 1997, WSPiZ IOiZ PWr, Warszawa (1997)
16. Schiff, J.L.: Cellular Automata: A Discrete View of the World. Wiley, Hoboken (2008)
17. Summerfield, M.: Rapid GUI Programming with Python and QT. Prentice Hall, Upper Saddle River (2007)
18. http://www.tiobe.com/index.php/paperinfo/tpci/Python.html
19. http://riad.usk.pk.edu.pl/rhk/odrodzenie/odrodzenie/odrodz6.html
20. http://www.money.pl/gospodarka/wiadomosci/artykul/awaria;w;usa;dwa; miliony;ludzi;wciaz;bez;pradu,180,0,1117364.html
21. Maiti, N.S., Ghosh, S., Chaudhuri, P.P.: Cellular Automata (CA) model for primality test. In: Wąs, J., Sirakoulis, G.C., Bandini, S. (eds.) ACRI 2014. LNCS, vol. 8751, pp. 146–155. Springer, Heidelberg (2014)
22. Wolfram, S.: Statistical mechanics of cellular automata. Rev. Mod. Phys. 55(3), 601 (1983)
23. Zelle, J.: Python Programming: An Introduction to Computer Science. Franklin, Beedle & Associates Inc., Wilsonville (2004)

Audio-Visual Systems

Facial Expression Analysis as a Means for Additional Biometric Security in Recognition Systems

Dustyn James Tubbs[✉] and Khandaker Abir Rahman

Saginaw Valley State University, University Center, MI, USA
{djtubbsl, krahman}@svsu.edu

Abstract. In the well explored domain of facial biometrics, methods which forgo traditional models of intruder detection can lead to a more robust system. One such method, which is outlined in this paper, is to utilize the movement of feature points over the course of an expression to make user authentication systems more secure. To do this, we developed a new algorithm, and used the process known as ranking, to describe facial expressions in a computationally cheap way. In our experiments, we performed 309,210 authentication attempts on 33 user profiles and achieved at best an error of only 3.4 %, with an average error of 33.28 %. Although such a system is not as accurate as common face biometric systems, we believe that this method can augment those systems to make them impervious to common attacks.

Keywords: Facial expression analysis · Biometrics · Feature points · Video analysis

1 Introduction

With common image/video authentication systems relying on matching an image against a set of user templates, potential information which can be used to identify a user, or deny an intruder, is lost. In addition, simply matching an image, or a set of images, against a template opens the authentication system up to a set of vulnerabilities such as:

1. Mask Attacks: A type of attack where an attacker fools an authentication system by wearing/using a print or screening of an authorized user's face as a mask. This attack is especially targeted toward systems who utilize liveliness of a user's eyes for validation.
2. Picture Attacks: A type of attack where an attacker fools an authentication system by presenting a picture of an authorized user. This attack is effective against systems that do not check for liveliness.
3. Replay Attacks: A type of attack where an attacker fools an authentication system by presenting a recording of an authorized user.

Although each of these particular attacks have been researched, and countered respectively, (Mask Attacks in [1, 2], Picture Attacks in [3, 4], Replay Attacks in [5]) this reactive way of approaching the problem of user authentication via images and

© Springer International Publishing Switzerland 2015
A. Dziech et al. (Eds.): MCSS 2015, CCIS 566, pp. 113–123, 2015.
DOI: 10.1007/978-3-319-26404-2_9

videos make it a game of how to best break the system with a given set of constraints. With the advent of social media, acquiring pictures of users to be used against such systems becomes almost a trivial task. This is not the most ideal method of approaching potential attacks on a biometric system when considering the vector of an attack is limited primarily by the creativity of the attacker.

Instead, it is our belief that better/more robust systems can be made via the introduction of other methods whose modalities are not the same. That is, by developing authentication systems which utilize more diverse information about aspects of a user, as opposed to the user's image itself, more secure methods of identifying legitimate users and attackers can form.

One such method, which is outlined in this paper, is to take into consideration the differences in how users make expressions. We believe that the dynamics of a facial expression provides a sufficiently unique signature to identify users and, consequently, deny attackers. In particular, we found that examining the amount that each facial feature point moves over the course of a sampling of an expression yields sufficient data to do this. Such a system is a necessary improvement, as taking into consideration the temporal characteristics of a user expression renders the system immune to the aforementioned vulnerabilities, who rely on static imagery in order to match users.

To validate our claim, we performed extensive experimentation where we analyzed user expressions from the six universal expressions: Angry, Disgusted, Happy, Sad, Surprised, and Scared, which we chose from their standardized use in popular databases [6]. Our results show that in analyzing facial expression movement over the course of an expression can yield a primitive authentication system with an acceptable error rate. As such, the contributions of this paper include:

- A novel method for biometric security based on facial expression by analyzing video. This new method utilizes the process known as ranking to describe and compare facial expressions. In addition, in developing this method we created a new algorithm which can be used for a more precise comparison of rankings. By doing so, we were able to prove that in comparing facial feature point movement for expressions, only few (for example five to ten which we used in our experiments) points truly matter.
- The results of extensive testing of this new method. This testing revealed that this ranking method of facial expressions is both regular in its performance, and reliable, which we demonstrate by performing 309,210 authentication attempts on 33 user profiles. These tests showed that our method has at best an error of 3.4 %, with an average error of 33.28 %.

2   Background

Within biometrics, there is a delicate balance of both convenience and intrusion in the implementation of an authentication system. Systems which are convenient, such as finger print analysis [7] or voice recognition [8], are equally weak in terms of the protection they offer [9, 10]. As such, it is usually advantageous for signal analysis systems to match user information without input other than an image, or set of images, from the user. This method reduces the potential avenues of attack, but opens potential complications for template matching. These complications include, but are not limited to: image lighting, user pose, and background activity. This trade off of environment limitation for data integrity, however, is one that allows for authentication systems with high success. Examples of these systems include iris detection [11] and facial recognition.

These image-based user authentication systems, too, have inherit weaknesses based on the premise of their foundation. Attacks on these systems, such as mask attacks, picture attacks, and replay attacks, focus on how deeply coupled the system is with superficial imagery. As such, there exists a niche for authentication systems who utilize more peculiar aspects of user imagery. One such system, which is what we are proposing, is one to utilize facial expression analysis for additional security for authentication.

There have been multiple studies on facial expression recognition systems, some of which utilize action units [12], static face imagery [13], neurofuzzy networks [14], and local binary patterns [15]. These systems, however, are insufficient to handle the challenges that are imposed by the advent of social media. Too readily can a potential attacker find a user's profile online and utilize a picture of the user for an attack. As such, there needs to be a system for authentication that cannot be readily fooled by an attacker with pictures of a user.

What we are proposing is a system to rank facial feature points (such as the corner of an eye or lip) movement during the course of an expression. In addition, the system we are proposing will not be built to analyze static imagery, but instead video sampling. It is our belief that such a system can produce computationally cheap results (via 2D feature point sampling) and sufficient accuracy for the purpose of rendering a facial biometric system immune to these kind of attacks.

In Sect. 3, we outline our experimental set up for data collection, as well as how much data we collected. In Sect. 4, we present our methodology for identification. In Sect. 5 we outlined how we performed testing, as well as the amount of authentication attempts that we performed. In Sect. 6, we present the results achieved from this testing. In Sect. 7, we present our analysis on our results and future works.

3 Experimental Setup

We chose to collect samples of the six universal expressions: Angry, Disgusted, Happy, Sad, Scared, and Surprised, for our experimentation. We chose these expressions in particular because, as present psychology suggests, they transcend both race and culture in their meaning.

To gauge the behavior of facial feature points over the course of an expression, static imagery would be completely insufficient to provide adequate information. Therefore, sampling of user expressions needed to be in the format of a video. To record these samples we utilized a Microsoft LifeCam Cinema which recorded in 720p HD at approximately 30 frames per second.

For a complete sample, we recorded a participant's face from a neutral expression, to a prompted expression, back to a neutral expression. We recorded samples from the participant in both a controlled environment where the lighting was controlled by way of a FalcoEyes LHD-5250 which concentrated five 28 Watt 5000–5500 Kelvin ~ 230 V/50 Hz light bulbs, with a white board background, and an uncontrolled environment where the lighting varied and the background activity varied. Samples from 42 participants were acquired in two locations on separate dates and times in the months of September 2014 and October 2014.

For each participant, we recorded 24 video samples, which consisted of two samples of each universal expression our controlled setting and our uncontrolled setting. With our total of 42 participants, we had at our discretion 1008 (24×42) video samples. Our participants consisted exclusively of university students and faculty between the ages of 18 and 40. Information on user ethnicity, gender, or if the user wore glasses, was not used to separate data.

4   Methodology

For security, our proposed methodology is on the basis of the following: analyze all facial feature point movement over the course of an expression sample and rank them in accordance to how far they move (accumulated Euclidian Distance of moving X-Y coordinates of feature point in frames) and match each point's movement to a user template. For example, if a particular point moved frequently it would be ranked higher than another which did not move as much. We believe such a ranking is sufficient to describe an expression, allowing us to generate a user profile by defining each of the universal expressions with a corresponding ranking. To validate, with this definition of comparison, is to merely compare rankings of an input sample against a user's template.

This simplistic method for authentication, which is easily broken down into discrete steps, is implemented in the following subsections where we disclose how we acquired feature point data from our samples (Sect. 4.1), why we chose feature point ranking (Sect. 4.2), and how we solved a limitation on present ranking systems (Sect. 4.3).

4.1   Locating Feature Points

The task for locating feature points in our expression samples, which was auxiliary to the question that we were asking, was accomplished by Noldus Facereader 5 [16]. Noldus would analyze a given video sample and, for each frame that it would identify a face, output the 2D location for 49 feature points. See Fig. 1 for examples of one frame of analysis given by Noldus.

4.2   Feature Point Ranking

With the task of locating feature points for the frames of each video sample handled in Section A, our goal now was to determine exactly how we would identify a user from an expression. With 49 feature points moving over the course of a sample, our inclination was that there would be a unique set of points that moved more frequently for

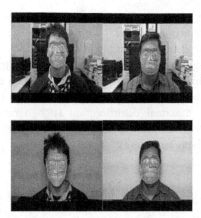

Fig. 1. Feature points of user expressions are captured using Noldus. Expression from participants are given as follows: Happy (top left), Sad (top right), Disgusted (bottom left), and Scared (bottom right).

one expression than another. Indeed, we felt as though the points that moved the most frequently would also distinctively vary between participants in our data set. As such, we created a ranking for the magnitude of each feature point's movement over the course of a sample, ranking higher points that moved more frequently. As a visualization aid, see Fig. 2 where this relationship given by the point's movement and a particular individual is undeniable to see.

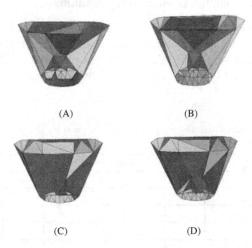

(A)   (B)

(C)   (D)

Fig. 2. A Delaunay Triangulation [17] of facial expression samples is made to visualize the differences between the samples. Triangles are colored on the basis of their point's movement. Points that move more frequently yield warmer colors. Figures A and B represent the expression of sad for Participant 29 in the controlled environment. Figures C and D represent the expression of sad for Participant 34 in the controlled environment. The similarities displayed are evident

With the practice of comparing rankings having been well established by Bergando, Gunetti, and Picardi in other research [18], we were almost ready to begin testing. In their research they compared rankings of equal sizes for their similarity. That is, they were comparing lists of attributes where the number of attributes in each list (for example, in our case, training and testing) were the same. To compare these rankings, one merely had to sum the displacement of indexes in one ranking as compared to another and divide by a maximal disorder that such a ranking can achieve. The equation for determining the maximal disorder of two equal sized rankings with length $|V|$, as given in [18], is given by Eq. (1):

$$\left(|V|^2\right) \text{ if } |V| \text{ is even; } \left(|V|^2-1\right)/2 \text{ if } |V| \text{ is odd} \tag{1}$$

This equation, however, is limiting in that it requires two rankings to have equal sizes. We wanted to have the ability to compare rankings of unequal sizes. Intuitively, this can be seen as wanting to weight a certain number of points higher in determining how close two expression rankings were. This coincides with our idea that only a certain set of points in a given expression ranking were highly active as compared to the rest of the points and can be used to describe the expression overall.

What this meant for us was a need to generate the highest disorder that could be achieved when comparing two rankings of unequal sizes, M and N. Our methodology for calculating this is found in the following section.

4.3   Generating Disorder for Unequal Sized Rankings

Given two sets of rankings M and N, such that M is a subset of N, It is possible to generate a disorder matrix such that each cell's value is determined by the absolute value of the index placement in M minus the index placement in N. As an example, given two rankings with $|M| = 6$ and $|N| = 7$, we could generate the disorder matrix in Table 1.

Table 1. A Disorder Matrix of $|M| = 6$ by $|N| = 7$

Indexes of M	Indexes of N						
	1	2	3	4	5	6	7
1	0	1	2	3	4	5	6
2	1	0	1	2	3	4	5
3	2	1	0	1	2	3	4
4	3	2	1	0	1	2	3
5	4	3	2	1	0	1	2
6	5	4	3	2	1	0	1

For Table 1, each data cell describes given a placement in M, if that corresponding indexed value was placed in N, what disorder would be created for that particular index. An example list exhibiting the behavior of having the maximum disorder achieved by this disorder matrix can be seen in Fig. 3. For this list, the maximum disorder is $6 + 5 + 4 + 3 + 2 + 1 = 21$. In order to provide a convenient method for calculating this for, we needed a generalize algorithm to calculate the maximum disorder that can be achieved for any arbitrary disorder matrix. Such an algorithm is given by Algorithm 1.

```
1      Algorithm 1:
       generateMaximumDisorder(DisorderMatrix)
Input: A disorder matrix DisorderMatrix created
by putting the absolute value of the column index
minus the row index in each cell.
Output: The maximum disorder that can be achieved
with the input DisorderMatrix
2    if DisorderMatrix is empty
3      return 0
4    let x be the maximum value found in Disor-
derMatrix
5 let submatrix be the sub matrix created by re-
moving the row and column that x is found in
6    return x + generateMaximumDisorder(submatrix)
```

Algorithm 1. The maximum disorder achieved from a given disorder matrix is found by finding the greatest value in the matrix and recursively summing it with the maximum values in the submatrices created by removing the row and column that the maximum value is found in.

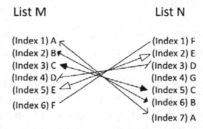

Fig. 3. An example listing of rankings M and N exhibiting maximum disorder is created via the disorder matrix given by Table 1.

5 Experiments

To begin the process of testing, we needed to define what data was needed to create a profile of a valid user. As stated in Sect. 3, we had 1008 video samples to utilize from 42 participants. As outlined in Sect. 4, we could create a ranking from an expression by sorting the set of feature points from a user based on the magnitude of their point's movement over the course of an expression sample.

Therefore, our definition of a valid user would one where we can determine a ranking of each universal expression. In addition, we decided that in creating the set of users for our testing that we wanted to separate samples created in a controlled and uncontrolled setting. We felt as though this would allow us to see the performance of our method more independent of our data set.

Out of the 42 participants from which we were able to sample expressions from, we were able to generate 33 complete profiles in each environment. Not every sample were we able to generate a complete set of facial feature points from every frame. Due to this, we had to strictly define the definition of a profile to be one where there existed a complete sample of which we could draw rankings from. It is because of this reason that we were only able to generate 33 profiles out of 42 participants.

Each user profile was trained off of the first sample for each universal expression in a particular environment, leaving the other sample for testing purposes. In order to test these user profiles, we provided both sample rankings, which were of the same expression from the same participant, and attacker rankings where were of the same expression from a different participant. The set of attacker rankings included expression rankings from participants of which a profile could not be generated.

For our controlled setting, we were able to generate rankings for 476 samples. For our uncontrolled setting, we were able to generate rankings for 461 samples. This discrepancy in the number of rankings for each environment is due to the reasons outlined above. Thusly, for an arbitrary set of user profiles, we were able to perform 30,921 authentication attempts (33 participants × 476 samples + 33 participants × 461 samples), with 792 (33 participants × 6 valid files × 2 environments) files being genuine attempts.

6 Experimental Results

To calculate the results of our experiment, we found for each perspective participant (33) in each environment (2), for each number of selected points (5, 10, ..., 49, chosen as the top **n** points in the ranking created by the magnitude of the feature point's movement), the Imposter Pass Rate (IPR), False Rejection Rate (FRR), and, consequently, the Equal Error Rate (EER) which is the interception of these two values. To do this, we iterated acceptance threshold values between 0 and 1 (which are descriptors of likeness of rankings, with 0 being a 100 % match and 1 being a complete mismatch) to see which samples were accepted. Stepping by 0.001, we were confidently able to generate the IPR and FRR for all users, in every environment, for any selected number of points.

To compute the overall performance of our methodology, we locate the EER for every participant over the course of the selected number of points. This is done twice, to demonstrate performance in each setting. Table 2 demonstrates the statistical trends of the EER for our method, while Fig. 4 graphically represents this data.

Table 2. I. Equal error rate (EER) statistics for each set of 33 users' profiles

Equal error rate	Selected number of points									
	5	10	15	20	25	30	35	40	45	49
User profiles created in the controlled setting										
Minimum	0.161	0.163	0.106	0.110	0.070	0.072	0.100	0.108	0.055	**0.034**
Maximum	0.587	0.666	0.666	0.663	0.666	0.666	0.666	0.666	0.666	0.666
Average	0.322	0.346	0.339	0.330	0.330	0.335	0.346	0.339	0.329	**0.312**
Standard Deviation	0.107	0.120	0.117	0.120	0.127	0.127	0.124	0.117	0.124	0.118
User profiles created in the uncontrolled setting										
Minimum	0.162	0.162	0.162	0.162	**0.164**	0.164	0.162	0.164	0.164	0.162
Maximum	0.663	0.665	0.670	0.703	0.665	0.661	0.665	0.685	0.668	0.665
Average	0.396	0.383	0.399	0.394	**0.382**	0.405	0.400	0.403	0.396	0.390
Standard Deviation	0.128	0.134	0.137	0.141	0.133	0.136	0.141	0.138	0.132	0.128

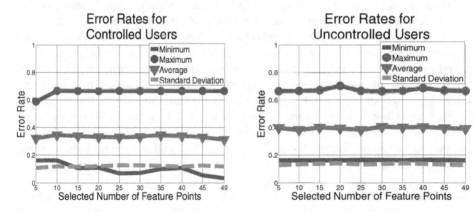

Fig. 4. The overall trends of the equal error rate for our method is demonstrated over the course of a selected number of feature points for controlled and uncontrolled users

7 Summary and Discussion

In conclusion, the methods and experimentation outlined in this paper represent a first step in the direction for user authentication via expression analytics over the course of a video sample. In developing our methodology, we created a novel algorithm for use in comparing rankings of unequal sizes. For testing our method, we collected 1008 video samples to generate 33 complete profiles of which 309,210 authentication attempts were made.

As is demonstrated by our results, feature point ranking as a means for user identification presents a fertile ground for further research. Users created in the controlled setting exhibited erroneous results in on average 31.33 % of attempts, with the best performance by a user attaining only 3.4 % of error with all 49 feature points selected. User profiles created in the uncontrolled setting exhibited erroneous results in on average 38.26 % of attempts, with the best performance by a user attaining only 16.4 % of error with only 25 feature points selected. See Fig. 4.

Although these numbers are the most ideal for each scenario, they're not too different from the average behavior exhibited. As can be demonstrated by Fig. 4, behavior from 5 points to 49 points varies only slightly over the course of testing. This demonstrates our hypothesis that only a few feature points truly matter over the course of a given expression ranking.

There are some interesting trends presented in our data that are impossible to ignore. For instance, take the maximum values for profiles created in our controlled setting. As outlined, the maximum reaches a certain point and stays static over the course of varying the selected number of feature points. So too, is this behavior showcased in the minimum values for users in our uncontrolled setting. In each case, we believe something interesting is at play. In the case of the maximum, we believe that the profile created who yielded this value most likely had an outlier sample that regularly caused an inflated amount of attacker samples to be accepted. Conversely, as in the case of the minimum, we believe that this user had the best sampling in terms of the quality of expressions trained off of and then given to our system. In both cases, values are well outside of one standard deviation from the average and should not be given too much weight.

Overall, the results given by our method are moderately successful, even if they are not as accurate as common image based biometrics. In the future, we believe that our method can at best be used to augment facial biometric systems who utilize imagery analysis for authentication. It has been proven that imagery analytics have high performance in terms of accuracy. By augmenting them with this system, they would be overall safer to use and more robust against attacks. Given the challenge of social media, an image/video of a user's face is relatively easy to find, a complete expression, however, is far more difficult for an attacker to find and use against the system, rendering it that much safer.

Acknowledgements. This research was supported by the Michigan Space Grant Consortium. We thank our colleagues in the College of Science, Engineering, and Technology at Saginaw Valley State University for their continued support. In addition, we thank the Undergraduate Research Program (UGRP) at Saginaw Valley State University for making our continued works possible. In addition, we thank the students at Saginaw Valley State University for their valuable data and Cody Brown, whose assistance was invaluable.

References

1. Kose, N., Dugelay, J.L.: Shape and texture based countermeasure to protect face recognition systems against mask attacks. In: 2013 IEEE Conference on Computer Vision and Pattern Recognition Workshops (CVPRW), pp. 111–116. IEEE (2013)

2. Kose, N., Dugelay, J.L.: Countermeasure for the protection of face recognition systems against mask attacks. In: 2013 10th IEEE International Conference and Workshops on Automatic Face and Gesture Recognition (FG), pp. 1–6. IEEE (2013)
3. Kim, G., Eum, S., Suhr, J.K., Kim, D.I., Park, K.R., Kim, J.: InBiometrics (ICB), 2012 5th IAPR International Conference on Face Liveness Detection Based on Texture and Frequency Analyses, pp. 67–72. IEEE (2012)
4. Määttä, J., Hadid, A., Pietikäinen, M.: Face spoofing detection from single images usingtexture and local shape analysis. IET Biometrics 1(1), 3–10 (2012)
5. Frischholz, R.W., Werner, A.: Avoiding replay-attacks in a face recognition system using Head-pose Estimation. In: AMFG 2003. IEEE International Workshop on Analysis and Modeling of Faces and Gestures, pp. 234–235. IEEE (2003)
6. Lucey, P., Cohn, J.F., Kanade, T., Saragih, J., Ambadar, Z., Matthews, I.: The extended Cohn-Kanade Dataset (CK +): a complete dataset for action unit and emotion-specified expression. In: 2010 IEEE Computer Society Conference on Computer Vision and Pattern Recognition Workshops (CVPRW), pp. 94–101. IEEE (2010)
7. Hong, L., Wan, Y., Jain, A.: Fingerprint image enhancement: algorithm and performance evaluation. IEEE Trans. Pattern Anal. Mach. Intell. 20(8), 777–789 (1998)
8. Reynolds, D.A., Rose, R.C.: Robust text-independent speaker identification using Gaussian mixture speaker models. IEEE Trans. Speech Audio Process. 3(1), 72–83 (1995)
9. Uludag, U., Jain, A.K.: Attacks on biometric systems: a case study in fingerprints. In: Electronic Imaging 2004, pp. 622–633. International Society for Optics and Photonics (2004)
10. Piotrowski, Z., Gajewski, P.: Voice spoofing as an impersonation attack and the way of protection. J. Inf. Assur. Secur. 2(3), 223–225 (2007)
11. Revenkar, P.S., Anjum, A., Gandhare, W.Z.: Secure iris authentication using visual (2010)
12. Tian, Y.L., Kanade, T., Cohn, J.F.: Recognizing action units for facial expression analysis. IEEE Trans. Pattern Anal. Mach. Intell. 23(2), 97–115 (2001)
13. Pantic, M., Rothkrantz, L.J.: Facial action recognition for facial expression analysis from static face images. Cybern. IEEE Trans. Syst. Man Cybern. Part B 34(3), 1449–1461 (2004)
14. Ioannou, S.V., Raouzaiou, A.T., Tzouvaras, V.A., Mailis, T.P., Karpouzis, K.C., Kollias, S. D.: Emotion recognition through facial expression analysis based on a neurofuzzy network. Neural Netw. 18(4), 423–435 (2005)
15. Shan, C., Gong, S., McOwan, P.W.: Facial expression recognition based on local binary patterns: a comprehensive study. Image Vis. Comput. 27(6), 803–816 (2009)
16. Noldus FaceReader 5. http://www.noldus.com/
17. Lee, D.T., Schachter, B.J.: Two algorithms for constructing a Delaunay triangulation. Int. J. Comput. Inf. Sci. 9(3), 219–242 (1980)
18. Bergadano, F., Gunetti, D., Picardi, C.: User authentication through keystroke dynamics. ACM Trans. Inf. Syst. Secur. (TISSEC) 5(4), 367–397 (2002)

Analysis of Urban Noise Frequency Characteristics Using a Smartphone

Paweł Tarsa[✉], Jacek Dańda, Jacek Wszołek, and Marek Sikora

AGH University of Science and Technology, Krakow, Poland
tarsa@student.agh.edu.pl,
{danda,wszolek,sikora}@kt.agh.edu.pl

Abstract. This paper describes an attempt to analyze frequencies of noise occurring in urban areas using an Android-based smartphone. The proposed solution enables audio writing to the device's memory, analysis on the device and transmission of results to the server. The article presents results of tests carried out in the city of Krakow.

1 Introduction

Urban development, contributing to development of local transport and industry, increases the intensity of sounds in a limited area to a level that can be described as harmful [1]. One of methods to reduce the noise level in areas particularly affected by this problem, thus ensuring the proper acoustic climate for urban residents is installation of noise barriers. It should be noted, however, that noise barriers are not an effective means of dampening of low frequency noise. Monitoring noise levels in urban areas is a necessity resulting from the requirements of the European Union [2].

The purpose of this publication is to demonstrate that it is possible to carry out rough, extensive measurements of spectrum characteristics of noise in urban areas, using low-cost, commonly available mobile devices.

This article is divided into 5 parts. Chapter 2 presents some issues related to the impact of specific frequency components of noise on human health, regardless of their intensity. Chapter 3 describes test methods used in this paper and the techniques used to validate the measurement system. In chapter 4, the obtained results are presented. Chapter 5 presents plans for further work in this area.

2 Impact of Frequency Noise Components on Human Health

Prolonged exposure to high noise level can lead to disorders that cause diseases such as hypertension, neurosis etc. [3]. A vexing noise also hampers any mental work and all forms of recreation. Due to the increasing number of anthropogenic sources of infrasound, especially in the urban environment, the impact of this frequency range for human health attracts an increasing interest [4]. In 2005, in the Institute of Occupational Medicine in Łódź, a group of volunteers were subjected to the influence of low frequency noise (10–250 Hz) at a level not exceeding 50 dB. Participants, which remained under

A. Dziech et al. (Eds.): MCSS 2015, CCIS 566, pp. 124–131, 2015.
DOI: 10.1007/978-3-319-26404-2_10

the influence of noise, committed multiple errors and worked less effectively than those not subjected to low frequency. Furthermore, participants under influence of noise had impaired cognitive function [5]. The results of these studies also show that exposure to infrasound can cause dysfunction of the human balance system, such as loss of balance or nystagmus.

Ultrasonic noise can also have adverse effects on the human body [6]. Ultrasonic noise is characterized by a spectrum in which the high frequency audible components are present, and low audible ultrasound of 10 kHz to 40 kHz. Research into effects of ultrasound noise on hearing organ is difficult, because ultrasound noise is usually accompanied by the audible noise. It is difficult to determine, whether changes in hearing are due to audible or ultrasonic noise only, or as a result of the simultaneous operation of both these components. Currently, common views are that as a result of nonlinear influence of ultrasound, subharmonic components of the sound cause pressure levels of the same order of magnitude as the basic component of the ultrasound. Therefore, this phenomenon may cause hearing impairment. A next negative effect of ultrasound is related to the vestibular organ in the inner ear, manifested by headaches, dizziness, imbalance, nausea, sleepiness during the day or excessive fatigue [6].

3   Method of Analysis

An important problem during the implementation of the work described in this paper was the choice of method for computation of the Fourier transform, which, as the basis one for the spectral analysis, has been selected from other transforms, e.g. piecewise-linear ones [7, 8]. Several different algorithms for calculating the DFT were also tested. Due to its high efficiency, *fftpack* library was used [9], which allows for calculation of the DFT for the 2048 elements sized vector for the audio signal sampled at 44 kHz, in the real time, on Android-based Samsung Galaxy S3 smartphone.

In order to simplify the analysis, it was assumed that as the dominant frequency band, the amplitude filter of 3 dB bandwidth was used. The procedure for detecting dominant band was based on finding the maximum values in coefficients obtained from the DFT. Next, number of samples that met the 3 dB criterion was determined. To calculate the energy associated with the selected band, the Parseval's theorem was used.

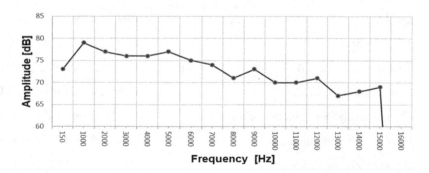

Fig. 1. Typical frequency responses of microphone

The frequency response of microphones in all devices used during the test were analyzed [10] with the use of the methodology described in [11]. An example of the frequency response of the Samsung Galaxy S3 smartphone in presented in Fig. 1. A similar procedure was also performed for tests based on recording and analyzing of sounds of selected frequencies.

4   Results

The presented results were obtained in separate research processes, at different times of the working day and on weekends, in the same places throughout the city. The measuring points were chosen based on maximum diversity in intensity and spectrum of noise, depending on the time of day. In the morning, usually the main factor generating the roadway noise were the combustion engines, with the clear low-frequency dominant High frequency component, caused as an effect of rotating wheels of vehicles (tire noise) had a low level due to traffic jams [12]. Noise registered in the afternoon usually was determined by both factors mentioned above. In the evening, smaller traffic, and a lower concentration of people resulted in a lower sound levels, and changes in the spectral characteristics of recorded sounds.

Analysis of the results show that the vast majority of the measured noise is dominated by the low-frequency range from 200 to 500 Hz, and the medium-frequency approx. 500 to 4 kHz [13]. The noise with the high-frequency dominant above 4 kHz, was observed only in the vicinity of construction sites.

Table 1. List of noise measurement points.

No.	Measurement point name	Location
1.	Opolska St., street side	50°09'13.4"N 19°92'51.3"E
2.	Opolska St., behind noise barriers	50°09'19.2"N 19°92'54.8"E
3.	Krowoderski Park	50°08'82.9"N 19°92'42.6"E
4.	Rydla St.	50°08'10.6"N 19°90'58.3"E
5.	Stańczyka and Armii Krajowej Crossroads	50°07'76.5"N 19°88'96.2"E
6.	Lea St.	50°07'36.2"N 19°89'58.0"E
7.	AGH Campus	50°06'80.7"N 19°90'72.4"E
8.	Czarnowiejska and Mickiewicza Crossroads	50°06'51.9"N 19°92'37.3"E
9.	Main Station in Kraków	50°06'82.8"N 19°94'68.6"E
10.	Floriańska and Św. Marka Crossroads	50°06'37.4"N 19°06'37.4"E
11.	Rynek Główny/Main Square	50°06'04.9"N 19°93'60.6"E
12.	Bulwar Czerwieński St.	50°05'37.8"N 19°93'12.0"E

The results of the measurements carried out at the points listed in Table 1 are indicated on the maps in Figs. 2, 3 and 4, for different times of day. Each measuring point is represented by a circle. Both the radius of the circle and the color depends on the dominant frequency recorded in a given measurement point. The meaning of color measurement points are shown in Table 2.

Table 2. Meaning of colors of measurement points from Fig. 1.

Dominant frequencies [Hz]	Color of the Measurement Point
0 - 150	
151 - 300	
301 - 550	
550 - 2kHz	
> 2 kHz	

Measurements carried out up to 600 m from the measurement point 1 and 2, i.e. at Opolska St., show that in the morning the dominant frequency is about 100 Hz lower than average dominant frequency of the urban noise. This is a result of frequent traffic jams in the morning, on the streets of Krakow. The main generators of noise in the traffic jams are vehicle engines, which generate sounds with the low frequency components, lower than 500 Hz. Diesel engines generate noise at frequencies lower than 200 Hz.

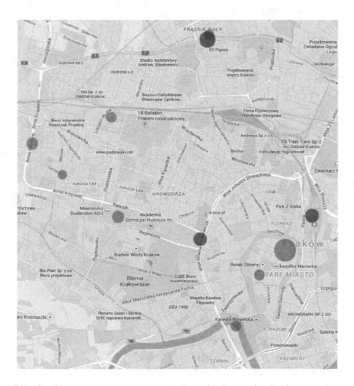

Fig. 2. The frequency characteristics of urban noise in the morning

Harmonics related to the tire noise, have less impact on the noise spectrum in the morning. The results of measurements obtained close to the footbridge over the Opolska St., became the basis for finding, that noise barriers have a significant effect on the spectral characteristics of the noise. Better suppression was observed for the medium and high frequencies. Measurements taken immediately before and behind the noise barriers on Opolska St. show the impact on the frequency spectrum of the urban noise. Sound recorded on the side of the street has the dominant frequency in the range 500 to 800 Hz, while signal registered behind the barriers is characterized by the dominant frequency in the range from 400 to 550 Hz. It should be noted that the power of the dominant band is decreased by about 10 dB, when compared to the power of the sound recorded from the Opolska St.. These results correspond to the efficiency of noise barriers with a height of 6 m [12].

For the measuring points 8 and 9, the frequency characteristics were similar to the measuring points 1 and 2, with the dominant low-frequency and mid-frequency noise. The high-frequency noise was observed in the location 10. It was associated with operation of construction machines with dominant frequency range of 8 kHz to 11 kHz.

Sounds recorded in location 3, had a fairly uniform frequency with the dominant components of 150 Hz. Spectra recorded in sections 4, 5, 6, 7, and 12 had the largest energy associated with the frequency band from about 300 to 550 Hz. Frequency characteristics of short recordings often show frequencies of large amplitude, outside the specified range. These amplitudes are related to specific incidents, for example with a screech associated with slipping tires.

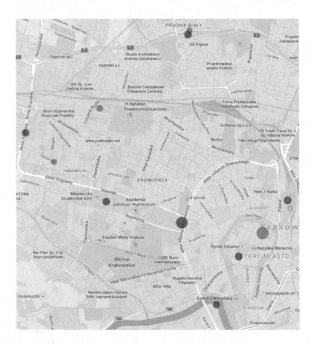

Fig. 3. The frequency characteristics of urban noise around noon

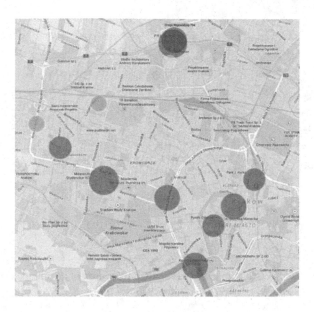

Fig. 4. The frequency characteristics of urban noise in the evening

Dominant components of noise in the measurement point 10 were of medium-frequency and high-frequency, when the equipment in the construction site was working.

In addition to measurements performed in the points specified in Table 1, sounds recorded at other, random places in the city of Krakow were analyzed. Based on over 200 measurements carried out in areas not included in Table 1, it was possible to observe, that noise that occurs e.g. in city buses has dominant frequencies in the range from 250 to 450 Hz. A siren of an ambulance was registered, too with the dominant frequency of approximately 1200 Hz. The observed amplitude of sound of the siren has local maximums at around 3500 Hz and 6500 Hz. Figure 5 illustrates the spectrum of an ambulance siren sound recorded with the smartphone. In the spectrogram shown in Fig. 6 the Doppler effect arising from movement of the vehicle is also visible.

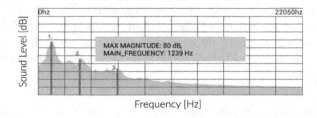

Fig. 5. The spectrum of sounds emitted by a siren of an ambulance

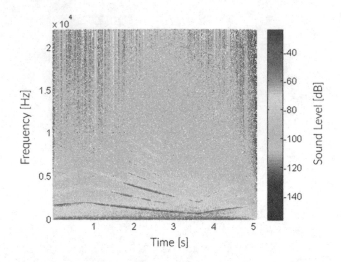

Fig. 6. Spectrogram of sounds emitted by a siren of an ambulance

5   Conclusions

The presented study demonstrated the possibility of using a mobile smartphone to perform qualitative noise tests in an urban environment, in a limited frequency range where the accuracy of the measurement is not critical. Performed tests confirmed the suitability of the proposed measuring system. It was observed that noise level in Krakow has the dominant components with the low and medium frequencies, and furthermore, as would be expected, the frequency spectrum depends on the time of day. The noise is virtually unchanged in the same time of working day, which results from the typical circadian rhythm of city life. The noise registered near congested roads and streets is dominated by the lower frequencies than in the case of roads without traffic jams. More-over, as expected, noise barriers significantly affect the noise spectrum, mainly suppressing the high and medium frequencies.

The further work on the proposed solution is planned. These plants are related to rebuilding the application and its networking interface to enable parallel measurements on multiple devices simultaneously. This solution will enable a dynamic creation of rough, qualitative, acoustic maps of cities. Therefore, observing the changes in noise characteristics without the need for expensive, dedicated research will be possible. Qualitative acoustic maps could allow public to draw attention to the problem of exposure to noise.

Acknowledgement.   This work was funded by the AGH University of Science and Technology within the statutory research grant 11.11.230.018

References

1. Inspekcja Ochrony Środowiska: Wojewódzki Inspektorat Ochrony Środowiska w Kielcach, Stan środowiska w województwie świętokrzyskim w roku 2001. Biblioteka Monitoringu Środowiska, Kielce (2002)
2. Parlament Europejski i Rada Unii Europejskiej, Dyrektywa Unii Europejskiej 2002/49/WE, Strasburg (2002)
3. Makarewicz, R.: Podstawy teoretyczne akustyki urbanistycznej. PWN, Poznań (1984)
4. Pawlas, K.: Wpływ infradźwięków i hałasu o niskich częstotliwościach na człowieka - przegląd piśmiennict. Podstawy i Metody Oceny Środ Pracy **2**(60), s.27–s.64 (2009)
5. Pawlaczyk-Łuszczyńska, M., et al.: The impact of low frequency noise on human mental performance. Int. J. Occup. Med. Env. Health **18**(2), 185–198 (2005)
6. Centralny Instytut Ochrony Pracy - Państwowy Instytut Badawczy, Hałas ultradźwiękowy. http://archiwum.ciop.pl/6542.html
7. Dziech, A., Belgassem, F., Aboukres, S., Nabout, A.: Periodic Haar piecewise linear transform. In: Proceedings of CESA 1996 IMACS/IEEE-SMC Multiconference, pp. 157–160 (1996)
8. Baran, R., Wiraszka, D., Dziech W.: Scalar quantization in the PWL transform spectrum domain. In: Proceedings of the International Conference on Mathematical Methods in Electromagnetic Theory, pp. 218–221 (2000)
9. Netlib Repository, FFTPACK. www.netlib.org/fftpack/
10. Wszołek, G.: Selected factors affecting uncertainty of all-weather microphones research. Arch. Acoust. **34**(4), s.547–s.557 (2009). ISSN 0137-5075
11. AudioCheck, White Noise. http://www.audiocheck.net/testtones_whitenoise.php
12. Turkiewicz, J., Wszołek, G.: Theoretical and experimental determination of the sound-absorbing property class of acoustic barriers. Acta Phys. Pol., A **125**(4-A), s.A-127–s.A-130 (2014). ISSN 0587-4246. Acoustic and biomedical engineering 2014
13. Mikulski, W., et al.: Hałas na stanowiskach pracy, http://neur.am.put.poznan.pl

Enhanced Method of Near Duplicate Detection for Red Carpet Photographs

Michał Grega^(⊠)

AGH University of Science and Technology, al. Mickiewicza 30,
30059 Krakow, Poland
grega@kt.agh.edu.pl

Abstract. The DEEP service is comprehensive new content discovery solution that offers fun, creative, modern way to discover information. Automated generation of content for DEEP relies on structured and unstructured sources of data and on multimedia databases. Unfortunately, using the Internet as a source for multimedia can result in the acquisition of so-called "Near Duplicates" — visually similar images. In this paper we propose an enhanced method of Near Duplicate detection for a special kind of photographs – images of celebrities commonly known as "red carpet" photographs. We have observed that near duplicates of such photos are most commonly crops of busts (head and upper torso) of the celebrity. We have combined an automated method for bust cropping with similarity computation and have obtained 95 % sensitivity and 99 % specificity for near duplicate detection.

Keywords: Image descriptors · Colour structure · Near duplicates · Query by example · QbE · MPEG-7

1 Introduction

Today so called Web 2.0, in which the consumer is at the same time the producer of the content, is omnipresent in form of blogs, video channels and audio podcasts. In recent years a new trend in content creation can be observed – the automated creation. Algorithms used for automated creation of content utilize commonly accessible and well structured data sources in order to produce on-demand content for the user.

For the past two years we have been working with an Israeli based company on a product called DEEP. According to its creators "DEEP is a comprehensive new content discovery solution that offers fun, creative, modern way to discover information. The service offers a multi-angle, highly visual and interactive way to experience various subjects, starting with movies, TV series and actors. Data curation and preparation for presentation are done automatically using DEEP's content discovery platform" [3].

The problem we have been tackling is of Near Duplicate (ND) detection and elimination from photograph database. Near Duplicates are photographs that

© Springer International Publishing Switzerland 2015
A. Dziech et al. (Eds.): MCSS 2015, CCIS 566, pp. 132–140, 2015.
DOI: 10.1007/978-3-319-26404-2_11

have almost the same content – come from the same photographic session or are a result of simple operations such as crop of a part of a photograph. The goal of our work is an algorithm that is capable of automated detection of near duplicate images for their elimination form a photograph database. What is also important is that the photographs considered are mostly so called "red carpet" photos, that is photographs of celebrities taken during events such as presented in Fig. 1.

The general problem of ND detection is well explored in numerous publications. A good overview of ND detection methods is provided in [6]. Low level image descriptors have many applications, such as in computer forensics [4], geolocalization [5], intelligent transportation systems [1] or in biomedical applications [2]. While working on the cited papers and analyzing available literature (e.g. [9] or [10]) we have observed, that the best results are obtained using a task–tailored algorithm rather than more general approach.

Fig. 1. Example of a red carpet image and its ND (image: creative commons by Keith Hinkle)

In our previous paper on the topic [3] we have selected a low level descriptor (Color Structure from the MPEG-7 standard [7]), experimented with the best distance threshold and analyzed part-to-part comparison methods. In this paper we propose a method that exploits a specific property of red carpet photos – fact, that many near duplicates are a crop of a bust of a person photographed. We have obtained better results than in our previously published algorithm, thus have decided to implement it in the DEEP system.

The rest of the paper is structured as follows. Section 2 presents our previous achievements in Near Duplicate detection. In Sect. 3 we present the principles of the proposed algorithm and in the following Sect. 4 – results obtain with use of this algorithm. The paper is concluded in Sect. 5.

2   Near Duplicate Detection

In our paper [3] we have proposed the first version of the algorithm. For the sake of the experiment we have prepared training and testing test sets of red carpet photographs. For reference we have also performed the tests using the external California ND database [6].

In the experiment we have identified the best performing MPEG-7 descriptor – Color Structure with a vector length of 256 values. We have also defined the L_1 distance metric for p, q image pair defined as:

$$d_{L1}(\mathbf{p}, \mathbf{q}) = \|\mathbf{p} - \mathbf{q}\|_1 = \sum_{i=1}^{n} |p_i - q_i| \tag{1}$$

Finally, in a set of experiments we have selected the threshold t value of $d_1(p, q)$ which discriminates between duplicate and non duplicate photographs. If $d_1 > t$ we consider the images to be different. Otherwise we consider them to be similar.

During this stage of research we have experimented with a set of possible image divisions by comparing parts of images to whole image. The method of image division was fixed – we have divided the image in 5 parts (Fig. 2).

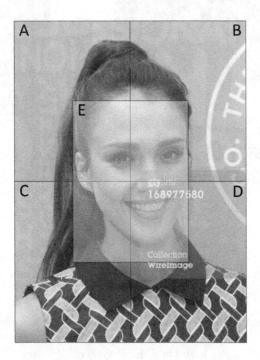

Fig. 2. Fixed image division method [3].

3   Enhanced Algorithm

In the presented research we have observed, that most of the near duplicates of red carpet photographs are crops on bust (torso and head) of the celebrity. In order to foster this knowledge we have made far going adaptation to our previous algorithm by comparing whole images and crops of busts. This concept is depicted in Fig. 3.

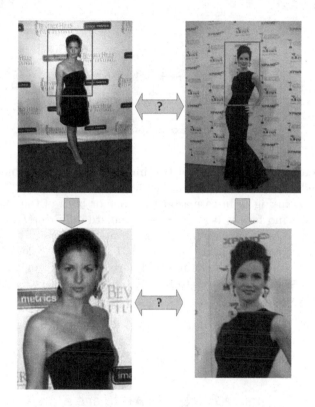

Fig. 3. Concept of ND detection using bust similarity. Image: Creative commons by Marthainsford and Andman8

First, we have created an algorithm that automatically extracts bust of a person from the image. The flow of the algorithm is presented in Fig. 4. In the first step we use Haar features in order to locate faces in both photographs using the method proposed by [8]. We have implemented a robust method of face detection that locates both faces and eyes in the image. We consider a region to be a "face" if only it contains at least one "eye". Once we have located the faces in the image we locate the largest one. This is justified by an assumption, that the photographer will make an attempt to compose the image in such a way, that the main person of interest is visually the largest in the image. Finally, we crop a bust (head and torso) from the input image. For selecting the cropping region we use the location of the face and estimate the size of the bust proportionally to the size of the face. As a result for each pair of input images I_1, I_2 we obtain a pair of busts B_1, B_2.

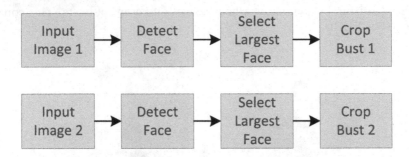

Fig. 4. Bust extraction algorithm

In order to assess the similarity of two images I_1, I_2 we crop busts from the images (denoted as B_1, B_2) and calculate their distance in pairs, following the pattern presented in Fig. 5. In case a bust for one or both of the images cannot be calculated (e.g. no face is detected) we calculate only $d_{L1}(I_1, I_2)$ using the algorithm proposed in [3]. In case busts were cropped successfully the distance d between images is calculated using Formula 2. The distance calculated this way is subsequently compared to the t threshold derived in our previous research. If $d(I_1, I_2) > t$ we assume the images to be different, otherwise we assume images to be near duplicates.

$$d(I_1, I_2) = \min(d_{L1}(I_1, I2),\ d_{L1}(I_1, B_2),\ d_{L1}(I_2, B_1),\ d_{L1}(B_1, B_2)) \qquad (2)$$

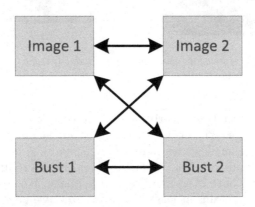

Fig. 5. Whole image and bust comparison algorithm

4   Results

In order to assess the results and compare them to our former solution [3] we have used traditional metrics used for the problem of binary classification. TP denotes the number of True Positives (similar images recognised as similar), FP denotes the number of False Positives (similar images recognised as not similar), TN denotes the number of true negatives (not similar images recognised as not similar) and FN denotes the number of False Negatives (not similar images recognised as similar). Precision, Sensitivity, Specificity and F-measure are calculated using the standard formulas for binary classification problems.

Also the same training and testing sets were used, so the results are fully comparable between the studies. The testing set consisted of 42 images, for which a correlation matrix was filed. Applying the property of symmetry to distance calculation ($d(I_1, I2) = d(I_2, I_1)$) this results in 903 possible comparison between images or 3612 comparisons in total (4 comparisons per image pair).

For assessing if a results of the algorithm is a false or true result we have manually created a correlation matrix. If we denote $A = a_{ij}$ as a correlation matrix than a_{ij} denotes similarity between ith and jth image. $a_{ij} = 0$ means, that the images i and j are not similar and $a_{ij} = 1$ means, that the images i and j are similar. Correlation matrices have always 1 on the main diagonal (as each image is similar to itself) and are symmetric as $a_{ij} = a_{ji}$ [3].

Table 1. Comparison of ND detection methods for red carpet photographs

	ND detection [3]	Enhanced ND detection
TP	53	56
TN	836	834
FP	8	10
FN	6	3
Sensitivity	0,89	0,95
Specificity	0,99	0,99
F–measure	0,88	0,9

Table 1 presents a comparison of results from our previous study [3] and obtained during the presented research for the red carpet images. We have managed to reduce the number of False Negatives (not similar images recognised as similar) with an increase of number of False Positives (similar images recognised as not similar). The overall metrics of sensitivity and F–measure have improved slightly and are above 95 %, which is a very satisfactory result for an automated classification method.

What is also worth mentioning is that slight increase in number of False Positives (by 2, which is 20 % overall) resulting in more significant decrease in number of False Negatives (by 3, which is 50 % overall) is acceptable from the point of view of the application. False Negatives (not similar images recognised as similar) cause images, that are not near duplicates to be removed from the database, which is a very undesired effect.

Presented algorithm comes at a cost of increased computational load. Haar cascades used for bust detection take a significant amount of time to compute. Comparing and averaging execution times for the algorithms without and with bust detection we have found, that the algorithm with bust detection is 30 times more time consuming than without this feature. There are two reasons for that effect. First, pre-trained Haar cascades for face and eye detection have to be loaded from the hard drive to the memory and Haar detection has to be performed. Second, each comparison of images with bust detection results in calculation of Colour Structure descriptors for four images instead of two in case of the algorithm without bust detection. In absolute values comparison of a pair of 1024×786 images without bust detection takes approximately 0,28 s while comparison of a pair of images with bust detection takes approximately 9 s.

Additionally, we have performed an experiment using the California Near Duplicate database [6]. This is a database of natural photographs taken by the author during his holiday. It is accompanied by a set of correlation matrices provided by the author and 9 other subjects, that have assessed similarity of the images in the set. Unfortunately, this database is anonymised by means of blurring the faces of persons in the images (Fig. 6). This renders our bust detection algorithm useless for this set, as it is face–detection dependant. Nevertheless we have run our former [3] and presented algorithms on the database. This experiment provided identical results for both algorithms confirming, that our new algorithm behaves correctly in case no bust is detected.

Fig. 6. Anonymized ND images from California ND database

5   Conclusions

In this paper we have proposed an enhanced method of near duplicate detection for red carpet images. The proposed method is an improvement to a method we have proposed previously in [3]. Near duplicate images of red carpet photographs are mostly crops of busts of actors depicted in those photographs. We use this property and propose a cross–check between images and automatically extracted crops of head and body.

Bust crop is executed using Haar cascades for detection of face and eyes. Based on the position and size of the face in the image a bust can be automatically cropped and used for the cross–check.

Our method improves the sensitivity of the algorithm by retaining its specificity. This comes at a cost of greatly increased computation time. This increased computation time is however still acceptable, as near duplicate removal can be set up as a background task for the database.

Our further research on the topic will focus on integration with the DEEP system and on optimization for improving execution times. We plan to implement multi–threaded execution of the algorithm and pre-loading of the Haar feature vectors in order to minimize the hard drive load.

Acknowledgements. The work was co-financed by The Polish National Centre for Research and Development (NCBR), as a part of the EUREKA Project IMCOP no. E! II/PL-IL/10/01A/2012.

References

1. Baran, R., Ruść, T., Rychlik, M.: A smart camera for traffic surveillance. In: Dziech, A., Czyżewski, A. (eds.) MCSS 2014. CCIS, vol. 429, pp. 1–15. Springer, Heidelberg (2014). http://dx.doi.org/10.1007/978-3-319-07569-3_1
2. Duplaga, M., Bułat, J., Leszczuk, M., Socha, M., Romaniak, P., Turcza, P.: The BRONCHOVID – computer system supporting bronchoscopy laboratory. In: Piętka, E., Kawa, J. (eds.) Information Technologies in Biomedicine. AISC, vol. 69, pp. 511–522. Springer, Heidelberg (2010). http://dx.doi.org/10.1007/978-3-642-13105-9_51
3. Eshkol, A., Grega, M., Leszczuk, M., Weintraub, O.: Practical application of near duplicate detection for image database. In: Dziech, A., Czyżewski, A. (eds.) MCSS 2014. CCIS, vol. 429, pp. 73–82. Springer, Heidelberg (2014). http://dx.doi.org/10.1007/978-3-319-07569-3_6
4. Grega, M., Bryk, D., Napora, M.: Inact-indect advanced image cataloguing tool. Multimedia Tools Appl. **68**(1), 95–110 (2014). http://dx.doi.org/10.1007/s11042-012-1164-3
5. Grega, M., Lach, S.: Urban photograph localization using the instreet application - accuracy and performance analysis. Multimedia Tools Appl., 1–12 (2013). http://dx.doi.org/10.1007/s11042-013-1538-1
6. Jinda-Apiraksa, A., Vonikakis, V., Winkler, S.: California-nd: an annotated dataset for near-duplicate detection in personal photo collections. In: Burnett, I.S. (ed.) QoMEX, pp. 142–147. IEEE (2013)
7. Manjunath, B., Salembier, P., Sikora, T.: Introduction to MPEG-7: Multimedia Content Description Interface. Wiley, New York (2002)
8. Viola, P., Jones, M.: Rapid object detection using a boosted cascade of simple features, pp. 511–518 (2001)

9. Xie, H., Gao, K., Zhang, Y., Tang, S., Li, J., Liu, Y.: Efficient feature detection and effective post-verification for large scale near-duplicate image search. IEEE Trans. Multimedia **13**(6), 1319–1332 (2011)
10. Zheng, L., Qiu, G., Huang, J., Fu, H.: Salient covariance for near-duplicate image and video detection. In: 2011 18th IEEE International Conference on Image Processing (ICIP), pp. 2537–2540, September 2011

Survey on Applications of Multimedia Technology to Examine Impact of Roadside Advertising on Drivers

Andrzej Czyżewski[1], Adam Korzeniewski[1(✉)], Piotr Odya[1],
Piotr Szczuko[1], and Bożena Kostek[2]

[1] Multimedia Systems Department, Gdańsk University of Technology, Gdańsk, Poland,
adamkorz@sound.eti.pg.gda.pl
[2] Audio Acoustics Laboratory, Gdańsk University of Technology, Gdańsk, Poland
bokostek@audioacoustics.org

Abstract. The correct location of ads, both static and moving, in close proximity of the roadway is an issue of high significance in the context of road safety. This publication aims to provide support in solving these issues by presenting a range of options for the implementation of extensive, multi-faceted research, using modern technology to allow an objective assessment of the risks arising from the presence of advertising spots in the roadway. The chosen research tools include the drivers' reaction tracking systems based on the use of advanced multimedia technology. These systems may be integrated in the actual vehicle, allowing for performing the tests in real-life conditions or as part of an extended driving simulator. In addition, a part of the proposed approaches to researching the problem is to check drivers' opinion using questionnaires and to analyze the traffic accidents taking place in close proximity to road advertising.

Keywords: Advertising · Billboard · Roads · Road traffic safety

1 Introduction

The absence of sufficiently detailed recommendations and rules governing the location of static and moving ads in the roadway and its immediate proximity in the context of road safety is an important issue for public roads managing entities. This situation can also be a source of potential problems in relations with companies managing this type of advertising media and, in certain circumstances may also affect the traffic. The absence of such rules is in contradiction with the Vienna Convention on Road Traffic of 8 November 1968, ratified by the Polish State 24 February, 1988. Article 4, Paragraph d, clause ii reads: "To install any board, notice, marking or device which might be confused with signs or other traffic control devices, might render them less visible or effective, or might dazzle road-users or distract their attention in a way prejudicial to traffic safety". The main goal of the proposed research, aimed at providing assistance in solving the problems mentioned above, is to provide methods to conduct extensive, multi-faceted experiments, using modern technology to allow both, an objective assessment of the risks arising from the presence of advertisements as well as subjective assessments obtained with the participation of experts from the fields of psychology and psychophysiology of

A. Dziech et al. (Eds.): MCSS 2015, CCIS 566, pp. 141–155, 2015.
DOI: 10.1007/978-3-319-26404-2_12

perception. For the proper implementation of the various stages of the research, the innovative research facilities should be designed and programmed, which among others should include the specialized equipment of the test vehicle, a driving simulator and traffic monitoring using advanced methods of image analysis. Due to the acquisition of data from many types of sources, e.g. from accident statistics and surveys psychological research, formulation of proposals will be possible following the aggregation of multidimensional data and intelligent, multidimensional analysis using knowledge mining methods in the form of the decision rules.

2   Related Works

The problem of the impact of advertisements placed in the roadway (or near) has been increasing for many years. Research conducted in other countries (e.g. USA) show that objects in the roadway and its close proximity have a significant impact on the behavior of drivers [28, 29]. This type of comprehensive studies have not been conducted on an adequate scale in Poland.

Driving is a complex process in which one can identify many elements affecting safety, including proper maneuvers, effective and purposeful control of the vehicle, comfort, and psychological and mental state of drivers. In this process there are objects interacting with each other in a physical way (vehicles, pedestrians, the lighting, the number of distracting objects, their location, types, sizes, etc.) and facilities consciously and unconsciously perceived by the user of the road, affecting its internal state (road signs, advertising) [1, 26, 30, 33]. In order to create the conditions for obtaining an exact description of the process, its in-depth research, evaluation of interaction and states, it is necessary to identify the key factors, entities, attributes and methods of an objective measurement. It is understood that driving a car is realized largely through the activities carried out reflexively, that is outside of conscious control of the driver. Any appearance of an unusual stimulus may, however, have a negative impact on the process as the capabilities of human information processing are in fact limited [2, 11]. The drivers' reaction are then delayed, which may contribute to the occurrence of a collision or accident. Roadway ads can focus the driver's attention and impair driving. Studies in various countries have shown that visual focus attracted off the road for more than two seconds significantly increases the risk of an accident [13]. Therefore, it is necessary to check whether the ads are able to attract the driver's attention and gaze for a long time. Hence, it is necessary to use an adequate eye tracking system that will evaluate the person's focus. These types of solutions based on the original vision tracking technology were used by the authors for determining the degree of focus, to establish communication with persons diagnosed as patients in a vegetative state [17, 18], control remote cameras by eye gazing, speech synthesis controlled by eye gazing [4, 14, 16]. In the literature one can also find numerous references to applications related to the assessment of drivers' behavior [10, 23].

Distracted attention can become an additional problem while driving, which is known and studied since the 60 s of the last century, occurring primarily in the conditions of cooperation between two senses of sight and hearing. It is defined as: changing the perception of the direction of the sound source, whose position does not coincide with its associated visual stimulus, also referred to as "image prox-imity effect" [6, 7]. It stems directly from the fact that the information provided by the sense of sight is the most crucial in building the human consciousness. This effect can be defined as the relationship between the position of a visual stimulus and the content of the stimulus and the focus of the eyes of a person in test and the effect of image distracting the attention [12, 19, 20, 21, 22]. The special attention will be paid to dynamic advertising, and especially the possible effects on the functioning of an organ of vision.

Sudden blindness due to rapid changes in the brightness can be dangerous even when the driver does not point the gaze towards the advertising. This applies particularly to the evening and night conditions and can cause dangerous situations. The research team at the Multimedia Systems Department of Gdansk University of Technology has expe-rience with visual tracking technology and its application, and among others, studies of attention and the distraction effect [14, 16, 17, 19, 20, 21, 22]. The impact of advertising on drivers is the new field of application of the developed solutions, which may enable effective use of similar technology in the field related to examining the impact of road-side advertising on drivers.

An important group of advertising media placed within a roadway are dynamic advertisements, using LED screens. Due to their brightness (5000 nits often exceeding) and volatility of the presented content, they seem to be one of the most significant threats to road users. The media LED lit advertising media owners displaying the spots prepared by the clients sometimes provide the guidelines for creating commercials for this type of media, for example, recommending the use of contrast, saturated colors, indicating that the size of the letters should be in the range of 10–15 % of the displayed image. At the same time they advise the use of fast image movements, a large amount of infor-mation at one time and white color on large surfaces, arguing it on the grounds of safety of road users. These assumptions, of a rather arbitrary character, require careful exper-imental verification.

3   Research Tools

It would be useful to use an experimental vehicle equipped with devices allowing for quantitative analysis of the impact of various factors distracting the driver. One of the most important elements of such a vehicle is a system that allows tracking of visual focus of the driver. This type of approach used to be adopted in similar studies, but with advances in eye-gaze tracking systems, it may be planned to measure, in addition to viewing direction, the preservation of the pupils to enable evaluation of the phenomenon of pupil accommodation and refraction lens. This is particularly important in the case of dynamic ads (LED), where, due to changes in the brightness of the presented content, eye function may be disordered. Such studies have so far been conducted in a very narrow range (mainly in simulators). Figure 1 illustrates the equipment of the experi-mental vehicle designed to enable the study of drivers' reaction while passing the road-side ads as well as photometric measurements and video recording of the pass for analytical purposes and use of the footage in a driving simulator.

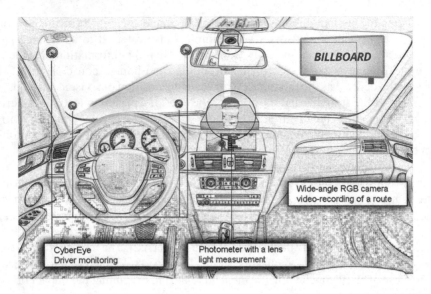

Fig. 1. Equipment of vehicle used to examine reaction, take measurements and video recording.

The results should be subjected to in-depth analysis, which in turn will help to establish guidelines for the deployment of preferred means of advertising media. Low-level MPEG 7 vision descriptors can be applied for the analysis of the displayed image. For example, the analysis of descriptors: Color Layout, and Scalable Color and Dominant Color will investigate occurrences of each color in advertising in both the RGB and YCbCr. It is also possible to appoint a representative component for each color space. In turn, the appointment of histograms (number of occurrences of a particular color in the block) will help to determine the dominant color [27]. In addition, the descriptors of shape and movement will be used in the study, so that it is possible to determine the correlation of the responses obtained in questionnaires completed by respondents, as well as those obtained from the measured parameters using a system of visual fixation, e.g. heat map and gaze plot [12, 19, 20, 21, 22]. For example, in the case of television advertising, one of the most important rules is a recommendation for the use of color in advertising material - EBU Technical Recommendation R103-2000 "Tolerances on "Illegal" colours in television" [5]. The range of available values in the YUV color space used in television systems is greater than the combinations which can be achieved in the actual deposit of basic RGB signals. If the YUV space signal is manipulated, it is possible for the illegal colors to appear. Television stations hedge against the occurrence of such colors by providing the ad creators with the Technical Documentation stating that in the event of a color inconsistency with the recommendations of the EBU R103, the ad will not be broadcast. Therefore, it seems important to examine these aspects in the context of illuminated advertising placed on billboards.

An important part of the study may also take place in a laboratory environment, where driving simulator (Fig. 2), should reflect the driving conditions. The content and the advertising parameters can be modified in a controlled manner, as well as common traffic events and threats will be simulated, including a pedestrian on the road, the driver blinded and glared by the advertising light and other relevant factors identified during the first stage of the study. Laboratory study may also use contact measurement of EEG signals, especially the P100 evoked potential associated with the operation of the center of vision in the brain. Simulation results should be compared with the results of the actual passes to determine the correlation degree existing between them.

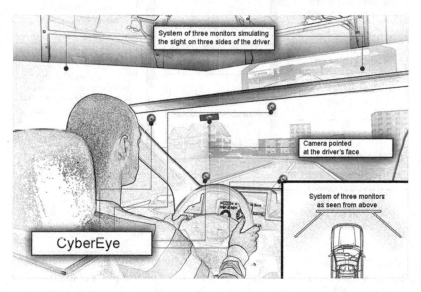

Fig. 2. Illustration of the driving simulator concept. Optional equipment is an EEG helmet.

4   Description of Research Methods

The proposed research methodology consists of seven stages. Figure 3 shows their themes and dependencies occurring between them. Finally, the research may be used to analyze the multilateral results and present conclusions in the form of guidelines and technical recommendations for the advertisement parameters and their location in relation to the roadway.

The factors and actors affecting the way of organizing and conducting experimental research can be definitely identified after further analysis, that is analysis of accidents in places with ads, analysis of the knowledge of behavioral psychology and psychophysiology of visual perception (with the participation of experts in the field), and identifying legal issues and administrative provisions. In Poland, the data on accidents and collisions can be downloaded from the System for Registration of Accidents and Collisions (SEWIK - http://sewik.pl). It should be noted that although holders of substantial supervision over the proper functioning of the system have the appropriate training and qualifications (according to their position), when interpreting the system data, it will be n0ecessary to take into account the errors occurring in the system (human factor) and the fact that some of the events are not reported to the police. Access to the system is public, but a login is required.

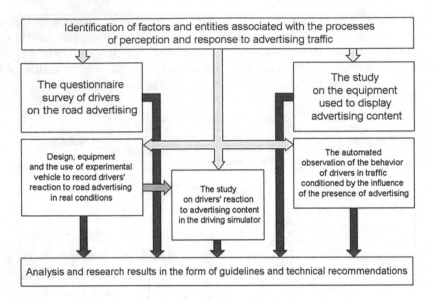

Fig. 3. The stages of the research and their interdependence

The data for analysis may also be pulled from the results of questionnaires collected among the drivers within the second stage of research. The polls content is in itself a significant research issue of an interdisciplinary character that requires the cooperation of specialists in the field of traffic engineering, police and psychologists. The task of this type has already been undertaken, as there are publications on research on similar subjects abroad [32], but a lack of the surveys relating to the specifics of the local traffic, the opinion of Polish drivers and professionals, requires for the issue to be looked at once again. The next phase of the work should focus on analysis of the amount of light emitted or reflected from advertising media [8]. Research in the field of perception shows that when within the field of sight an object is visibly brighter or darker than its surrounding, the visual attention is directed at it involuntarily. At dusk, the driver's eyes compensate for low-light, becoming more sensitive to light, resulting in even greater susceptibility to distraction or dazzle [24]. Since ones can expect that innovative methods of image analysis, the study of reaction and the combined multidimensional data processing will provide a large number of results, the last stage of testing should be devoted for their analysis and on the basis of which, the guidelines and technical recommendations should be formulated, becoming the project deliverables.

4.1 Identification of Factors and Entities Associated with the Processes of Perception and Response to Advertising Traffic

In the context of identifying these factors and entities, among others, the following parameters should be examined:

- driver-related physical (visual acuity, vision correction if used, seat height, distance from the windscreen, the optical horizon height above the plane of the roadway) [36];
- driver-related behavioral (degree of focus, viewing direction, the eyesight retention time on the elements of the scene, reaction time);
- vehicle (windshield size, height of the seat above the road surface, the instantaneous velocity of a ride);
- road (turn, tilt, number of lanes, road type, road signs present in a given place and their distribution in relation to the vehicle and billboards, topology of intersections and junctions, green belts width) and traffic (flow, liquidity, the effect of traffic lights)
- the weather and sunlight;
- history of accidents broken down by type of event, time of day, year [34] and location [9].

A set of parameters of the road ads is important in future studies, including the list expected attributes that can be developed during the study.

- the content (images, text, elements size, and their emotional character);
- dynamic content (changes in color, contrast, flicker, movement character, the size of moving elements);
- orientation and position relative to the road;
- uniformity, directionality and strength of light.

The instantaneous driver behavioral traits should be pre-tested, such as eye fixation point tracking (recording objects that attract attention and the time they fixed the eyesight), the activity of the optic tract and the response to the stimulus (P100 potential in EEG measuring), response times (the time to start braking after noticing threats). Interdependencies and relationships of cause and effect between the various factors and actors can be identified by means of observation, surveys and statistical analysis carried out within the remaining steps of the study.

4.2   The Questionnaire Survey of Drivers on the Road Advertising

Creating a survey is one of the critical stages of an overall study. The prepared questionnaire should be correlated with laboratory tests (examination of respondents in conditions of a virtual, simulated test environment, ad sizes and controlled parameters) and with the measurements taken in real-life conditions. For this reason, the questionnaire questions should refer to the circumstances of the place, i.e. urban area, industrial area, built-up area outside the city, green area–park, type of road (fast road, highway, country road, etc.), distance from the road, the angle of the billboards in relation to the road, road topology: the straight section of the road, the curvature; varying weather conditions; time of day/night. Another part of the survey should include the questions regarding the content of the displayed ad, its colors, the frequency of the scene changes within a single ad, and between advertisements. In addition, questions should also refer to the respondent's assessment of vision (normal vision, in case of defected vision, the type of defect, in case of corrected vision, glasses or contact lenses worn by the driver), sensitivity to light, etc. The element common to surveys, laboratory and real-life tests should be the answer that would determine the extent to which the LED advertising impacts the eyesight distraction effect. The use of the point of visual fixation tracking system in the will allow to examine the impact of the LED ads on perception.

4.3 The Study on the Equipment Used to Display Advertising Content

This step allows to examine the luminance of currently used advertising panels, depending on the location and the time of day or night [8, 24]. In the case of dynamic ads (LED screens) the evaluation should be subjected to the light emitted by the screen directly, in the case of traditional advertising it should be the light reflected from the surface of the billboard. The photometer with appropriate lenses should be used for the luminance tests. The measurements are done in two ways: by using the luminance measurements adapter and without it. A proper adapter allows for precise luminance measurement results for a small angle of light, which means that a photometer without and adapter may turn out to be more practical. The methodology involves the use of light meter to measure the total light in a particular location with the tested advertising media lights switched on and off. Then, using appropriate transformations, one can get the difference in the level of luminance scenes from the carrier and without it, which expresses the luminance of the advertising media. The described method is insensitive to small changes in the angle of measurement, which significantly improves the measurement process. Additionally, the original concept for measuring the luminance of advertising media is to use the cameras recording the inside of the vehicle. Changing the parameters of the recorded image while maintaining a constant level of exposure will allow to determine the desired luminance levels. This method, as experimental, however, requires verification and comparison with the assessments carried out on the basis of the indication of a light meter. In addition to measuring the luminance of advertising space, the physical dimensions and location in relation to the road should also be measured. All measurements should be performed at different times of the day and night to cover the widest possible range of variation of the whole scene. One should also take into account the limited angles of illumination of the LED screens (typically approx. 120 degrees horizontally and 50 degrees vertically).

4.4 Design, Equipment and the Use of Experimental Vehicle to Record Drivers' Reaction to Road Advertising in Real Conditions

A number of test runs are required to conduct a research related to the driver's perception of static and dynamic advertising, during which the driver's reactions are measured and recorded (for further analysis) journey parameters (e.g. change of speed). An experimental vehicle is indispensable for the realization of the research. The vehicle should be equipped with the following:

- contactless eye tracker enables the evaluation of the driver's visual point of focus and concentration over time, pupil diameter will also be analyzed in order to assess the process of accommodation and refraction of the eye;
- photometer used to assess ambient light and the intensity of light coming from the dynamic ads;

- stereoscopic image-recording camera in front of a car will allow to overlay the recording on the information gathered using the eye tracker (such as the eyesight points of focus);
- set of high-resolution cameras, enabling 360 degree image recording around the car. The images will be then used during the tests in the simulator and to assess the traffic;
- camera recording the driver's face - for the purposes of assessing the driver's behavior;
- GPS logger to monitor the route and record the drive parameters (e.g. speed, lane changing frequency);
- accelerometer to record data on braking and acceleration of the vehicle;
- LTE based system for data transfer to enable the transmission of data in real time.

Research should be based on relatively large group (e.g. 60 drivers) divided into three categories:

- young drivers - at the age of 18–30 years, not more than 10 years holding the license;
- mature driver - at the age of 30–60 years, driving license for more than 10 years;
- elderly drivers - over 60 years of age, as shown by research in this age group there is a deterioration of cognitive properties, which may mean that they the exposure to the road advertising may affect them in a different way [38].

Test rides must include the different categories of roads that can be chosen in a way that would allow to record the driver's behavior. Because of the involvement of the driver's attention and the fatigue related to it, it can be assumed that one of the routes will lead in an urban area, the other outside the urban area, including fast roads or motorways. The length of the route may be approx. 15–20 km for the urban area and approx. 40–50 km for the area outside the city. For each route and each driver, rides should take place both during the day and night. Each route must be selected in such a way that the driver has passed a certain number of ads of each type. The billboard airtime purchase should also be planned so that messages of specific content and color can be displayed in order to get the results of reference.

Since the tests will take place on existing public roads and in the presence of other vehicles, it does not seem possible to maintain constant conditions (e.g. the amount of traffic, traffic jams) for all drivers. However, by recording images from the camera recording the image around the vehicle and GPS data, it will be possible to take into account the traffic as one of the parameters affecting the results obtained.

4.5 The Study on Drivers' Reaction to Advertising Content in the Driving Simulator

The purpose of this step is to provide a laboratory environment to emit the stimulus and measure the subject's reaction. The test environment can be recreated inside the vehicle (windshield, steering wheel and pedals, instruments, made on a 3D printer or purchased) and the vehicle environment (engine sound emission and projection of preformatted imagery o large-format monitors, auto-stereoscope monitors that do not require glasses to project 3D content or projectors in front of and at the sides of the cab). The measurement of a conscious reaction might be determined by pressing the button, brake, etc., at a notion of a road sign, pedestrian, changing lights, or a hazard. On the other hand, visual fixation test and EEG-P100 evoked potential may be employed to measure the unconscious response. The following should be tested and determined:

– the impact of the billboard light glare (time and emissions) on the duration of readaptation to twilight and night vision [26, 30, 31, 36, 37];
– minimal duration of a correct perception of the content of the traffic sign after the perception of the visual stimuli of advertising [1, 33];
– influence of the advertisement content on the traffic signs comprehension and assessment of the situation on the road [26, 30].

Visual stimuli can come from two sources:

– video recordings of the ride on the selected route, recorded using the system developed in the previous stage, merged into a high resolution panoramic image, surrounding the person in test;
– interactive driving simulation, close to real virtual environments, which allow one to modify elements of the road, visibility conditions, content, advertising and other aspects.

In case of a virtual environment, some routes can be prepared (at least 10), that would playback the previously recorded actual road segments. This would allow to compare the results obtained for the footage and the virtual stimulus and to determine the correlation with the data collected during the actual traffic passing. The test procedure and method of selection of stimuli should be developed that would reduce the effects of memorizing the route and road signs so that the same person could participate repeatedly in the study.

The elements and time the test person focuses on should be determined using an eye tracking device, for example. CyberEye [15]. It would resolve the issue the attracting object identification, despite the constant movement present in the displayed image. Analysis of the data will provide an objective measure of the degree of attention on the road and the time of distraction caused by the objects on the roadside. The second measurement will use the visually evoked potentials - signals recorded on the scalp using electrodes. Typically, in order to determine the activity of the brain related to processing visual stimulus (for example in the diagnosis of intersection of the optic nerve, glaucoma, multiple sclerosis) recording the most dominant wave with a latency of about 100 ms and a positive sense. This study enables objective evaluation of the optic tract and brain response to the stimulus. Subjective aspects, e.g. comprehension of the scene (road signs, situation on the road) can be measured using input devices: such as the steering wheel, pedals (including braking in response to the threat) and touch screen with a list of ones' choice (such as questions about the content of the sign) to study the conscious perception of the characters after stimulus presentation. At the same time, the P100 potential measurement will determine the relationship between the elongation of conscious perception, advertisement parameters and the complexity of the scene.

4.6   The Automated Observation of the Behavior of Drivers in Traffic Conditioned by the Influence of the Presence of Advertising

The aforementioned objectives of the research can be achieved based on the methods of computer vision processing imagery provided by the cameras observing the traffic in the vicinity the advertising media. The acquired signals are correlated with the signals from the system tracking the point of visual fixation and cameras mounted on the vehicle. This approach enables the analysis of driver behavior, not only in terms of units (per driver), but also as a whole (traffic, creating traffic jams because of advertising set near the road). Analysis of images from the cameras will determine both the flow of traffic near the billboard advertising, as well it will make it possible to determine the degree of how busy the roadway is. Driver behavior can be modeled using a set of parameters such as distance between the vehicles and the average speed. These parameters can be changed in the neighborhood of advertising. This way, it is possible to detect behaviors such as slowing down in the area of the billboard, unconscious turning in the direction of advertising, or delayed responses to light signals emitted by traffic lights. It would be useful to have experience in the analysis of traffic and spotting events that may be occur it [35] as well as in modeling the behavior of objects in the area supervised by a camera monitoring system [3, 25]. In particular, one should examine the reactions of drivers to solid black background media, simulating a non-operating billboard.

4.7   Analysis and Research Results in the Form of Guidelines and Technical Recommendations

Cumulative analysis of results should be an erudite, but not exclusively, as is ay be possible to use advanced methods of data analysis, namely statistical and intelligent methods based on the of knowledge mining. The latter approach is justified by the multidisciplinary nature of research, the results of which will have a diverse form and nature, ranging from data derived from extensive questionnaires, through the analysis of the accident, the measurements of technical parameters advertising displays and defining descriptors of the broadcast advertising material, to the results of biometric tests in simulated and actual conditions and data from monitoring of the traffic surrounded by ads.

5   Experiment Guidelines

Implementation of the research will enable the construction of driving simulator, development of multimodal data analysis algorithms and to investigate the impact of advertising on the roads on the perception of the driver. These elements can provide the environment for the further development of research on perception and behavior. For testing purposes, the recordings from the cockpit of the vehicle were conducted (sample scene of the recording is shown in Fig. 4), however they were not subjected to a thorough analysis, yet.

The test results could be used to settle the problem of administrative location of static and dynamic advertising in the roadway and its immediate proximity. In the case of dynamic ads, it will also allow to specify the rules for emission of the content and the panel brightness in order to avoid not only excessive attraction of driver's attention, but also blinding the driver, especially in unfavorable conditions when that easily lead to a situation that requires urgent accommodation of the eye. Emphasis should be placed on recommendations on the four most common types of advertising media:

- static billboard 6 × 3 m in size (area of 18m2);
- static billboard 5,04 × 2,38 m in size (area of 12m2);
- LED advertising - typical medium of this type has an area of approx. 20–30m2 and a resolution in the range from 576 × 288 to 640 × 480;
- backlit panels also known as citylights- medium sized 1,2 × 1,8 m, backlit, placed mostly on bus stops.

Fig. 4. Frame of the recording made during a sample test

The main assumption relating to the prospects of the implementation developed under the above research guidelines is to collect a knowledge on advisable ways to present advertising content, in order to increase traffic safety. The most important entity - human, is the primary recipient of the results of such research, through an indirect impact on the protection of life and health, potentially reducing the fatigue caused by driving.

Acknowledgements. The authors wish to express their gratitude to Mr. Pawel Spaleniak, an employee of the Multimedia Systems Department at Gdansk University of Technology, for the concept sketches used in this publication (Figs. 1 and 2).

References

1. Castro, C., Martos, F.J.: Effect of background complexity in perception of traffic signs: the distracting effect of advertisements in the proximity of the sign. General Psychology (1998)
2. Cooper, P.J., Zheng, Y., Richard, Ch., Vavrik, J., Heinrichs, B., Siegmund, G.: The impact of hands-free message reception/response on driving task performance. Accid. Anal. Prev. **35**, 23–35 (2003)
3. Czyżewski, A., Lisowski, K.: Employing flowgraphs for forward route reconstruction in video surveillance system. J. Intell. Info. Syst. **43**(3), 521–535 (2014)
4. Czyżewski, A., Łopatka, K., Kunka, B., Rybacki, R., Kostek, B.: Speech synthesis controlled by eye gazing. In: 129th Convention of the Audio Engineering Society, Paper No. 8165, San Francisco, USA, 4.11.2010 - 7.11(2010)
5. EBU Technical Recommendation R103-2000 "Tolerances on "Illegal" colours in television"
6. Gardner, M.B.: Proximity image effect in sound localization. J. Acoust. Soc. Amer. **43**, 163 (1968)
7. Gooding, L.: The effect of viewing distance and disparity on perceived depth, SPIE Proc. Stereoscopic Displays Appl. II **1457**, 259–266 (1991)
8. Rea, M.S.: IESNA Lighting Handbook. Illuminating Engineering Society of North America, New York (2000)
9. Interaktywna mapa wypadków i baza danych (Interactive map of accidents and database), (in Polish) Polskie Obserwatorium Bezpieczeństwa Ruchu Drogowego: https://www. obserwatoriumbrd.pl
10. Inman, V.W., Balk, S.A., Perez, W.A.: Traffic Control Device Conspicuity, National Highway Traffic Safety Administration, Report No. FHWA-HRT-13-044, August 2013
11. Kang, J.J., Bian, Z., Andersen, G.J.: Crash Risk: Eye Movement as Indices for Dual Task Driving Workload. In: Proceedings of the Fifth International Driving Symposium on Human Factors in Driver Assessment, Training and Vehicle Design, pp. 356–362. Big Sky, USA (2009)
12. Kaszuba, K., Kostek, B.: Brain-computer interaction based on EEG signal and gaze-tracking information. Elektronika **5**, 21–26 (2012)
13. Klauer, S.G., Dingus, T.A., Neale, V.L., Sudweeks, J.D., Ramsey, D.J.: The impact of driver inattention on near-crash/crash risk: an analysis using the 100-car naturalistic driving study data, National Highway Traffic Safety Administration, Report No. DOT HS 810 594, April 2006
14. Kulasek, Ł., Kunka, B., Czyżewski, A.: Badanie rozpoznawania twarzy przez człowieka z wykorzystaniem systemu śledzenia fiksacji wzroku Cyber-Oko (The study facial recognition by humans with a tracking system using visual fixation Cyber Eye). Elektronika **1**, 29–31 (2011). (in Polish)
15. Kunka, B.: System śledzenia punktu fiksacji wzroku jako narzędzie wspierające badania korelacji wzrokowosłuchowych (Fixation point tracking system vision as a tool to study the correlation wzrokowosłuchowych) Rozprawa doktorska (Doctoral thesis in Polsih), Politechnika Gdańska, promotor Prof. Bożena Kostek (2011)
16. Kunka, B., Czyżewski A., Kostek B.: Concentration tests. An application of gaze tracker to concentration exercises. In: 1st International Conference on Computer Supported Education, p. 66. Lizbona, Portugalia, 23–26 March 2009
17. Kunka, B., Czyżewski, A., Kwiatkowska, A.: Awareness evaluation of patients in vegetative state employing eye-gaze tracking system. Int. J. Artif. Intell. Tools (IJAIT), **21**(2), 1–11 (2012)

18. Kunka, B., Czyżewski, A., Kwiatkowska, A.: Interaction with post-comatose patients employing video-based eye-gaze tracking system; XVIII Krajowa Konferencja Biocybernetyki i Inżynierii Biomedycznej, Gdańsk, Polska, 10–12 October 2013

19. Kunka, B., Kostek, B.: Objectivization of audio-visual correlation analysis. Arch. Acoust. **37**(1), 63–72 (2012)

20. Kunka, B., Kostek, B.: New aspects of virtual sound source localization research. Audio Eng. Soc. **61**(5), 280–289 (2013)

21. Kunka, B., Kostek, B.: Exploiting audio-visual correlation by means of gaze tracking. Int. J. Comput. Sci. Appl. Multimedia Appl. Process. **7**(3), 104–123 (2010)

22. Kunka, B., Kostek, B., Kulesza, M., Szczuko, P., Czyzewski, A.: Audio-visual correlation analysis employing gaze-tracking and quality of experience methodology. Hum. Comput. Interact. Knowl.-Based Environ. Spec. Issue Intell. Decis. Technol. J. Intell. Decis. Technol. **4**(3), 217–227 (2010)

23. Lappi, O., Pekkanen, J., Itkonen, T.H., Pursuit eye-movements in curve driving differentiate between future path and tangent point models. PLOS ONE, **8**(7), July 2013

24. Lewin, I.: Digital Billboard Recommendations and Comparisons to Conventional Billboards. Lighting Sciences, Inc., Scottsdale (2009)

25. Lisowski, K., Czyzewski, A.: Modelling object behaviour in a video surveillance system using Pawlak's Flowgraph. In: Dziech, A., Czyżewski, A. (eds.) MCSS 2014. CCIS, vol. 429, pp. 122–136. Springer, Heidelberg (2014)

26. Molino, J.A., Wachtel, J., Farbry, J.E., Hermosillo, M.B., Granda, T.M.: The effects of commercial electronic variable message signs (CEVMS) on driver attention and distraction: an update. US Department of Transportation, Federal Highway of Transportation (2009)

27. Multimedia Description Schemes. http://mpeg.chiariglione.org/standards/mpeg-7/multimediadescription-schemes. (data dostępu 29 March 2015)

28. Perez, W.A., Bertola, M.A., Kennedy, J.F., Molino, J.S.: Driver visual behavior in the presence of commercial electronic variable message signs (CEVMS), National Highway Traffic Safety Administration, Report No. FHWAHEP-11-014, March 2011

29. Perez, W., Bertola, M.A.: The effect of visual clutter on driver eye glance behavior. In: Proceedings of the Sixth International Driving Symposium on Human Factors in Driver Assessment, Training and Vehicle Design, pp. 180–186. Lake Tahoe, USA (2011)

30. Perez, W.A., Bertola, M.A., Kennedy, J.F., Molino, J.A.: Driver visual behavior in the presence of commercial electronic variable message signs (CEVMS). US, Department of Transportation, Federal Highway of Transportation (2012). http://www.fhwa.dot.gov/real_estate/oac/visual_behavior_report/final/cevmsfinal.pdf

31. Polska norma PN – EN 13201:2007 Oświetlenie dróg (the Polish norm concerning lighting of roads)

32. Sisiopiku, V.P., Islam, M.M., Wittig, S., Welburn, S.C., Stavrinos, D.: Perceived and real impacts of digital advertising billboards on driving performance. In: Proceedings of the 5th International Conference on Applied Human Factors and Ergonomics AHFE 2014, pp. 19–23. Kraków, Poland, July 2014

33. Summala, H., Hietamäki, J.: Drivers' immediate responses to traffic signs. Ergonomics **27**(2), 205–216 (1984)

34. Symon, E.: Statystyki wypadków. (Statistics of accidents – in Poland) Wydział Ruchu Drogowego, Biura Prewencji i Ruchu Drogowego KGP (2015). http://statystyka.policja.pl/download/20/156960/Raportroczny2014r.pdf

35. Szwoch, G., Dalka, P.: Detection of vehicles stopping in restricted zones in video from surveillance cameras. In: Dziech, A., Czyżewski, A. (eds.) MCSS 2014. CCIS, vol. 429, pp. 242–253. Springer, Heidelberg (2014)

36. Śmigacz, A.: Badania kierowców – kontrastometria. (Examination of Polish drivers) Expert Medyczny (3) (2002). http://www.emedyk.pl/artykul.php?idartykul_rodzaj=72&idartykul=590
37. Tarnowski, A.: Widzenie zmierzchowe a bezpieczeństwo na drogach. Transport samochodowy (1), Wydawnictwo ITS, Warszawa (2012). http://www.its.waw.pl/transportsamochodowy/Numer_1_2012,0,3091,1.html
38. Wang, D.-Y.D., Entsminger, S.: Age and Attentional Capacity. In: Proceedings of the Fifth International Driving Symposium on Human Factors in Driver Assessment, Training and Vehicle Design, pp. 427–432. Big Sky, USA (2009)

Biometric Applications

Static Audio Keystroke Dynamics

Patrick Bours[1]($\boxtimes$), Eva Kiktová[2], and Matúš Pleva[2]

[1] Gjøvik University College, Gjøvik, Norway
patrick.bours@hig.no
http://www.nislab.no/

[2] Department of Electronics and Multimedia Communications, Technical University
of Košice, FEI TU Košice, Letná 9, 041 20 Košice, Slovak Republic
{eva.kiktova,matus.pleva}@tuke.sk
http://www.kemt.fei.tuke.sk

Abstract. In this paper we investigate the accuracy of an identification scheme based on the sound of typing a password. The novelty of this paper lies in the comparison of performance between timing based and audio based keystroke dynamics data in both an authentication and an identification setting. We collected data of 50 people typing the same given password 100 times, divided into 4 sessions of 25 typings, and tested how well the system could recognize the correct typist. When training with data of 3 sessions and testing with the remaining session we achieved a maximal accuracy of 97.3 % using cross validation. Repeating this with training with 1 session and testing with the 3 remaining sessions we achieved an accuracy of still 90.6 %. The results show the potential of using Audio Keystroke Dynamics information as a way to identify users during log on.

Keywords: Biometrics · Keyboard dynamics · Acoustical analysis · Authentication · Identification

1 Introduction

Password systems are widespread and used many times on a daily basis. The main advantage is the easy usage, but that advantage is often offset because users select weak passwords and hence the password system becomes weak. Analysis on a database of 32M leaked passwords [1] has shown that users select passwords that can be easily broken by a dictionary attack. Biometric systems provide higher security, but generally at the cost of an expensive sensor. Keystroke Dynamics (KD) is a way to combine passwords and biometrics at no additional costs, because this is a device already present at a laptop or computer. Keystroke Dynamics does not so much look at what a user types, but how a user types. So far, the most used features in KD are timing related features, as this information is easiest to collect [2,3]. The Operating System (OS) of a computer can provide information on when a key is pressed down (down time) and when it is released (up time). In some research also key pressure [4,5] has been considered for KD features. This will however require a special keyboard, which means that the advantage of no extra costs is lost.

© Springer International Publishing Switzerland 2015
A. Dziech et al. (Eds.): MCSS 2015, CCIS 566, pp. 159–169, 2015.
DOI: 10.1007/978-3-319-26404-2_13

Relatively little research has been done using the sound produced when typing on a keyboard [6–9]. In this paper we will investigate this area and see if we can identify the user by the sound of typing his/her password. The novelty of this paper lies in the fact that will compare the performance of "classical" timing based KD with the relatively new audio based KD. Our comparison is both with respect to authentication as well as identification. Most laptops and desktop computers do have a microphone and camera present, hence it will be relatively easy to collect audio information. The remainder of this paper is organized as follows. In Sect. 2 we will give an overview of the research done in Keystroke Dynamics with the focus on using audio information. We will also provide some additional information on how audio typing information can be used. Section 3 will describe the setup of our experiment as well as describe the data that is collected. Sections 4 and 5 will provide the description of how the analysis on our data has been performed as well as the results of this analysis. We conclude this research with a discussion of our results and topics for future research in Sect. 6.

2   State of Art

Keystroke Dynamics is a behavioural biometric modality that is used to authentication or identify individuals based on their typing rhythm [2]. The major advantage of KD as a biometric is that it can be software based and no extra hardware is required. Most KD systems used key-up and key-down timing information from which the duration and latency features can be derived. Duration is a single key feature and represents how long that key had been kept down (i.e. the elapsed time between key-down and key-up of that particular key). Latency is a feature of 2 consecutive keys and represents the time that the keyboard is not used, i.e. the time between key-up of the first key and key-down of the second key. Alternative definitions of latency exist but this is not relevant for this paper. Note that latency can be negative, if the second key is pressed before the first is released. In [10] a comparative study of statistical and machine learning approaches has been conducted on a common database to see what analysis technique performs best. On a database of 51 persons and 400 samples per person, the best performing analysis method was using the Scaled Manhattan Distance, with a 9.6 % Equal Error Rate.

In some research [4] it has shown that including key pressure will lead to better performance results. This, however, requires specialized hardware to measure this kind of information. If KD is performed on a tablet with a touch screen, then such information is available. In our research we will not focus on pressure or touch screens. We will exhibit the fact that the sound of typing is different for different persons. Some people gently press each key separately, while others might type fast and hit keys hard. It has been noted before that the sound of typing differs per person, and, per key typed. This information can be used to either recognize the person that is typing, or what this person is typing. Early research was mostly focused on retrieving the text from the keystroke audio [11–13]. Interestingly, it is not just the sound that can be recorded, but also the vibration of a laptop screen [14], due to the typing on the keyboard, can be captured by a laser microphone and be used to reconstruct the typed text. An assumption that is often made is that the user types English text, and no typing corrections are considered.

Little research has been done in using the typing audio for authentication or identification of people. To the best of our knowledge is this first investigated in [6], where the authors combine keystroke timing information with typing sound information. In their investigation they experiment participants needed to type the password "kirakira". Audio data was collected through a separate microphone placed at the base of the laptop keyboard. Ten users all provided 10 typing samples, and of these samples 5 were used to train a Self Organizing Map (SOM), while the other 5 were used for testing. They evaluated the performance of the system in an authentication setting. In a follow-up publication [7] they used Supervised Pareto SOM to improve their results. The main difference between the research in [6,7] and our research threefold. First of all do we use a different analysis technique on the audio data, furthermore do we compare performance between timing KD and audio KD and finally is our dataset much larger (50 versus 10 users and 100 versus 10 samples per user). The overlap lies in the fact that they, just as we, have used a fixed password, i.e. we considered static authentication in both cases.

In [9] the authors extend their initial work [8] on keystroke sound. They investigate not the possibility for static authentication, but concentrate on continuous authentication [15] to see how the sound of typing can be used. They collected audio data of 50 persons, typing either a fixed text (i.e. the first paragraph of "A Tale of Two Cities" by Charles Dickens, containing 613 characters, shown on screen) or a free text (i.e. they were tasked to type a half page email to family without further instructions on the content). Audio data was collected using the microphone of an inexpensive webcam mounted at the top of the laptop screen, where the microphone was directed towards the keyboard. The authors obtain an EER of approximately 11 % in their experiments. They also briefly looked at an identification setting where they obtained a rank-1 accuracy of approximately 75 %. The main differences with the research from Roth et al. is that they focus on long texts, i.e. on continuous authentication, while our focus is on short passwords, i.e. static authentication.

The contributions in this paper can be summed up as follows:

- Collection of a database of timing and audio related information (see Sect. 3 for more details);
- Comparison of authentication and identification performance between timing based KD and audio based KD.

3   Data Collection

Because there exist no publicly available dataset for our purposes, we did have to collect our own data. The setup for our data collection is similar to what is done in the works from Dozono et al. [6] and Nakakuni et al. [7] and from Roth et al. [8,9]. The difference with [6,7] is the size of the collected database and with [8,9] is the amount of data per sample. We focus on the password scenario where all users type the same password. The password used is the word "password" and the participants in the experiment cannot see what they type. This is enforced by moving the screen away from the participants and only the experiment supervisor can see what the participant types. Each of the 50 participants (10 female, 40 male, average age 26, mainly staff and students of Gjøvik University College) has to type the password 100 times, divided into 4 session of 25 times. The experiment supervisor checked how many correct typings of the password occurred in each session and stopped the participants after the session. In between sessions the participants could relax a few minutes before they continued to the next session. The experiment took place in a semi-controlled environment, where there was no background noise, but noise from neighboring rooms could not be controlled, only recorded. Generally speaking the noise level from adjacent rooms was very low during the full experiment. In our experiment we used a simple webcam microphone (Logitech model QuickCam

Fig. 1. Experiment setup used to collect the audio data

Pro 9000) to collect the typing sound of a desktop keyboard (DELL model SK-8135). The webcam and keyboard were placed in an area marked by tape, indicating also the location of the microphone of the webcam. The distance between the keyboard and the microphone was approximately 10 cm and the microphone was placed near the middle of the keyboard. Minor moves of the equipment could have appeared, but no large movements were possible. One major difference between our research and related research is that we have used a desktop keyboard instead of a laptop keyboard. Figure 1 shows the setup that was used in the experiment.

Besides the audio data collected we also the timing information from the typing data. This data will be used to calculate the performance for static timing based KD to see the difference in performance when compared to the audio typing data.

The password is 'password' and coded as $k_1, k_2, ..., k_8$, e.g. $k_5 = $ 'w' and $k_3 = k_4 = $'s'. The data from user i ($i = 1..50$) collected in typing j ($j = 1..25$) of session l ($l = 1..4$) is:

1. The key-down timings: $t^{down}_{i,j,l,m}$ for $m = 1..8$;
2. The key-up timings: $t^{up}_{i,j,l,m}$ for $m = 1..8$;
3. The audio file $S_{i,j,l}$ for the full typing of the password.

From the key-down and key-up timings duration and latency can be calculated. More precisely we have:

1. $dur_{i,j,l,m} = t^{up}_{i,j,l,m} - t^{down}_{i,j,l,m}$ for $m = 1..8$; and
2. $lat_{i,j,l,m} = t^{down}_{i,j,l,m+1} - t^{up}_{i,j,l,m}$ for $m = 1..7$.

Durations and latencies are used to measure the performance of the timing based KD system and will be used to compare against the performance of the audio KD system.

An graphical representation of one audio file is given in Fig. 2. We can clearly distinguish the sound produced by each pressing down and releasing of a key. This particular user had relatively high latencies (distance between key release of one key and key down of the next key), except between the two s'es. Various other users typed faster, resulting into some negative latencies, meaning that the sound of the key down of the next key was recorded before the sound of the key up of the current key.

4   Data Analysis

This section is split into two parts. In the first part we will focus on the baseline analysis based on the timing information, while the second part focuses on performance for audio related information.

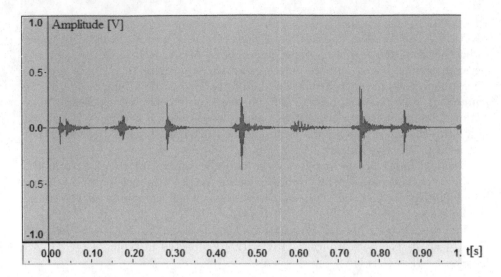

Fig. 2. Example WAV file for typing 'password'

4.1   Timing Based Analysis

We have used the collected timing information to calculate the duration and latency features for all 100 typings of each of the 50 participants. We used 1 session for training and 3 sessions for testing, and used cross validation to assure that all 4 sessions are used for training. Alternatively we used 3 sessions for training and 1 for testing in a similar setup. We evaluated the performance of the system both for authentication and for identification. The template of a user consisted of the mean and standard deviation for each of the 8 durations and 7 latencies [2]. The distance metric used is the Scaled Manhattan Distance (SMD) as this is the best performing distance metric according to [10]. If a template is denoted by $T = ((\mu_1, \sigma_1), (\mu_2, \sigma_2), \ldots, (\mu_{15}, \sigma_{15}))$ and the test input is denoted by $t = (t_1, t_2, \ldots, t_{15})$, then the Scaled Manhattan Distance is equal to:

$$d(T, t) = \sum_{i=1}^{15} \frac{|\mu_i - t_i|}{\sigma_i}.$$

4.2   Audio Based Analysis

According to the previous setup the acoustic data were split into a training and a testing set. To capture the nature of the acoustic signal, the MFCC (Mel-Frequency Cepstral Coefficients) features were applied [16]. Figure 3 shows the MFCC features for a single typing of a user (i.e. for a recorded audio file). These features were extracted from 25 ms Hamming windows with a $10ms$ frame shift. The Mel-filter bank was created by 26 filters and the final number of cepstral coefficients was set to 12. We also used log energy, and first and second time derivatives of the 12 static coefficients as features. One signal frame was finally described by a 39 dimensional MFCC feature vector (MFCC_{EDA}). The Hidden Markov Model (HMM) based approach was employed for the classification. Each user was modeled by *ergodic* HMMs from 1 to 7 states and from 1 to 1024 PDFs (Probability Density Functions). All user models were created and evaluated in off-line tests (using the HTK toolkit [17]), but generally 5, 6 and 7 states achieved worse results compared to HMMs with a lower number of states, therefore these results are not presented here. In the authentication setting we used a number of frames and log energy for normalization of the recognition score (log probability of the particular model).

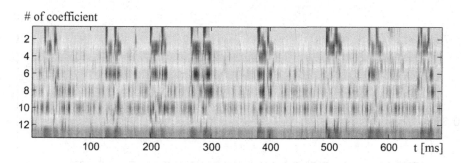

Fig. 3. Example of 13 static MFCC features for one user

5   Results

In this section will we present the results from our analysis. As in the previous section will this section also be divided into two parts, one for the results related to the timing based analysis from Sect. 4.1 and one for the results related to the audio based analysis from Sect. 4.2.

5.1   Timing Based Results

The obtained Equal Error Rate (EER) when using 1 session for training and 3 for testing was equal to 14.4 %, which dropped to 11.7 % when 3 sessions were used for training and 1 for testing.

When evaluating in an identification setting, with the same template and distance metric as above, we obtained a rank 1 accuracy of 56.7 % when using 1 session for training and 64.6 % when using 3 sessions for training. For the last case the full Cumulative Matching Curve (CMC) is given in Fig. 4.

We clearly see that the identification accuracy is not very high and only increases slightly when using three sessions for training and the remaining session for testing. The EER for authentication is at an acceptable level, certainly given the fact that it is a short password (only 8 characters, i.e. 15 features) and that it is a common English word that most likely is easy to type for all participants.

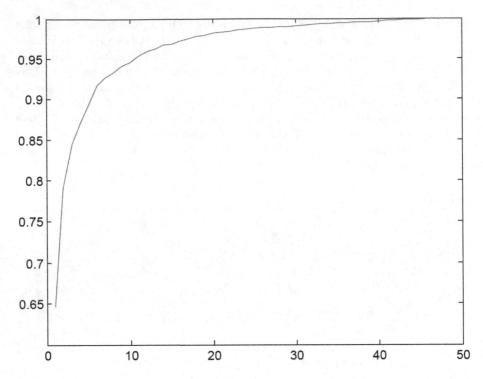

Fig. 4. CMC curve for 3 training sessions and 1 test session

5.2 Audio Based Results

We first evaluated the audio information for authentication purposes. However, when using a single session for training and the remaining three sessions for testing, we found that the EER was as high as 21.1 %. Even when using 3 sessions for training and the last session for testing did not improve these results significantly, as the EER only decreased to 19.1 %. These results obviously are too low for practical purposes, and in particular these are lower than the results we obtained based on the timing data.

When using the audio based information in an identification setting, we noticed that the results were much better. The accuracy did highly depend on the number of PDFs and the number of HMMs used. Table 1 gives a partial overview of the accuracies obtained for various values of the number of PDFs used and various HMM states. The table shows the results when using 3 sets for training and 1 for testing. It can be seen that the best result is obtained for 3 HMM states in combination with using 128 PDFs, but other settings give results that are almost as high.

We have done a similar test, but now using only a single session for training the system, while the other 3 sessions are used for testing. In this case the results are significantly lower, as can be seen in Table 2. We also note, when comparing the two tables, that the range of accuracy values is much broader when using only 1 session for training.

Table 1. Accuracy results when using 3 sessions for training and 1 for testing

# PDFs \ # HMM	1	2	3	4	5
64	94.6	95.7	96.8	94.9	92.7
128	96.0	96.8	97.3	96.6	94.4
256	96.9	97.0	96.7	96.2	94.4
512	97.2	95.6	92.8	92.2	90.0
1024	96.1	83.4	71.5	62.0	70.8

Table 2. Accuracy results when using 1 session for training and 3 for testing

# PDFs \ # HMM	1	2	3	4	5
64	88.3	89.6	90.0	86.5	81.7
128	90.6	88.5	86.2	82.9	77.1
256	90.0	76.7	65.4	59.1	58.1
512	83.5	39.1	26.0	25.1	29.2

5.3 Comparison

In this section we will make a comparison between the performance results based on timing information compared to the audio information

What we can clearly observe is that audio and timing information perform differently. Most noticeable is that timing information performs significantly better in an authentication setting, while in an identification setting the performance of audio information is much better. Given the high performance of audio KD data in case of identification we do assume that we must be able to gain a better performance also for authentication. The main hurdle is at this moment that the distance scores need to be normalized.

6 Conclusions and Future Work

We have conducted an experiment to investigate if timing information or acoustic information of typing a password would give a better performance, both for authentication and for identification.

From the above analysis we see that acoustic information obtained from typing a password does not provide high quality data for authentication purposes. When using the timing information obtained at the same time, our performance is significantly higher (11.7 % compared to 19.1 % Equal Error Rate).

It is interesting to notice that for identification purposes this conclusion needs to be reversed, as the rank-1 accuracy based on the timing data is only 64.6 % while it is 97.3 % for audio based data.

The above observation leads to an interesting question, that will be pursued in future research. It will be very interesting to see what the performance and accuracy of the system will be if we apply fusion of the timing and audio information.

In this paper we have used a restricted setting, where a fixed keyboard and microphone is used and background noise was reduced as much as possible. These settings are in line with similar research on acoustic keystroke dynamics. Any variation of these settings is worth investigating, as well as an extension to a continuous setting, where audio produced while typing on a keyboard can be used to confirm that no change of user has occurred.

Thanks

We would like to thank all the anonymous participants of the experiment who spend their time so that we could obtain the data that is used in the analysis described in this paper.

Acknowledgments. This publication is supported partially (50 %) by the Project implementation: University Science Park TECHNICOM for Innovation Applications Supported by Knowledge Technology, ITMS: 26220220182 project supported by the Research & Development Operational Programme funded by the ERDF & partially by ITMS: 26220220141 project (50 %).

References

1. Imperva. Consumer password worst practices. Technical report, The Imperva Application Defense Center (ADC) (2010)
2. Banerjee, S.P., Woodard, D.L.: Biometric authentication and identification using keystroke dynamics: a survey. J. Pattern Recogn. Res. **7**(1), 116–139 (2012)
3. Teh, P.S., Teoh, A.B.J., Yue, S.: A survey of keystroke dynamics biometrics. Sci. World J. **2013**, 1–24 (2013)
4. Rao, K.R., Anne, V.P.K., Sai Chand, U., Alakananda, V., Navya Rachana, K.: Inclination and pressure based authentication for touch devices. In: Satapathy, S.C., Avadahani, P.S., Udgata, S.K., Lakshminarayana, S. (eds.) ICT and Critical Infrastructure: Proceedings of the 48th Annual Convention of CSI - Volume I. AISC, vol. 248, pp. 781–788. Springer, Heidelberg (2014)
5. Tasi, C.-J., Chang, T.-Y., Cheng, P.-C., Lin, J.-H.: Two novel biometric features in keystroke dynamics authentication systems for touch screen devices. Secur. Commun. Netw. **7**(4), 750–758 (2013)
6. Dozono, H., Itou, S., Nakakuni, M.: Comparison of the adaptive authentication systems for behavior biometrics using the variations of self organizing maps. Int. J. Comput. Commun. **1**(4), 108–116 (2007)

7. Nakakuni, M., Dozono, H., Itou, S., Mastorakis, N.E., Poulos, M., Mladenov, V., Bojkovic, Z., Simian, D., Kartalopoulos, S., Varonides, A., et al.: Adaptive authentication system for behavior biometrics using supervised pareto self organizing maps. In: Proceedings of the 10th WSEAS International Conference on Mathematical Methods, Computational Techniques and Intelligent Systems (MEMECTICS08), vol. 10, pp. 277–282 (2008)
8. Roth, J., Liu, X., Ross, A., Metaxas, D.: Biometric authentication via keystroke sound. In: 2013 International Conference on Biometrics (ICB), pp. 1–8. IEEE (2013)
9. Roth, J., Liu, X., Ross, A., Metaxas, D.: Investigating the discriminative power of keystroke sound. IEEE Trans. Inf. Forensics Secur. 10(2), 333–345 (2015)
10. Killourhy, K.S., Maxion, R.A.: Comparing anomaly-detection algorithms for keystroke dynamics. In: IEEE/IFIP International Conference on Dependable Systems & Networks, 2009. DSN'09, pp. 125–134. IEEE (2009)
11. Asonov, D., Agrawal, R.: Keyboard acoustic emanations. In: 2004 Proceedings of IEEE Symposium on Security and Privacy, pp. 3–11, May 2004
12. Wu, L., Bours, P.: Content reconstruction using keystroke dynamics: preliminary results. In: 2014 Fifth International Conference on Emerging Security Technologies (EST), pp. 13–18, September 2014
13. Zhuang, L., Zhou, F., Tygar, J.D.: Keyboard acoustic emanations revisited. ACM Trans. Inf. Syst. Secur. (TISSEC) 13(1), 3 (2009)
14. Barisani, A., Bianco, D.: Sniffing keystrokes with lasers/voltmeters. In: Proceedings of Black Hat USA (2009)
15. Bours, P.: Continuous keystroke dynamics: a different perspective towards biometric evaluation. Inf. Secur. Tech. Rep. 17, 36–43 (2012)
16. Kiktova, E., Lojka, M., Pleva, M., Juhar, J., Cizmar, A.: Comparison of different feature types for acoustic event detection system. In: Dziech, A., Czyżewski, A. (eds.) MCSS 2013. CCIS, vol. 368, pp. 288–297. Springer, Heidelberg (2013)
17. Young, S.J., Evermann, G., Gales, M.J.F., Hain, T., Kershaw, D., Moore, G., Odell, J., Ollason, D., Povey, D., Valtchev, V., Woodland, P.C.: The HTK Book, version 3.4. Cambridge University Engineering Department, Cambridge, UK (2006)

Continuous User Verification
via Mouse Activities

Khandaker Abir Rahman[✉], Ryan Moormann, Danielle Dierich,
and Md. Shafaeat Hossain

Saginaw Valley State University, 7400 Bay Road,
University Center, MI 48710, USA
{krahman,remoorma,dgdieric}@svsu.edu, hossainm3@southernct.edu

Abstract. Behavioral biometrics such as mouse dynamics are gaining
attention these days to address the limitations of conventional verification systems. In this paper we present a novel method to continuously
verify a user via their mouse activities. Our method, based on comparing
mouse activities against a simple statistical profile, was tested over 76,500
mouse activities collected from 45 users. A total of 354,375 genuine and
impostor verification attempts have been performed by deploying 175
different verifier setups. In our experiments, we achieved an impressive
low Equal Error Rate (EER) of 6.70 %. On average the EER was 13.42 %.
We opine that, our method can complement regular verification systems
and can better serve for continuous verification purpose because of its
simplicity.

Keywords: Mouse dynamics · Behavioral biometrics · Continuous
verification

1 Introduction and Background

In the wake of growing concern over security that came about with the increasing
involvement of technology such as computer, internet, multimedia in our lives, it
is becoming more important than ever to continuously verify who a user actually
is. Among the existing methods to continuously verify a user, behavioral traits
(e.g., keystroke dynamics, mouse dynamics, and web usage patterns) are now
under the spotlight. For continuous verification, behavioral traits are promising
because they can be gathered without inconveniencing the user and even from
a remote location. Among the traits, mouse dynamics is gaining attention since
mouse activities are one of the most common activities a user performs and
that ensures a reasonable supply of samples which is mandatory for continuous
verification. Another benefit of authenticating a user based on mouse activities
is, unlike many other biometric features, there is no extra equipment needed.
Just the mouse that is normally already connected to a computer.

While relatively new, user authentication with mouse activities does have existing research. The research already done, however, has limitations. The majority

© Springer International Publishing Switzerland 2015
A. Dziech et al. (Eds.): MCSS 2015, CCIS 566, pp. 170–181, 2015.
DOI: 10.1007/978-3-319-26404-2_14

of the existing research was done with a relatively small population. Using a small population when conducting research can affect the results of that research. Another limitation present in existing research is high Impostor Pass Rate (IPR). When testing for authentication, the amount of false acceptances should be as close to 0 % as possible. Having higher IPR and False Rejection Rates (FRR) leaves room for improvement on the research already conducted.

We see high IPR and FRR occurring with multiple accounts of previous research done in this area [1–3]. One of these research procedures only took into account mouse curves when authenticating a user [3]. This could be the reason they saw such high IPR and FRR rates, successful authentication is more difficult to achieve when only a few characteristics are used to build a user profile.

There has been some previous research done with very promising results. However, while the research in [4] saw IPR at only 0.43 % and FRR at 1.75 %, the population size used was very low, they only used 11 subjects when conducting their research. While the results they achieved are more successful than the majority of other research done in this area, their low subject count raises questions about how reliable their system may be. When using a broader subject count, there is a possibility that these low IPR and FRR percentages would no longer be as low as originally recorded. It is hard to tell reliability when such a small population is being used. One study done in [5] that saw very low IPR and FRR rates at 0.55 % and 3 % respectively, only 10 subjects were used to calculate these results. These subjects were also studied over a long period time, making the system much more accurate. This method may be difficult to implement on a larger group of people to get results that accurate. Another instance in [6] where this research saw low IPR and FRR rates (just over 2 %) also had a relatively low subject count. This research used a slightly larger number of subjects, 22, but even that number is still relatively low to see accurate results for large populations of people.

Promising research that has been done so far in [1] used 37 subjects, saw higher IPR and FRR rates at slightly under 10 %, and needed only 11.8 s to authenticate a user. While the IPR and FRR rates are lower than most other research with a similar authentication time, they are still higher than what is desired. If lower IPR and FRR rates could be achieved at an even faster authentication time, the practicality of using mouse movements to authenticate users would increase. Another instance of promising results found in [7] saw an EER of 1.3 %. However, they came to this conclusion based on of research done on keystroke dynamics, saying that larger sample sizes make chances of two users having similar characteristics increases significantly.

The most promising existing mouse dynamic authentication research achieved IPR at 0 % and FRR at 0.36 % in [8]. However, their method relies on relatively heavy computation. Another research procedure showed in [9], had users use the mouse to login as if unlocking a combination lock. They saw successful results with low IPR and FRR. Another research procedure in [10] had users draw a complex figure with the mouse to login. They saw a 93 % successful verification rate with their research. While the results of mouse authentication through the use of a mouse to draw a pattern to login into a system are promising, it is not as practical as a continuous verification system would be. Drawing a pattern with the mouse is more easily replicated than a user's specific and unique everyday normal use of the mouse.

Our research on mouse dynamic user authentication addresses the limitations talked about. We have used a larger population base to take our samples from to stabilize our accuracy. With our research, we have taken a larger variety of mouse characteristics into consideration when measuring the uniqueness of a user's mouse characteristics. Using a larger amount of mouse characteristics can build a more complete and specific profile for each user.

Contribution of this work follows:

- We propose a simple method of user verification using mouse dynamics. Unlike existing methods which rely on sophisticated calculations, our method uses basic statistical information. A light weight system such as ours, is more suitable for continuous verification in real time.
- We performed 354,375 rigorous tests under 175 experimental setups. Our dataset containing mouse activities collected from 45 users, was large enough for a sustainable test result. Our system, showed impressive results with EER as low as 6.70 %.

We organized the paper as follows. In Sect. 2 we discuss data collection. In Sect. 3 we present the feature extraction method. In Sect. 4 we discuss the experimental setup. In Sect. 5 we present our results and analysis. We conclude in Sect. 6.

2   Data Collection

We wanted our data set to include movements that were natural to best simulate the day-to-day actions a user would perform on the computer in a real situation. This is to have a more relevant set of data that our authentication method would see in a more practical environment. To do this, we asked a class of students to record their mouse movements. The students were instructed to perform any activity on the computer they normally would for an hour period.

In order to log the mouse activity of users we created a simple mouse logger. The logger was a small piece of software that ran on the windows operating system. The logger, when run on a machine, logged the position of the cursor using the windows method GetCursorPos(), the state of the left and right mouse buttons (up or down), and a timestamp every 15.6 ms. 15.6 ms being the average default timer resolution that windows supports. The resulting log was then placed into a text file. We then screened the samples and removed samples with very few (0 to 10) movements and samples that weren't an hour long. Post-screening we had 45 valid user samples and left around 76,500 mouse activities for our experiments. Our samples consisted of university students' mouse activities collected from late November 2014 to early December 2014. Table 1 shows some statistics of collected samples.

Table 1. Overview of the samples collected

Activity	Maximum	Minimum	Average
Left clicks	716	37	547.84
Right clicks	690	0	122.8
Double clicks	1282	1	181.64

3   Methodology

So far, we have outlined the source of our data and the essential idea that we are trying to attain. In this section we will define the steps we took to create a system capable of authenticating a user based on their mouse movements alone. We will define exactly which features in the mouse data we consider as well as how we create a profile of a user based on their own mouse data which accurately represents that user. Finally, we explain how the profiles which we created for each user are able to verify whether a set of mouse movements are likely to have originated from it's own user.

3.1   Feature Extraction

In order to classify a test sample we needed some way to compare test samples and training samples. To do this we used features that are found in our definition of a mouse movement. The features, defined in Table 2 and visualized in Fig. 1, were found to be unique among users. In total we had six features and three sub-features. The double click length feature is interesting in that it contains three sub features allowing each sample to provide a unique set of features even if the entire length of the double clicks happen to be the same between the testing and training sets.

We defined a mouse movement as a period of cursor movement followed by a click. This isn't to say that a click without any prior movement is not considered a mouse movement. It would be a mouse movement with zero speed, acceleration, and jerk.

If the cursor sustains no action (movement or clicks) for a period of 500 ms or longer we classify that period and any preceding cursor movement as a pause. This allows for periods where a user is not concentrating on moving the mouse with intent while not having it affect periods where a user is moving the mouse with intent. We do not use pauses for classification in our method. If a mouse movement ends in a pause instead of a click we could define that as a partial mouse movement. Research has gone into studying these partial movements [7]. However, we do not consider these partial movements in our classifier because their occurrences, while abundant, degrade the accuracy of the final result. While they may hold unique identifying information about a user its more difficult to tell if the partial mouse movement came from purposeful movement (e.g. shaking the mouse to wake up the screen) or accidental movement (e.g. knocking into the mouse with your elbow.)

Table 2. Descriptions of the features used

Feature	Description
Left click length	The length of a single click from the first record the mouse button is found to be down to the first record the mouse button is found to be up
Right click length	
Double click length	Split into 4 sub-features: Total Length and intervals 1,2, and 3
	Total length: The time between the first record the mouse is found to be down and the first record the mouse is found to be up after the second click
	Interval 1: The first single left click length in a double click
	Interval 2: The time between the first record of the left mouse button being found up after the first click to the first record of the left mouse button being found down for the second left click
	Interval 3: The second single left click length in a double click
	Note: A visualization of the intervals in Fig. 1
Speed	Distance the cursor travelled divided by the total time of the movement up until the click
Acceleration	Change in Speed over time
Jerk	Change in Acceleration over time

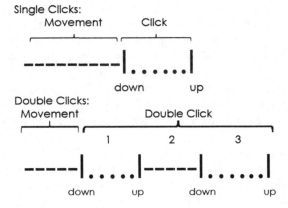

Fig. 1. A visual representation of the click features. Dashes representing no button activity, dots representing periods where the mouse button is down, and vertical bars representing the first record that the mouse button has changed state.

3.2   Outlier Filtering

For our setup we first went through each of the user samples and extracted each of the features from each mouse movement. To remove rare cases of features far from the normal, we implemented an outlier removal scheme. We define a mouse feature to be an outlier if it is more eccentric than 66 % of the population of the same mouse features for a single user. For example, if we are looking to find if a particular mouse feature F is an outlier we use the algorithm described in Algorithm 1.

Algorithm 1. Determines if a single feature F is an outlier from the rest of the population of its own kind. $featurePopulation$ is an array of same-typed features from a testing sample that F is also a member of.

1: **procedure** IsAnOutlier(F)
2:      $count \leftarrow 0$
3:      **for each** $feature$ in $featurePopulation$ **do**
4:          **if** $|F - feature| > R$ **then**
5:              $count \leftarrow count + 1$
6:      **if** $count \div featurePopulation_{size} \geq .33$ **then**
7:          **return** True
8:      **else**
9:          **return** False

We defined a variable R, for each mouse feature, a number large enough to include most of the population while small enough to remove the noise from the data. We found optimal values for our R values after extensive experimentation we will describe later on.

We created a simple algorithm for determining if a particular record of a mouse feature is an outlier outlined in Algorithm 1. For a given set of mouse features from a training sample (the $featurePopulation$), we compared each feature in the $featurePopulation$ against every other feature of the same type, i.e. a Single Left Click Length feature is only compared to every other Single Left Click Length feature. Then a simple tally is kept of how many of the features in the $featurePopulation$ have a distance greater than R as shown on line 4 and 5 of Algorithm 1. On line 6 we simple restate that if the if the tally is greater than 33 % of the $featurePopulation$ we claim the feature F is an outlier and discard it from the training set.

3.3   Verification

To authenticate a user based on their mouse movements, we analyze six mouse features over the course of a sample. Our method is a simplistic user-authentication model. We create a profile based on a user's past behavior then test further samples against that profile to determine if the sample we test with is close enough to the previous profile to be considered the same user. In a real world set-up the method would look similar to Fig. 2. Instead, we use half of the recorded mouse movements as a test set for a user and the other half are used to train the user's profile. We then split the edited list of features into a testing set and a training set. For each file we create user profiles based on half of the user's

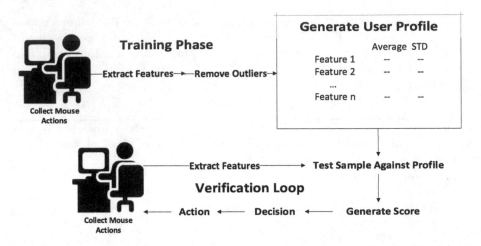

Fig. 2. An overview of continuous verification with mouse movements. In the training phase a user creates a profile based on their mouse movements (the average and standard deviation of each mouse feature). The profile is used to represent a user in the verification phase where features from live mouse movements can be verified against the profile in order to determine if the live mouse movements came from the user who created the profile. If the verifier determines that the live mouse movements are illegitimate an action can be taken. (e.g. logging the user out, creating a log of the incident, etc.)

sample (about 50 mouse movements on average for our samples). The profiles being simply the averages and standard deviations of each of the mouse features. The mouse movements from the sample that we did not use for the profile go into the user's testing set. Using a simple classification scoring method we can see how well a user profile and a testing set of data match up. For our entire set of data we took every user profile and tested each against every testing set. Our custom testing method generated a score for each test between 0 and 1 based on a simple scoring formula

$$score = \frac{\text{Number of Accepted Features}}{\text{Total Number of Features}} \tag{1}$$

1 being a perfect match and 0 being a complete mismatch. It should be noted we accept a particular feature if

$$lowerBound \leq featureValue \leq upperBound, \text{where,}$$
$$lowerBound = AVG_{Train} - M * STD_{Train} \tag{2}$$
$$upperBound = AVG_{Train} + M * STD_{Train}$$

We tested by comparing each of the mouse movements in a testing set against the users profile. If the features in the mouse movement are within M standard deviations of the corresponding means in the user profile then the test gets a point. The total amount of points accrued is divided by the total amount of mouse movements in the file to generate the score.

4   Experimental Setup

We had a few parameters where it was not immediately apparent what we should set them as. For the R variables we needed values that can discriminate mouse feature values that are too eccentric while keeping as much unique data as possible. To solve this we wrote a script that ran the feature extraction and verification programs and found the EER over an array of values for each parameter to determine the optimal values for those parameters where the EER is at its lowest. We found that an M value of 1.9, a Single Click R of 20 ms, and a Double Click R of 185 ms to produce the lowest EER for our set of data. By varying the parameter value we experimented with 175 (5 Single Click $R \times$ 5 Double Click $R \times$ 7 M Values) different experimental set-ups. Note that we do not use any R parameter for the other features since they show less variance. In total, we experimented with 354,357 verification attempts (45 users $\times$ 45 users $\times$ 175 experimental setups) (Table 3).

Table 3. The values used for our parameters for testing.

Parameter	Values tested
Single click R value	15 20 25 30 25
Double click R value	175 180 185 190 195
M value	0.7 1 1.3 1.6 1.9 2.2 2.3

5   Experimental Results and Analysis

To calculate the results of our experiment we took each users profile and tested that against every other set of testing data. Therefore, for experimental setup, we generated 2025 (45 $\times$ 45) verification scores. We then calculated the False Reject Rate (FRR) and Impostor Pass Rate (IPR) values for varying threshold values from 0 to 1 with a stepsize of 0.01. We plotted 1000 FRR and IPR values as shown in each subfigure in Fig. 3. For space constraint, we show FRRs and IPRs for four experimental setup out of 175 setups. In each subfigure, the EER is marked as the crossover point between FRR and IPR curves. In total, we generated 175 EERs from all setups. In Table 4, 35 EER values generated by varying double click R and M values when single click value set to 20 ms, are listed. In Fig. 4, EER values are shown for four other single click R values. From the figures, our observations are as follows:

- The Lowest EER achieved is 6.70 % (see Fig. 4(c)) when M= 2.2, single click R=20 ms and double click R=185 ms. Average EER is 13.19 % and standard deviation is 5.77 %.
- Among the parameters, M is found to have greater influence on accuracy (see the curves in each sub-figure in Fig. 4). This urges to explore setting up the M value for each user separately rather than deploying generic one.

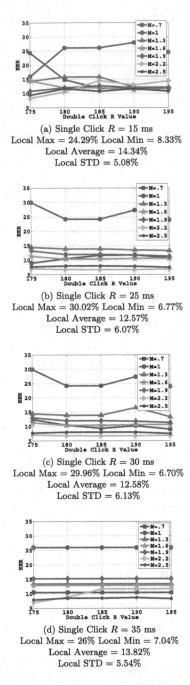

(a) Single Click $R = 15$ ms
Local Max = 24.29% Local Min = 8.33%
Local Average = 14.34%
Local STD = 5.08%

(b) Single Click $R = 25$ ms
Local Max = 30.02% Local Min = 6.77%
Local Average = 12.57%
Local STD = 6.07%

(c) Single Click $R = 30$ ms
Local Max = 29.96% Local Min = 6.70%
Local Average = 12.58%
Local STD = 6.13%

(d) Single Click $R = 35$ ms
Local Max = 26% Local Min = 7.04%
Local Average = 13.82%
Local STD = 5.54%

Fig. 3. Scatter plots of EER over the ranges of the parameter values we chose. The X-axis is Double Click R-Values, the Y-axis is the EER. Each plot is a separate Single Click R value. Global Max = 30.02 % Global Min = 6.70 % Global Average = 13.19 % Global STD = 5.77 %

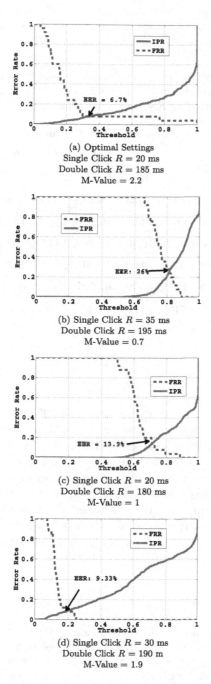

Fig. 4. Plots of the IPR and the FRR for four different parameter settings. The point at which the IPR and FRR intersect is the Equal Error Rate (EER).

- Single click R value also show some level of influence on accuracy. EERs in Fig. 4(b, c) are lower than EERs in Fig. 4(a, d). It is worth mentioning that, number of single clicks are found to be far more than other activities.

Table 4. The EER rates found across multiple parameter values. Each column is a separate double click R value while each row is a separate M value. The entire table is tested against one single click R value set to 20 ms.

Double click R values

	175	180	185	190	195
.7	14.86%	10.53%	9.33%	9.33%	8.99%
1	30.02%	24.23%	24.23%	27.37%	24.00%
1.3	14.46%	13.90%	10.40%	13.56%	13.33%
1.6	11.35%	10.40%	10.40%	10.59%	11.81%
1.9	13.35%	12.00%	12.00%	11.81%	11.36%
2.2	13.36%	6.77%	6.70%	6.75%	6.88%
2.5	7.71%	8.00%	8.00%	7.89%	7.50%

(M values)

6   Conclusion

Our comprehensive experiment which comprises 354,357 verification attempts carried over 45 users, shows the effectiveness of our method. On average, the EER we found was 13.42 %. The lowest EER was found to be 6.70 %. In the future, we want to test our method on more user samples with finer control over the environment the users manipulated the mouse in so as to ensure our method is characterizing the differences between users and less between environments. To improve accuracy even further, we want to set the parameter values (especially M) for each users separately instead of adopting generic values. We believe that, a simple system with impressive accuracy such as ours, can easily be considered for continuously verify system users in real time.

References

1. Shen, C., Cai, Z., Guan, Z., Du, Y., Maxion, Y.: User authentication through mouse dynamics. IEEE Trans. Inform. Forensic Secur. **8**(1), 16–30 (2013)
2. Jorgensen, Z., Yu, T.: On mouse dynamics as a behavioral biometric for authentication. In: Proceedings of the 6th ACM Symposium on Information, Computer and Communications Security - ASIACCS 2011, pp. 476–482 (2011)
3. Schulz, D.: Mouse Curve Biometrics. In: 2006 Biometrics Symposium: Special Session on Research at the Biometric Consortium Conference (2006)

4. Pusara, M., Brodley, C.: User re-authentication via mouse movements. In: Proceedings of the 2004 ACM Workshop on Visualization and Data Mining for Computer Security - VizSEC/DMSEC 2004 (2004)
5. Shen, C., Cai, Z., Guan, X., Sha, H., Du, J.: Feature analysis of mouse dynamics in identity authentication and monitoring. In: 2009 IEEE International Conference on Communications (2009)
6. Ahmed, A., Traore, I.: A new biometric technology based on mouse dynamics. IEEE Trans. Dependable Secure Comput. 4(3), 165–179 (2007)
7. Zheng, N., Paloski, A., Wang, H.: An efficient user verification system via mouse movements. In: Proceedings of the 18th ACM Conference on Computer and Communications Security - CCS 2011, pp. 139–150 (2011)
8. Nakkabi, Y., Traore, I., Ahmed, A.: Improving mouse dynamics biometric performance using variance reduction via extractors with separate features. IEEE Trans. Syst. Man Cybern. A 40(6), 1345–1353 (2010)
9. Syukri, A.F., Okamoto, E., Mambo, M.: A user identification system using signature written with mouse. In: Boyd, C., Dawson, E. (eds.) ACISP 1998. LNCS, vol. 1438, pp. 403–414. Springer, Heidelberg (1998)
10. Revett, K., Jahankhani, H., de Magalhães, S.T., Santos, H.M.D.: A survey of user authentication based on mouse dynamics. In: Jahankhani, H., Palmer-Brown, D., Revett, K. (eds.) Global E-Security. CCIS, vol. 12, pp. 210–219. Springer, Heidelberg (2008)

Experiments and Deployments

The Concept of Co-operation
of INSIGMA Event Reporting System
with National Emergency Notification System

Damian Duda[✉], Tomasz Podlasek, Piotr Pyda, and Andrzej Stańczak

Military Communication Institute, Zegrze Południowe, Poland
{d.duda,t.podlasek,p.pyda,a.stanczak}@wil.waw.pl

Abstract. The paper presents the concept of integration of INSIGMA Event Reporting System (INSIGMA ERS) and national emergency notification system, SPR in polish (System Powiadamiania Ratunkowego). The concept is based on the logical interface between systems as a tool of proposed integration. The resulting integration may present the synergy effect which would provide faster and timely delivery of emergency information from society to public security services. It may significantly increase the security of citizens.

The exemplary performance results show the large potential for optimisation of reporting as well as transmission process.

Keywords: Emergency notification system · Event reporting · Co-operation

1 Introduction

The objective of INSIGMA project is to design and implement sophisticated information system for detection and identification of threats as well as monitoring and identification of mobile objects. The project is conducted by three universities, AGH University of Science and Technology, Military University of Technology, University of Computer Engineering Telecommunication as well as by Military Communication Institute. There are three task groups defined, which embrace following research areas: (1) design of automatic observation and recording of mobile objects parameters, their data transmission and archiving, personal identification of their users, (2) threat detection and road traffic analysis with visualization on dynamic map, (3) person and threat detection based on use of mobile terminals and advanced monitoring, searching of persons, data and multimedia content.

The primary data sources intended for INSIGMA system are intelligent cameras and road traffic sensors, e.g. inductive loops, light-sensitive detectors, passive acoustic sensors, etc. installed in pre-planned locations.

Intelligent Information System for Global Monitoring, Detection and Identification of Threats (INSIGMA). Work has been co-financed by the European Regional Development Fund under the Innovative Economy Operational Program, INSIGMA project no. POIG. 01.01.0200-062/09.

© Springer International Publishing Switzerland 2015
A. Dziech et al. (Eds.): MCSS 2015, CCIS 566, pp. 185–194, 2015.
DOI: 10.1007/978-3-319-26404-2_15

However, there is a significant requirement to collect data from areas outside the range of fixed sensors. This need motivated the project team to develop a model and a prototype of mobile sensors as a supplement of stationary infrastructure. For this purpose the terminal, i.e. mobile phone, with appropriate application program was proposed. The application was developed which allows sending of messages with information about current threats, road accidents and other dangerous events from the user of terminal to the INSIGMA system. A graphical and textual interface is offered to the user, presenting structured menu-driven form to enter the data. The developed terminal software is made as an Android application program. The software provides the user interface, background map and communication facilities to INSIGMA system. The tabular input form is customised according to the type of accident selected and is linked with the INSIGMA's ontological classification of events.

The server part of software collects, processes and stores messages from users. The function is provided by modules, adapted to the needs of INSIGMA's event processing subsystem.

The paper is focused on presenting the concept of co-operation of designed and implemented INSIGMA ERS and national emergency notification system. There are presented: short characteristics of national emergency notification system, concept of co-operation between systems in question, description of INSIGMA ERS and exemplary results of laboratory tests.

2   The National Emergency Notification System

The national emergency notification system SPR [1] is a part of the national rescue system (pol. Krajowy System Ratownictwa, KSR). It should be noted that KSR consists of state emergency medical service (pol. Państwowe Ratownictwo Medyczne, PRM), state fire service PSP (pol. Państwowa Straż Pożarna,), the Police (in polish Policja), etc.

The main elements of the SPR are:

- National IT Network for "112" call emergency number (in polish Ogólnopolska Sieć Teleinformatyczna na potrzeby obsługi numeru 112, OST 112) [2],
- Emergency Call Centre (pol. Centrum Powiadamiania Ratunkowego, CPR),
- Focal Point of the System of Emergency Centres (pol. Centralny Punkt Systemu Centrów Powiadamiania Ratunkowego, CP SCPR),
- Localisation and Information Platform with a Central Database (pol. Platforma Lokalizacyjno-Informacyjna z Centralną Bazą Danych, PLI CBD),
- Emergency Notification IT System (pol. System Informatyczny Powiadamiania Ratunkowego, SIPR),
- Command Support Systems (pol. System Wspomagania Dowodzenia, SWD) of the Police, PRM, PSP etc.,
- Information System of the Main Office of Geodesy and Cartography (pol. System Informatyczny Głównego Urzędu Geodezji i Kartografii, SI GUGiK),
- Central Map Module (pol. Centralny Moduł Mapowy, CMM).

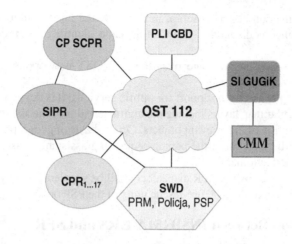

Fig. 1. Functional diagram of the SPR

Functional diagram of the SPR is shown in the Fig. 1. The task of the SPR is to provide an information, so that it will be possible to arrive of appropriate rescue units to the person requesting of assistance.

The process of handling the alarm notification in the SPR is presented in the Fig. 2.

The notice of an event requiring the intervention of emergency or ordinal services is done by dialing 112 or another emergency number. Checking the location of the person requesting assistance shall take place in the PLI CBD, and then the alarm signal from the phone is redirected over the 112 OST network to the appropriate CPR for localization of event.

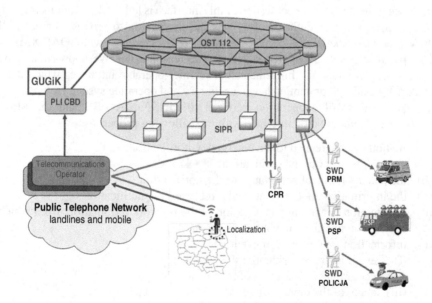

Fig. 2. The process of handling the alarm notification in the SPR

After the connection has been setup, in the CPR the phone number of the person requesting assistance is displayed. The Calling Line Identification Presentation functionality is used.

The operator sends the message over the 112 OST network to the Police, PSP and/or PRM command posts.

The digital map is used as a support for public services. It is developed and updated by GUGiK. Particular map layers include the characteristics of the site, the layout of the streets and the location of the relevant objects. On the basis of geographical coordinates corresponding to the location of the person requesting assistance, visualization of this location is presented automatically.

Information received by the CPR dispatcher shall be supplemented by additional data and redirected to the Police patrol, fire-rescue units of the PSP or ambulances of the PRM.

3   Cooperation Between INSIGMA ERS and SPR

According to the Ministry of Administration and Digitization of Poland decree [3] it is formally possible to co-operate between SPR and other information systems using interfaces, which are developed as a part of its open architecture. Because of above there is possible to connect SPR and INSIGMA ERS systems using interface called "other systems", which is shown in the Fig. 3.

When a user of the INSIGMA system would like to report an event, he/she opens the ERS Client application and fill-in data into the data-entry form, with structured description of the event. These data are sent to Traffic Intensity Data Repository (TIDR) and further to other modules of INSIGMA system. Thanks to the fact, that it is possible to use the SPR's interface to "other systems", the information from INSIGMA system can be shared with SPR. However, the technical details of interface are not covered in the legal documents. It seems the technical specification of this interface is left to SPR Administrator, i.e. it is "site/implementation defined". This was the motivation to propose, based on the INSIGMA project experiences, the Web Services (WS) technology with SOAP/XML and WSDL specifications as an integration "glue". The reason is that WS allows to automate the process of designing and implementation of inter-operable interfaces which do not depend on a specific programming language, library and operating system features.

The prerequisite of cooperation between the INSIGMA ERS and the SPR is providing the communication interface with the following properties:

1. information or data related to the emergency notification:
   (a) unique identifier of the notification;
   (b) the date and time of acceptance of the notification;
   (c) the information about operator who received the notification;
   (d) information concerning the location of the network termination, from which a connection to emergency number was made;
   (e) information on the place of event, including:
       (i)   event address (residential if available),
       (ii)   geographic coordinates of the event,
       (iii) name of the object where the event takes place,
       (iv)   information about the building in which the event takes place;

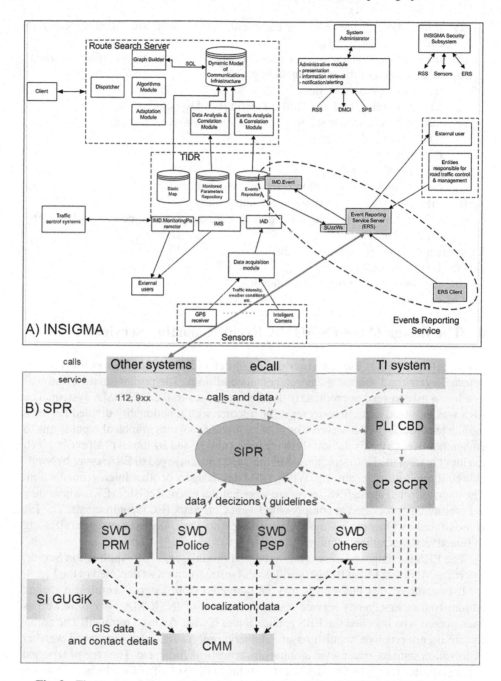

Fig. 3. The proposed concept of cooperation between SPR and INSIGMA ERS systems

(f) information on the nature of the event, according to a detailed directory of events;

(g) information about emergency entity or entities, which were reporting the alarm;

(h) a description of the event, including:
   (i)   the number of victims,
   (ii) other relevant data or information related to notification;

(i) data of person who is sending notification message, including:
   (i)   name and surname,
   (ii)   phone number,
   (iii) localisation data;

(j) confirmation of notification received by operator;

(k) information about the status of the notification;

(l) information on the state of the dial-up connection to the person declaring the notification;

2. notification message should contain:
   (a) ID of the voice record,
   (b) the content of the original notification.

4 The Design of the INSIGMA Event Reporting Service

The INSIGMA ERS is used as a user-driven source of information about observed and detected events and abnormal environmental conditions. The primary assumption was to allow a user to send appropriately detailed messages to the INSIGMA system. The ERS was designed as a client-server infrastructure with functionality divided between mobile terminal and ERS server. The client software provides graphical input forms to gather the necessary information about the type, subtype and attributes of an event. Next, the input is formatted into structured SIP message and conveyed to ERS server by available communications means, e.g. Wi-Fi, GSM data transfer or other Internet connection. The data collected at the ERS server are stored at the Event Registry (ER), where they are preliminary processed to comply with Event Correlator (EC) requirements. The ER is monitored by Operator's Console, which presents the collected messages, allowing to selectively check them, confirm or reject.

The ERS is composed of several functional modules, i.e. SIP Application Server, Interface Modules, Event Registry and access infrastructure, as depicted in the Fig. 4.

It is assumed that the reports may be delivered from external entities, e.g. road administrators, emergency service operator, the user of INSIGMA system as well as each person who installed the ERS application in his/her Android terminal. The architecture do not preclude acquisition of automatic reports e.g. from unmanned weather observation stations, water level monitoring, acoustic sensors, etc. The type of reported event is limited by the INSIGMA Event Ontology (IEO) [4]. The Graphical User Interface (GUI) of ERS reflects the contents of IEO too. The GUI provides input forms for the following event attributes:

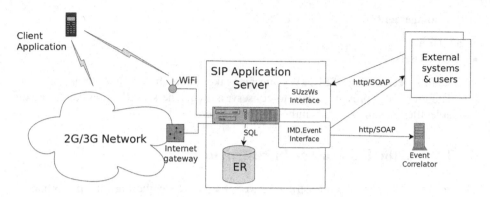

Fig. 4. The structure of INSIGMA ERS

– type of event,
– subtype of event,
– geolocation of event,
– event details,
– occurrence time of event.

The part of the design and development processes were two Web Services-base interfaces, IMD.Event and SUzzWs. They form one-way communications channels from ERS to EC and from external systems to ERS accordingly. The IMD.Event is a kind of internal interface, thus it will be not described further. The second, SUzzWs interface, provides the functional API to the ERS event registry. Until now following methods are available in SUzzWs:

Events management:

– addEvent
– sendEvent
– sendEvents

Events searching:

– findEvent
– findAllEvents
– findEventsByCircle
– findEventsByUser
– findEventsByType
– findEventsByRect
– findEventsOnDate
– findEventsInDateRange

User management:

- addUser
- findAllUsers

The full specification of SUzzWs interface takes about three hundred lines of XML text data and is not presented here to conserve space. The specification can be made available after the contact with authors of this paper.

5   Tests in the Laboratory Infrastructure

The tests conducted in the infrastructure were focused on gathering time performance metrics. The results provided in this paper give the Total Service Latency - T_{SL}. T_{SL} is defined as:

$$T_{SL} = T_{Ack} - T_{Sent}$$

where:

- T_{Sent} – is the time when the report was sent from ERS terminal;
- T_{Ack} – is the time when the acknowledgement of reception was received at ERS terminal.

For testing the ERS server the SIPSAK tool was used [5] with specially crafted SIP message. The content of the testing SIP message was as following:

Header Data:

```
MESSAGE sip:211@sozz.wil.lab SIP/2.0
… [cut for brevity]
Content-Length: 597
```

Payload Data:

```
<?xml version="1.0" encoding="UTF-8"?>
<EventNotification>
<Author>
… <!-- Origin of information -->
</Author>
<EventType>WeatherDifficulties</EventType>
<EventSubType>Rain</EventSubType>
… <!-- More attributes if necessary -->
<Position>
…
</Position>
<EventStartTime>1423233073006</EventStartTime>
<Description></Description>
</EventNotification>
```

The results of tests are gathered for two cases:

- 2 Mbps, high quality link, PER = 0
- 2 Mbps, degraded quality link, PER = 0.1

PER means Packet Error Rate. The confidence level was assumed at 0.98. The results are collected in the Table 1.

Table 1. The results of Total Service Latency measurements

The nominal Packet Error Rate on link	Total Service Latency [ms]	Mean number of timeouts per single transmission
0	85 ± 16.8	0
0.1	115 ± 19.5	11

Subtracting the double serialization time on 2 Mbps link, i.e. 2×3.9 ms, the mean T_{SL} was about 77 ms. For the degraded case the T_{SL} increased to about 107 ms. It was observed that on average one of ten messages was re-transmitted.

The content of SUzzWs messages was omitted to conserve space in the paper. However, it can be accessed on request from authors.

6   Summary

The paper presents the short descriptions of INSIGMA ERS and national emergency notification system – SPR. These covers the emergency call handling procedures and its external interface to other systems. The interface is the basis of proposed integration of SPR and INSIGMA Event Reporting System. The synergy effect is expected as a result of integration. It would provide faster and timely delivery of emergency information from society to public security services. It may significantly increase the security of citizens.

The exemplary performance results show the large potential for optimisation of reporting as well as transmission process.

The further work are focused on technical issues of interoperability between INSIGMA ERS and National Emergency Notification System. It was observed, that potential customers do not limit transmission options to cellular infrastructure, but dedicated wireless transmission methods without infrastructure are in the area of interest.

References

1. Ustawa o systemie powiadamiania ratunkowego, (The Act on Emergency Notification System) Dz. U. 2013 poz. 1635, 18 czerwca 2013 (only available in polish)
2. OST 112 – ogólnopolska sieć teleinformatyczna na potrzeby obsługi numeru alarmowego 112, (Polish National IT Network for "112" call emergency number), Centrum Projektów Informatycznych, Warszawa (2012) (only available in polish)

3. Rozporządzenie Ministra Administracji i Cyfryzacji i Cyfryzacji ws. wymagań funkcjonalnych dla systemu teleinformatycznego i interfejsu komunikacyjnego oraz warunków współpracy SPR z Policją, Państwową Strażą Pożarną oraz dysponentami zespołów ratownictwa medycznego, (Ordinance of the Minister of Administration and Digitization of Poland about functional requirements for information system and communication interface and terms of cooperations between the SPR and the Police, PSP and staffs emergency medical service holders), Dz. U. 2014 poz. 1159, 21 sierpnia 2014 (only available in polish)
4. Szwed, P., Chmiel, W., Śliwa, J., Gleba, K.: Ontology for data representation in monitoring system (pol. „Ontologia do reprezentacji danych w systemie monitoringu"), INSIGMA – Technical report, D2.4, December 2011
5. SIPSAK – SIP Swiss Army Knife, http://sourceforge.net/projects/sipsak.berlios/. Accessed June 2015

Learning Fuzzy Cognitive Map for Traffic Prediction Using an Evolutionary Algorithm

Wojciech Chmiel and Piotr Szwed$^{(\boxtimes)}$

AGH University of Science and Technology, Kraków, Poland
{wch,pszwed}@agh.edu.pl

Abstract. The motivation for the presented work was the need for solution allowing efficient estimation of traffic parameters in based on sparse measurements covering a small fraction road segments within large urban road network. The solution was intended to be deployed within the Dynamic Map, an important component of the INSIGMA system used for route planning and traffic control. We have chosen to base the estimation model on Fuzzy Cognitive Maps (FCM) formalism and apply an Evolutionary Algorithm to learn the model parameters. The main argument in favor of FCM is their simplicity and the speed of calculations that can be required for real-time updates of traffic parameters. This paper discusses a novel evolutionary algorithm for FCM learning and demonstrates feasibility and efficiency of such approach by giving results of tests performed on road networks of various size.

Keywords: ITS · Traffic prediction · Evolutionary algorithm · Fuzzy Cognitive Maps

1 Introduction

Integration of Intelligent Transportation Systems (ITS) with urban traffic infrastructure is considered a most promising avenue of development of modern cities. ITS are combinations of various underlying technologies: sensing, data interpretation, communications, information integration and control assembled together to reach the most prominent goals: safety, mobility and environmental performance.

The system developed within INSIGMA project [6] is an ITS offering such services as collection and storage of traffic data originating from various types of sensors including cameras [14], and GPS devices [28,29], personalized and dynamic route planning [9,27], vehicle tracking and traffic control. Capabilities of INSIGMA system would not be fully described without mentioning such advanced traffic surveillance functions, as make and model recognition of cars [4,5] and license plate recognition [15].

This work is supported by the European Regional Development Fund within INSIGMA project no. POIG.01.01.02-00-062/09.

A. Dziech et al. (Eds.): MCSS 2015, CCIS 566, pp. 195–209, 2015.
DOI: 10.1007/978-3-319-26404-2_16

The key component responsible for storing static and dynamic data related to urban traffic within INSIGMA system is the Dynamic Map [6,27]. It can be considered a complex information system composed of spatial databases, as well as a set of software modules responsible for data collection, interpretation and provision. The Dynamic Map uses internally semantic representation of traffic parameters relying on the system ontology [25,36] and offers ontology based access method for various clients [27]. The ontology defines unambiguously numerous types of measured parameters including average traveling times for road segments, maximum speeds for current traffic conditions, maneuver time at crossroads or queues length for selected lanes. Availability of such readings depends on installed and integrated sensors and their capabilities, whose semantic descriptions are incorporated into the Dynamic Map.

The challenging problem for interpretation of data stored in the Dynamic Map by various clients is their sparsity. Taking as a reference the Kraków city, whose road network comprises about 5000 road segments, it is hard to imagine that such fixed sensors as cameras or inductive loops would virtually cover the whole urban area. It is more likely to assume that the traffic monitoring system would be installed at a few dozen of selected main roads and crossroads yielding a set of *observable* traffic parameters. For the majority of secondary roads, smaller streets reaching main city arteries their traffic conditions cannot be effectively monitored.

To discuss this concept, we refer to Fig. 1 showing an excerpt of a map comprising a main road with separated lanes and a number of secondary roads reaching it. Assuming that two sensors are installed at locations marked as A and B, we expect that there are dependencies between the measurements at point A and the part of road network marked with dash line, as well as the measurements at point B and at road segments marked with solid line. Hence, abstracting of their exact semantics, traffic parameters attributed to road network can be divided into two sets: observable (measured) and unobservable. For such application as dynamic route planning based on information in the Dynamic Map, the later that should be estimated (predicted) by applying a certain model capturing causal dependencies between them (see Fig. 1b).

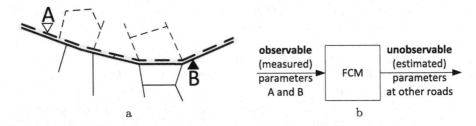

Fig. 1. A partial map with indicated sensors A and B and a concept of the traffic parameters estimation system

In this paper we propose to apply Fuzzy Cognitive Maps (FCM) to express dependencies between traffic intensity at points, where its is measured and other roads that are not monitored. The main argument in favor of FCM is their simplicity and the speed of calculations (basically a multiplication of vector by a sparse matrix) that can be required for real-time updates of traffic parameters. For FCM leraning and validation we used data generated by the traffic simulator SUMO [17]. SUMO (Simulation of Urban MObility) is a free and open traffic simulation framework allowing to model road vehicles, public transport and pedestrians.

The deployment of the solution based on FCM within the Dynamic Map included the following steps:

1. Various traffic conditions were simulated using the off-shelf mature traffic simulator SUMO. As an option, actual traffic measurements can be performed in field for selected roads (in the vicinity of sensor locations).
2. Traffic data (time series) for all road segments in the analyzed road network were collected.
3. Prospective locations, where sensors are to be installed were selected. Then the road segments were divided into two sets: the first comprised elements, for which the traffic parameters are to be measured, the second those, for which they should be estimated
4. An initial FCM structure reflecting the topology of road network was proposed and its parameters were learned with dedicated evolutionary algorithm.
5. Finally, the developed FCM model was applied in the operational system (the Dynamic Map).

Due to limited space we focus here on the step 4 from the above workflow. In particular, we discuss the construction of FCM learning algorithm, as well as we report results of experiments.

The paper is organized as follows: next Sect. 2 discusses various traffic prediction methods and defines the FCM. It is followed by Sect. 3, which discusses a novel evolutionary FCM learning algorithm. In Sect. 4 results of experiments are given. Section 5 provides concluding remarks.

2   Related Works

This section discusses traffic prediction models, as well as provides an introduction to the Fuzzy Cognitive Maps formalism.

2.1   Traffic Prediction Methods

The need of reliable and fast traffic prediction methods emerged with the recently observed development of ITS. The methods can be divided into two groups [10]: *classical*, which are based on statistical approaches combined with flow models, and *data-driven* using such machine learning models as Artificial Neural Networks (ANN) [33,34], Support Vector Regression (SVR) and fuzzy systems. The later group seems to be dominant in the recent publications. In [10] ANN is applied to forecast traffic patterns in Budapest based on data originating from

Vissim simulator. Similarly, in [37] ANN was used for prediction, however, the described method comprises clustering both in spatial and temporal domain to group traffic influence points within the road network. SVR combined with a radial basis kernel was applied in [2]. The article [19] discusses a novel SVR method coupled with the Kalman filter. In [12] hybrid fuzzy rule-based system was used for the modeling and short-term forecasting of traffic flow in urban arterial networks and a Genetic Algorithm was used to learn membership functions.

Examples of classical methods are given in [11], where unified models for network-wide traffic prediction based on partial least squares method and its tensor variants were proposed or [22], which describes enhanced Autoregressive Integrated Moving Average (ARIMA) and Historical Average methods applied to predict traffic conditions, in particular, to predict congestion caused by accidents.

2.2 Fuzzy Cognitive Maps

Cognitive maps were first proposed by Axelrod [3] as a tool for modeling political decisions, then extended by Kosko [16] by introducing fuzzy values. A large number of applications of Fuzzy Cognititive Maps (FCM) were reported, e.g. in project risk modeling [18], risk assessment related to IT security [30–32], crisis management and decision making, analysis of development of economic systems and the introduction of new technologies, academic units development [26], ecosystem analysis [21], signal processing and decision support in medicine. A survey on Fuzzy Cognitive Maps and their applications can be found in [1] and [23].

FCMs are directed graphs whose vertices represent concepts, whereas edges are used to express causal relations between them. A set of concepts $C = \{c_1, \ldots, c_n\}$ appearing in a model encompasses events, conditions or other relevant factors. A system state is an n-dimensional vector of concept activation levels ($n = |C|$) that can be real values belonging to $[0, 1]$ or $[-1, 1]$.

Causal relations between concepts are represented in FCM by edges and assigned weights. A positive weight of an edge linking two concepts c_i and c_j models a situation, where an increase of the level of c_i results in a growing c_j; a negative weight is used to describe the opposite rapport.

Causal relations between concepts in FCM can be represented by $n \times n$ influence matrix $E = [e_{ij}]$, whose elements e_{ij} are weights assigned to edges linking c_i and c_j or have 0 values, if there is no link between them.

Figure 2 gives an example of an FCM graph, whose vertices were assigned with concepts c_1, c_2, c_3 and c_4, whereas the edges were assigned with linguistic weights defining mutual influences. Corresponding E matrix is defined by (1). The selection of values corresponding to linguistic values is arbitrary; in the example the values: -1, -0.66, -0.33, 0, 0.33, 0.66 and 1 were used.

$$E = \begin{bmatrix} 0 & 0 & 0 & 0 \\ 1 & 0 & 0 & -0.33 \\ 0.66 & 0.33 & 0 & 0 \\ 0 & 0.66 & -1 & 0 \end{bmatrix} \tag{1}$$

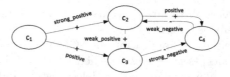

Fig. 2. An example of FCM graph. Vertices are assigned with concepts, directed arcs with linguistic weights of specifying influence.

Reasoning with FCM consists in building a sequence of states:

$$\alpha = A(0), A(1), \ldots, A(k), \ldots$$

starting from an initial vector of activation levels of concepts. Consecutive elements are calculated according to the formula (2). In the $k+1$ iteration the vector $A(k)$ is multiplied by the influence matrix E, then the resulting activation levels of concepts are mapped onto the assumed range by means of an *activation* (or *splashing*) function.

$$A_i(k+1) = S_i(\sum_{j=1}^{n} e_{ij} A_j(k)) \tag{2}$$

The selection of the activation function depends on assumptions regarding the calculation model, in particular the selected range and the decision to use continuous or discrete values. Multiplication of an n-dimensional square matrix E, both containing elements whose absolute values are bounded by 1, results in a vector having elements in $[-n, n]$. Values from this interval should be mapped by an activation function into the range $[-1, 1]$ (or $[0, 1]$) preserving monotonicity and satisfying $S(0) = 0$ (or $S(0.5) = 0.5$ in the second case.)

In the further analysis we used a popular sigmoid activation functions were used:

$$S(x) = \frac{1}{1 + \exp(-\beta x)} \tag{3}$$

Basically, a sequence of consecutive states $\alpha = A(0), A(1), \ldots, A(k), \ldots$ is infinite. However, it was shown that after k iterations, where k is a number close to the rank of matrix E, a steady state is reached or a cycle occurs. Hence, the stop criterion for the reasoning algorithm in the k step is the following:

$$\exists j < k \colon d(A(k), A(j)) < \epsilon, \tag{4}$$

where d is a distance and ϵ a small value, e.g. 10^{-2}.

A sequence of states α can be interpreted in two ways. Firstly, it can be treated as a representation of a dynamic behavior of the modeled system. In this case there exist implicit temporal relations between consecutive system states and the whole sequence describes an evolution of the system in the form of a *scenario*. Under the second interpretation the sequence represents a non-monotonic fuzzy inference process, in which selected elements of a steady state are interpreted as reasoning results (outputs). An occurrence of a cycle can be treated as a form of undecidability.

A common task related to applications of FCM is learning. For the majority of cases, the set of concepts is C is established by experts, and the goal of the learning process is to align responses of modeled system and FCM by tweaking the weights in the matrix E. Selection of learning methods and fitness functions depend on whether a user is interested in mimicking dynamic behavior of the analyzed system or rather aligning output values of selected concepts in a steady state [23]. We will discuss the second approach in more detailed manner, as it was employed in our research.

Let $A_1^S, \ldots A_m^S$, where $m \leq n$ denote values of output (or decision) concepts determined in a reasoning process performed according to the formula (2). While defining a fitness function a common approach [24] consists in making assumption that for an input vector it would be possible to appoint strict bounds $[A_i^{min}, A_i^{max}]$ in which the obtained values of A_i^S should lay. The bounds can be defined by experts participating in the learning process or originate from observations.

Under this setting, the fitness function expresses a penalty for leaving the bounds. It is given by (5), the symbol H denotes the Heaviside function: $H(x) = 0$, if $x < 0$ and $H(x) = 1$, if $x \geqslant 0$.

$$\varphi(E) = \sum_{i=1}^{m} H\left(A_i^{min} - A_i^S\right) \left|A_i^{min} - A_i^S\right| + \sum_{i=1}^{m} H\left(A_i^S - A_i^{max}\right) \left|A_i^S - A_i^{max}\right| \quad (5)$$

The survey by Papageorgiou [23] reports more then 20 FCM learning algorithm falling into three groups: population based (e.g. genetics algorithm, PSO, memetic PSO, Tabu search), Hebbian-based and hybrid. Due to limited space we refer the reader to the included bibliography.

3 Evolutionary Algorithm for Learning of Fuzzy Cognitive Maps

In this section we describe FCMEVOL, an evolutionary algorithm developed for learning FCM expressing dependencies between traffic intensity at road segments.

A solution in FCMEVOL is represented as the vector of real numbers and the algorithm uses a specialized set of pseudo-genetic operators. As crossover operators $BlendAlphaCrossover$ (BAC) with randomly chosen α value and $BlendAlphaBetaCrossover$ (BABC) with $\alpha = 0.5$ and $\beta = 0.75$ are applied [35]. The mutation (RM) operator changes a randomly picked element in solution vector (normal distribution). Additionally, in FCMEVOL local optimization (LO) algorithm was implemented.

The knowledge, accumulated in the search process for the problem solution, is encoded as a set P of solutions called population, where $M = |P|$ is the population size. The evolution of the population with use of genetic operators realizes the search process within EA. Every genetic operator generates new solutions (offsprings) on the basis of old solutions (parents).

Selection mechanism implemented in FCMEVOL [7] algorithm exploits the modified approach to selection schema proposed by Michalowicz [20] called *modGA*. The modification with respect to the classical genetic algorithm is the following: in the *modGA* a new population is formed by selecting from the old population independently r, $1 < r < M$, solutions to be parents and r solutions to die. These selections are performed based on the fitness of solutions: a solution with a better than average performance has a higher chance to be selected as a parent, solutions with a worse than average performance have higher chances to be selected to die. Then, a new population consists of $(M - r)$ solutions from the old population (all solutions except these selected to die) and r offspring of the r selected parents; i.e. r selected solutions undergo transformations by means of genetic operators. This way, in course of one iteration (one generation) only r, $r < M$, solutions are selected and processed.

For FCM weights selection a special type of the evolutionary algorithm was used, called BREADTH_DEPTH, which implements mechanisms preventing from premature convergence. In course of one iteration initially one genetic operator is randomly chosen and then r, $r \in \{1, 2\}$, solutions are selected from the population and processed: one solution if mutation operator is chosen and two in case of crossover operator. Thus, the algorithm also belongs to the class of Steady State EA and in this way it has all features of the *modGA*. We assume that the population set P is linearly ordered in accordance with the solution's fitness by means of objective function $\varphi(x)$: the best population permutation ($x_{best} = \mathrm{argmin}\, \varphi(x) : x \in P$) has number 1, the worst ($x_{worst} = \mathrm{argmin}\, \varphi(x) : x \in P$) has number $\alpha = |P|$. Besides, to simplify genetic search process and save the computation time, the parents are selected from the population P by means of random-uniform sampling mechanism and the generated offspring is inserted between other in accordance with its fitness.

Let us notice that the best population permutations have the chance to be selected more frequently, then other permutations and in this way these solutions become *super individuals*. Such super individual has a large number of offspring and this, due to the constant size of the population, prevents other individuals from contributing an offspring in the next generations. In some generations a super individual can eliminate desirable 'chromosomal material', what leads to a rapid convergence to the local optimum. To avoid this shortcoming we introduced the *tabu* mechanism [8]. We assumed, that at the first stage of the evolutionary search process called BREADTH, a number of best population permutations, l_{top} top-solutions, can not be chosen as parents. It is most likely that in this case the evolution search process can be performed in the whole search space. In the second stage of genetic search process, called DEPTH, the genetic search process is enhanced to the space regions connected with the best population permutations for local tuning. Thus, in this stage, the mutation operator is replaced by a local optimization (hill climbing) procedure and some number of worst population permutations, l_{end} solutions, are tabu and cannot be chosen as parents.

The implemented FCMEVOL algorithm follows the main idea of BREAD-RTH_DEPTH search process. On the other hand the number of algorithm parameters is decreased. In this way the adjustment of the algorithm for solution of the problem instance is much easier. In FCMEVOL, instead of two stages of the search process like in BREADRTH_DEPTH search, we split the population P, by one algorithm parameter m, into two parts and limit application of the unary genetic operators to definite area of the population.

During experiments the presented FCMEVOL algorithm (Algorithm 1) had the following parameters: λ - the population size, L - total iteration number, m - population split number and genetic operator selection probabilities $p_{RM}, p_{BAC}, p_{BACB}, p_{LO}$. Thus the expected numbers of genetic operators application, during the whole search process, are: $RM - L \cdot p_{RM}$, $BAC - L \cdot p_{BAC}$, $BACB - l \cdot p_{BACB}$, $LO - L \cdot p_{LO}$.

Algorithm 1. FCMEVOL algorithm.

Require $\varphi(\cdot), p_{LO}, p_{RM}, p_{BAC}, p_{BACB}, m, L, \lambda$.

Step 1. Initialize population with λ random solutions.

Generate randomly λ solutions, as well as compute objective function $\varphi(x)$ for each solution. Set up the initial population P ordering the generated permutation by function $\varphi(x)$, so that the first permutation, permutation in the population P is the best one and the last permutation λ is the worst, i.e., $x_{worst} = argmax\varphi(x) : x \in P$.

Step 2. Selection of crossover operator.

Choose randomly one pseudo-genetic operator from the set BAC, BACB, where selection probabilities of the operators are: $p_{BAC}, p_{BACB} = 1 - p_{BAC}$ as well as select randomly, with uniform distribution, and copy two solution - parents from the population P. Using chosen crossover operator generate two offspring x^1, x^2 of the parents and insert them between other population P solutions in accordance with objective function $\lambda(x^j), (j = 1, 2)$ value. Remove two worst (last) permutations from the population P.

Step 3. Mutation.

Sample randomly number $\gamma \in [0, 1]$ and if $\gamma < p_{RM}$, then chose one permutation from the items $[1, m]$ of the population P, modify it by the use of mutation operator RM and insert between other population solutions in accordance with objective function value.

Step 4. Local optimization.

Sample randomly number $\gamma \in [0, 1]$ and if $\gamma < p_{LO}$ then chose one permutation from the items $[m+1, \lambda]$ of the population P, improve it by use of local optimization operator LO and insert between other population solutions in accordance with objective function value.

Step 5. Check the stop condition.

After L iteration return $x_{approx} = \operatorname{argmin} \{\varphi(x) : x \in P(x)\}$

---

4   Experiments

In this section we discuss results of experiments performed using FCMEVAL. The traffic data were generated using the space-continuous traffic simulator - SUMO (Simulation of Urban MObility) developed by the Institute of Transportation Systems in German Aerospace Center [17]. SUMO models the movement of every single vehicle in the streets, assuming that its behavior depends on both: the vehicle's physical abilities to move and the driver's controlling behavior. SUMO allows also to introduce detectors into road segments and collect statistical data during simulations, including average speed, occupancy, waiting time, travel time and density.

The developed FCM model of a traffic network followed a simple rule: each road segment was represented by a concept. Hence, for a network comprising n road segments, the FCM would contain n concepts and at most $n \cdot (n-1)$ weights expressing influences. It should be noted that some values of mutual influences could be equal zero, which means no influence between concepts.

As the goal function, the function $\varphi(E)$ defined by the formula (5) was used. The bounds $[A_i^{min}, A_i^{max}]$ for individual road segments were established by performing multiple simulations for several time slots characterized by different traffic properties (flow directions, traffic intensity). There were selected 12 basic time slots and for each of them 12 simulations were made. The collected data allowed to establish reference values of $[A_i^{min}, A_i^{max}]$ bounds.

4.1   Experiments on a Small Road Network

In this case a small network with 15 single carriageway was used. For this network 10 car routes were generated with variable flow intensity (Table 1). Three experiments were carried out using the traffic network defined on Fig. 3. In the experiment case detectors are presented on subset of edges $E_{ded} = \{U, W, X, Y, Z\}$.

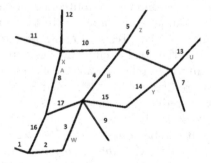

Fig. 3. Small network used in tests

The FCMEVOL algorithm was used with the following control parameters (which were determined during several preliminary tests): the population size

Table 1. Routes and traffic volumes in map presented in Fig. 3.

Route nr	Edges	Volume [cars/s]	Route nr	Edges	[cars/s]
1	1-2-3-4-5	0.25-3	6	5-4-3-2-1	0.33-2
2	9-4-5	0.33-2	7	1-2-3-15-14-13	0.33-2
3	9-4-6-7	0.33-2	8	7-13	0.33-2
4	12-10-4-9	0.33-2	9	1-16-17-4-5	0.33-2
5	1-16-8-12	0.33-2	10	1-16-8-11	0.33-2

$\lambda = 60$, the number of algorithm iteration - $L = 100$, the local optimisation probability - $p_{LO} = 0.1$, the random mutation probability - $p_{RM} = 0.2$, *BlendAlphaCrossover* pseudo-genetic operator probability - $p_{BAC} = 0.6$, *BlendAlphaCrossover* pseudo-genetic operator probability - $p_{BACB} = 0.4$, the split population parameter $m = 20$.

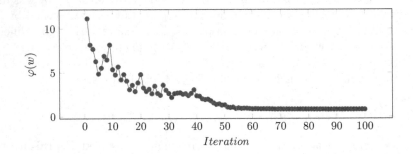

Fig. 4. FCM learning process for the traffic network presented in Fig. 3

Results returned by the trained FCM network were compared with the data collected from SUMO. Table 2 summarizes outcomes of three tests performed: using the data applied in the learning process (Test#1), using randomly generated data for low traffic intensity (Test#2) and high intensity (Test#3). The investigated parameter was the road occupancy, i.e. percentage of lane length covered by vehicles. Columns O_S refer to values collected from the SUMO simulator, whereas O_{FCM} to results yielded by learned FCM.

For the first test average difference between results obtained using SUMO (reference values) and FCM is about 9%, the biggest is about 18% and the smallest is about 1.35%. It can be noted that in Test#2 that average difference between results obtained using SUMO (reference values) and FCM is about 11%, the biggest is about 31% and the smallest is about 5%. For the third test the average difference between results obtained using SUMO (reference values) and FCM is about 20%, the biggest is about 38% and the smallest is about 2%.

Table 2. Test results of prediction traffic volumes (occupation) using FCM

Lane	Test#1		Test#2		Test#3	
	$O_{S_{avr}}$ [%]	O_{FCM} [%]	$O_{S_{avr}}$ [%]	$O_{FCM_{avr}}$ [%]	$O_{S_{avr}}$ [%]	$O_{FCM_{avr}}$ [%]
U in direction 14	58.25	55.45	45.07	62.54	75.31	42.91
U outside map	30.83	25.17	19.80	28.78	50.27	12.35
W in direction 2	17.03	26.58	15.11	10.01	28.13	37.52
W in direction 4	75.34	57.38	60.69	43.00	84.38	65.28
X in direction 12	35.16	43.28	8.13	2.10	53.13	55.17
X in direction 16	70.52	89.21	51.79	82.97	87.64	50.49
Y in direction 13	17.23	33.64	14.43	9.57	28.44	68.15
Y in direction 15	50.27	48.92	31.17	20.46	61.73	56.62
Z in direction 4	22.12	18.84	6.07	19.47	25.18	11.22
Z outside map	8.52	0.44	4.38	11.35	10.17	13.48

4.2   Learning FCM Network on Example of Kraków City Map

In this test a map of part of Kraków with 682 road segments was used. The corresponding FCM network has 682 vertices and 464 442 edges. To reproduce the real situation six types of vehicle was used: passanger, bus, motorcycle, delivery transport/trailer and passenger/sedan. For each vehicles, appropriate values of acceleration, length and maximal speed were defined.

Similarly to the test cases described in Sect. 4.1, three experiments were carried out using the traffic network defined on Fig. 5. In the experiment virtual detectors were placed at subset of edges $E_{ded} = \{A, B, C, D, E, F, GH, I, J\}$.

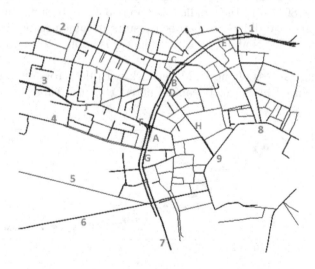

Fig. 5. Large road network - city of Kraków

Table 3. Test results of prediction traffic volumes (occupation) using FCM for the network presented in Fig. 5.

Lane	Test#1 $O_{S_{avr}}$ [%]	O_{FCM} [%]	Test#2 $O_{S_{avr}}$ [%]	$O_{FCM_{avr}}$ [%]	Test#3 $O_{S_{avr}}$ [%]	$O_{FCM_{avr}}$ [%]
A	34.15	41.78	26.79	89.80	51.32	16.80
B	37.13	39.34	32.35	17.81	58.22	2.28
C	26.64	20.51	24.92	21.60	38.72	16.88
D	55.13	32.39	38.17	45.61	79.43	10.37
E	16.83	24.27	18.22	100	30.10	25.65
F	74.82	79.95	68.21	81.26	95.23	29.10
G	41.28	45.54	27.84	36.56	52.37	12.50
H	52.33	61.74	31.76	42.68	59.45	8.59
I	18.35	24.33	12.43	26.91	32.03	13.11
J	18.98	25.23	10.02	19.36	22.62	17.21

For learning FCM, FCMEVOL algorithm was used with the same control parameters values as in Sect. 4.1. The trained FCM network was tested for prediction of traffic intensity for three test cases corresponding to those performed in the case of the small network (Table 3).

For Test#1 it can be observed that average difference between results obtained using SUMO (reference values) and FCM is about 7.71 %, the biggest is about 22.74 % and the smallest is about 2.21 %. In the second test the average difference between results obtained using SUMO and FCM is about 11 %, the biggest is about 80 % and the smallest is about 3.32 %. Results for Test#3 are the following: average difference between results obtained using SUMO (reference values) and FCM is about 36 %, the biggest is about 69 % and the smallest is about 4.45 %.

The learning process of the FCM network with detectors on E_{ded} subset of edges was presented in Fig. 6. It can be noted that the value of the objective

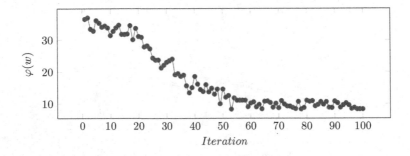

Fig. 6. FCM learning process for the road network of city Kraków

function, at the end learning process, is significantly greater than in case of presented on Fig. 4. It is because the size of the traffic network and the number of elements summed in the objective function is much bigger.

5   Conclusions

The motivation for the presented work was the need for solution allowing efficient estimation of traffic parameters in based on sparse measurements covering a small fraction road segments within large urban road network. The solution was intended to be deployed within Dynamic Map, an important component of the INSIGMA system used for route planning and traffic control. We have chosen to base the estimation model on Fuzzy Cognitive Maps formalism and apply FCM learning techniques to determine the model parameters.

This paper discusses a novel evolutionary algorithm FCMEVOL for FCM learning and demonstrates feasibility and efficiency of such approach. In our experiments we have used SUMO simulator to generate learning data for networks of various sizes, as well as to generate test data for various traffic scenarios.

Due to a certain similarity of FCM to ANN, the proposed approach is close to intensively investigated data-driven traffic prediction methods based on neural networks [10,13,37]. However, for the network learning an evolutionary algorithm is used, what is more common for fuzzy traffic models [12].

Due to the problem complexity and the relative simplicity of the FCM, the obtained results sometimes differs from real traffic. We may conclude, however, that any estimation method would inherently involve a tradeoff between accuracy and real-time performance. In this light, FCM offer a real advantage: once learned, the traffic estimation can be performed really quickly and in most cases at accepted level of accuracy.

References

1. Aguilar, J.: A Survey about fuzzy cognitive maps papers (Invited Paper). Int. J. **3**(2), 27–33 (2005)
2. Asif, M., Dauwels, J., Goh, C., Oran, A., Fathi, E., Xu, M., Dhanya, M., Mitrovic, N., Jaillet, P.: Unsupervised learning based performance analysis of n-support vector regression for speed prediction of a large road network. In: 2012 15th International IEEE Conference on Intelligent Transportation Systems (ITSC), pp. 983–988, September 2012
3. Axelrod, R.M.: Structure of Decision: The Cognitive Maps of Political Elites. Princeton University Press, Princeton (1976)
4. Baran, R., Glowacz, A., Matiolanski, A.: The efficient real- and non-real-time make and model recognition of cars. Multimedia Tools Appl. **74**(12), 4269–4288 (2015)
5. Schlichter, B.R., Svejvig, P., Andersen, P.E.R.: Value creation from public health-care IS. In: Bergvall-Kåreborn, B., Nielsen, P.A. (eds.) TDIT 2014. IFIP AICT, vol. 429, pp. 1–15. Springer, Heidelberg (2014)
6. Chmiel, W., et al.: Contribution of the INSIGMA project to the field of intelligent transportation systems. In: Dziech, A., Czyżewski, A. (eds.) MCSS 2014. CCIS, vol. 429, pp. 58–72. Springer, Heidelberg (2014)

7. Chmiel, W., Kadłuczka, P.: A multi-phase diversification method of population in the evolutionary algorithm. Automatyka 151(1), 195–202 (2008)
8. Chmiel, W., Kadłuczka, P., Kwiecień, J., Pukocz, P., Filipowicz, B.: Strategic planning optimisation using tabu search algorithm. In: Advances in Decision Sciences and Future Studies. KICSS 2013 : Looking into the Future of Creativity and Decision Support Systems, Kraków, Poland, vol. 2, p. 69–74, Nov 2013
9. Chmiel, W., Kadłuczka, P., Ernst, S.: A multicriteria model for dynamic route planning. In: Dziech, A., Czyżewski, A. (eds.) MCSS 2011. CCIS, vol. 149, pp. 174–182. Springer, Heidelberg (2011)
10. Csikos, A., Viharos, Z.J., Kis, K.B., Tettamanti, T., Varga, I.: Traffic speed prediction method for urban networksan ann approach. In: 2015 International Conference on Models and Technologies for Intelligent Transportation Systems (MT-ITS), pp. 102–108. IEEE (2015)
11. Dauwels, J., Aslam, A., Asif, M.T., Zhao, X., Vie, N.M., Cichocki, A., Jaillet, P.: Predicting traffic speed in urban transportation subnetworks for multiple horizons. In: 2014 13th International Conference on Control Automation Robotics & Vision (ICARCV), pp. 547–552. IEEE (2014)
12. Dimitriou, L., Tsekeris, T., Stathopoulos, A.: Adaptive hybrid fuzzy rule-based system approach for modeling and predicting urban traffic flow. Transp. Res. Part C: Emerg. Technol. 16(5), 554–573 (2008)
13. Dougherty, M.S., Cobbett, M.R.: Short-term inter-urban traffic forecasts using neural networks. Int. J. Forecast. 13(1), 21–31 (1997)
14. Głowacz, A., Mikrut, Z., Pawlik, P.: Video detection algorithm using an optical flow calculation method. In: Dziech, A., Czyżewski, A. (eds.) MCSS 2012. CCIS, vol. 287, pp. 118–129. Springer, Heidelberg (2012)
15. Janowski, L., Kozłowski, P., Baran, R., Romaniak, P., Glowacz, A., Rusc, T.: Quality assessment for a visual and automatic license plate recognition. Multimedia Tools Appl. 68(1), 23–40 (2014)
16. Kosko, B.: Fuzzy cognitive maps. Int. J. Mach. Stud. 24, 65–75 (1986)
17. Krajzewicz, D., Erdmann, J., Behrisch, M., Bieker, L.: Recent development and applications of SUMO - Simulation of Urban MObility. Int. J. Adv. Syst. Meas. 5(3&4), 128–138 (2012)
18. Lazzerini, B., Mkrtchyan, L.: Analyzing risk impact factors using extended fuzzy cognitive maps. IEEE Syst. J. 5(2), 288–297 (2011)
19. Lippi, M., Bertini, M., Frasconi, P.: Short-term traffic flow forecasting: an experimental comparison of time-series analysis and supervised learning. IEEE Trans. Intell. Transp. Syst. 14(2), 871–882 (2013)
20. Michalewicz, Z.: Genetic Algorithms + Data Structures = Evolution Programs (2Nd, Extended Ed.). Springer-Verlag New York Inc., New York (1994)
21. Ozesmi, U., Ozesmi, S.: Ecological models based on people's knowledge: a multistep fuzzy cognitive mapping approach. Ecol. Model. 176(1–2), 43–64 (2004)
22. Pan, B., Demiryurek, U., Shahabi, C.: Utilizing real-world transportation data for accurate traffic prediction. In: 2012 IEEE 12th International Conference on Data Mining (ICDM), pp. 595–604. IEEE (2012)
23. Papageorgiou, E.: Learning algorithms for fuzzy cognitive maps: a review study. IEEE Trans. Syst. Man Cybern. Part C: Appl. Rev. 42(2), 150–163 (2012)
24. Parsopoulos, K.E., Papageorgiou, E., Groumpos, P.P., Vrahatis, M.N., et al.: A first study of fuzzy cognitive maps learning using particle swarm optimization. In: The 2003 Congress on Evolutionary Computation, CEC 2003, vol. 2, pp. 1440–1447. IEEE (2003)

25. Sliwa, J., Gleba, K., Chmiel, W., Szwed, P., Glowacz, A.: IOEM - ontology engineering methodology for large systems. In: Jędrzejowicz, P., Nguyen, N.T., Hoang, K. (eds.) ICCCI 2011, Part I. LNCS, vol. 6922, pp. 602–611. Springer, Heidelberg (2011)
26. Szwed, P.: Application of fuzzy cognitive maps to analysis of development scenarios for academic units. Automatyka/Automatics 17(2), 229–239 (2013)
27. Szwed, P., Kadluczka, P., Chmiel, W., Glowacz, A., Sliwa, J.: Ontology based integration and decision support in the insigma route planning subsystem. In: Ganzha, M., Maciaszek, L.A., Paprzycki, M. (eds.) Federated Conference on Computer Science and Information Systems - FedCSIS 2012, Wroclaw, Poland, 9–12 September 2012, Proceedings, pp. 141–148 (2012)
28. Szwed, P., Pekala, K.: An incremental map-matching algorithm based on hidden markov model. In: Rutkowski, L., Korytkowski, M., Scherer, R., Tadeusiewicz, R., Zadeh, L.A., Zurada, J.M. (eds.) ICAISC 2014, Part II. LNCS, vol. 8468, pp. 579–590. Springer, Heidelberg (2014)
29. Szwed, P., Pekala, K.: Map-matching in a real-time traffic monitoring service. In: Kozielski, S., Mrozek, D., Kasprowski, P., Małysiak-Mrozek, B. (eds.) BDAS 2014. CCIS, vol. 424, pp. 425–434. Springer, Heidelberg (2014)
30. Szwed, P., Skrzynski, P.: A new lightweight method for security risk assessment based on Fuzzy Cognitive Maps. Appl. Math. Comput. Sci. 24(1), 213–225 (2014)
31. Szwed, P., Skrzynski, P., Chmiel, W.: Risk assessment for a video surveillance system based on Fuzzy Cognitive Maps. Multimedia Tools Appl., 1–24 (2014). http://link.springer.com/article/10.1007%2Fs11042-014-2047-6, doi:10. 1007/s11042-014-2047-6
32. Szwed, P., Skrzynski, P., Grodniewicz, P.: Risk assessment for SWOP telemonitoring system based on fuzzy cognitive maps. In: Dziech, A., Czyżewski, A. (eds.) MCSS 2013. CCIS, vol. 368, pp. 233–247. Springer, Heidelberg (2013)
33. Tadeusiewicz, R.: New trends in neurocybernetics. Comput. Methods Mater. Sci. 10(1), 1–7 (2010)
34. Tadeusiewicz, R., Chaki, R., Chaki, N.: Exploring neural networks with C#. CRC Press, Boca Raton (2014)
35. Takahashi, M., Kita, H.: A crossover operator using independent component analysis for real-coded genetic algorithms. In: Proceedings of the 2001 Congress on Evolutionary Computation, vol. 1, pp. 643–649 (2001)
36. Wojnicki, I., Szwed, P., Chmiel, W., Ernst, S.: Ontology oriented storage, retrieval and interpretation for a dynamic map system. In: Dziech, A., Czyżewski, A. (eds.) MCSS 2012. CCIS, vol. 287, pp. 380–391. Springer, Heidelberg (2012)
37. Zhang, B., Xing, K., Cheng, X., Huang, L., Bie, R.: Traffic clustering and online traffic prediction in vehicle networks: a social influence perspective. In: 2012 Proceedings IEEE INFOCOM, pp. 495–503, March 2012

Author Index

Printed in the United States
By Bookmasters